T0304832

# Praise for *The 5 Principles of Parenting*

"What Aliza does is come in and teach us how to individually handle how we raise children as well as ourselves. Her process is empowering and not based on just one person's opinion. It seems impossible for one human to know so much research, and yet her hard work has paid off for all of us. She eschews judgment and helps us all quiet the inner voices of doubt and get into problem-solving mode. I simply don't know what I would do without her wisdom. She is my go-to for how we all, including ourselves, *Raise Good Humans*!"

—**Drew Barrymore**

"Dr. Aliza Pressman's excellent (and long anticipated) book, *The 5 Principles of Parenting*, reflects her warmth, humor, depth of knowledge, and no-nonsense approach to raising good humans (see what I did there?). In the first half, Dr. Pressman sets up the why of the science; the second half gives parents flexible, bite-size examples of the how. I finished this book feeling more competent, empowered, and calm; how often can you say that when thinking about parenting? Thank you, Aliza—I love this book!"

—**Jennifer Garner**

"Imagine receiving practical wisdom based on solid, cutting-edge science about how you can raise your kids to be thoughtful, emotionally balanced, compassionate, and engaged citizens of the world. That's what you have here. Aliza Pressman's magnificent guide . . . will be something to turn to again and again in the privilege and journey of being a parent. Enjoy!"

—**Daniel Siegel, MD,** *New York Times* **bestselling coauthor of** ***Parenting from the Inside Out, The Whole-Brain Child,*** **and** ***The Power of Showing Up*** **and author of** ***Brainstorm, Aware,*** **and** ***The Developing Mind***

"With deep compassion, simplicity, and insight, this book powerfully conveys the science behind raising good humans. It is filled with practical tools that any parent can start utilizing on their journey toward raising resilient children."

—**Dr. Shefali Tsabary, bestselling author of** ***The Conscious Parent: Transforming Ourselves, Empowering Our Children***

"*The 5 Principles of Parenting* is the one book parents can turn to for every stage of development. Dr. Aliza Pressman masterfully translates the science into the practical realities of being a parent and provides clear strategies every parent can use."

— **Lori Gottlieb, *New York Times* bestselling author of *Maybe You Should Talk to Someone* and cohost of the *Dear Therapists* podcast**

"In a time when there's a lot of noise and advice about parenting and child development, Dr. Aliza Pressman is a rare find. She is at once a credible expert, practical, accessible, and beloved. Respected by colleagues and parents alike, Dr. Pressman's work is impactful and powerful, influencing how this generation of parents thinks about and cultivates their children's development."

— **Tina Payne Bryson, LCSW, PhD, coauthor of multiple bestsellers, including *The Whole-Brain Child* and *No-Drama Discipline***

"Here, at last, is the book parents have been waiting for! Dr. Aliza Pressman distills decades of developmental research into sound and practical guidance that addresses the real questions and concerns that all parents face. Brimming with warmth and wisdom and free from fads and fear, this book belongs in the hands of everyone who cares for or about children."

— **Lisa Damour, PhD, author of *Untangled*, *Under Pressure*, and *The Emotional Lives of Teenagers***

"This book is a gift to parents. . . . Relax, build your relationships, enjoy your parenting."

— **Alan Sroufe, professor emeritus at the University of Minnesota and author of *A Compelling Idea: How We Become the Persons We Are***

YOUR ESSENTIAL GUIDE
*to* RAISING GOOD HUMANS

# *the* 5 principles *of* parenting

# Dr. Aliza Pressman

First published in the USA in 2024 by SIMON ELEMENT,
a trademark of Simon & Schuster, Inc.

First published in the UK in 2024 by Headline Home, an imprint of
HEADLINE PUBLISHING GROUP

2

Cataloguing in Publication Data is available from the British Library

Hardback ISBN 978 1 0354 1594 6
Trade paperback ISBN 978 1 0354 1597 7
eISBN 978 1 0354 1595 3

Offset in 11.98/15.04pt Arno Pro by Jouve (UK), Milton Keynes

Printed and bound in Great Britain by Clays Ltd, Elcograf S.p.A.

Headline's policy is to use papers that are natural, renewable and recyclable
products and made from wood grown in well-managed forests and other controlled
sources. The logging and manufacturing processes are expected to conform to
the environmental regulations of the country of origin.

HEADLINE PUBLISHING GROUP
An Hachette UK Company
Carmelite House
50 Victoria Embankment
London EC4Y 0DZ

www.headline.co.uk
www.hachette.co.uk

*To Penelope and Vivian:*
*You've taught me all the important things I know.*

*And now that you don't have to be perfect, you can be good.*

—John Steinbeck, *East of Eden*

CONTENTS

# Contents

# *the* 5 principles *of* parenting

# Grounding Your Parenting in the Science of Child Development

*Trees exhale for us so that we can inhale them to stay alive.*
—MUNIA KHAN

## Welcome to *The 5 Principles of Parenting*

The research is conclusive. There are five principles we all need to get fluent in if we want to raise good humans. They are:

+ Relationships
+ Reflection
+ Regulation
+ Rules
+ Repair

These are the Five Rs that lead to resilience—to humans who can weather life's storms and stay true to their values. Because *fluency* means being able to easily implement these principles in your day-to-day life, this book is organized in a way that will show you why these principles matter and will teach you how to engage with them in virtually any context.

The first half of this book covers everything you'll need to know about the big-picture science of parenting, and the second half shows you how to apply that science to the most common dilemmas parents present to me in my practice as a developmental psychologist and guide.

You'll notice that we're not going to go through the principles one by one but, rather, take an approach of total immersion. By the end of this book, you'll find that you not only know exactly what these terms refer to but you'll also be able to use them with ease and eloquence.

## How I Got Here

My love affair with developmental psychology started before I became a mom.

What makes us become who we are, from our earliest moments and over time? How can parents and communities best shelter the newcomers? What can go wrong? How can we heal from mistakes? I found it fascinating that there was a whole field of study exploring the answers to these questions.

Twentieth-century Swiss philosopher and psychologist Jean Piaget spent much of his professional career watching and listening to children to discover the secrets of the mind. In a thought-leap considered radical at the time, he observed that children aren't just empty vessels waiting to be filled with knowledge, but also active builders of their own education—little scientists constantly creating and testing their theories of their worlds. This made so much sense to me. As parents, we do that, too! We're not just empty vessels in need of being filled up with expert know-how. We bring all our own histories and experiences to parenting. We're parent-scientists, constantly testing strategies to see if they make our lives in our unique families' experiences easier. Through *Relationships*, self- and co-*Regulation*, *Reflection*, *Rules*, and *Repairs*, we become active builders of our own family dynamics.

Each of our ideas of what makes for a good human is unique. There are literally *millions* of ways to be a good human. As such, there are *millions* of ways to be a good parent. Parenting asks us to interrogate and reflect on what *we* think "good" means.

Developmental psychology can help.

As a developmental psychologist engaged in the science of how we get to be who we are and how we change over time, I always draw from the research. But research is dynamic; all scientific studies are conducted in some context, and that context isn't your unique family. Your personal experience is valuable. Your cultural and family traditions are meaningful. Some of your quirks are probably strengths unique to your situation.

Some parents read absolutely everything, and some reject "expert" advice across the board. But I've learned with all things in parenting: there's a space between—and for me, that's what this book is about. When we focus on our **Relationships** within our families, when we take time for **Regulation** and **Reflection**, when we're clear about **Rules**, and when we make a habit of **Repair** after mistakes, we find that space between micromanagement and chaos.

Extreme ideas may seem comforting at times, like there's some way to "win" at parenting if only you and your child conduct yourselves just right. Like, *Oh good, there's a clear answer. All my worries about raising a good human can be put to rest.* I get that. The illusion of total certainty has incredible appeal. But as you may have already learned the hard way, extremes are unsustainable. The middle road might not seem as sexy or as black-and-white, but trust me—it's an easier road to stay on.

So much of parenting can feel like a one-and-done challenge— if we don't get attachment right with our newborns, we and they are doomed to lifetimes of feeling alienated. Not true! Research on attachment shows that attachment *relationships* are dynamic. And like all relationships, attachment relationships can be mended, shifted, and built upon. It's called *repair*, and it's one of my five principles of parenting. Not only can mistakes be met with repairs and do-overs, but these mistakes and repairs can actually strengthen our relationships. As you read this book, I want you to let your ears perk up whenever we come to one of these Five Rs: **Relationships**, **Regulation**, **Reflection**, **Rules**, and **Repair**. The Five Rs lead to that elusive sixth R we're all hoping and building toward: Resilience.

We don't have to be perfect parents the moment our kids are born—or ever. The science shows us that our own learning curves are key to the whole process of raising good humans. So much of the expectation in parenting is that we're going to raise our children to be good and well adjusted—that *their* development is the only outcome we should be invested in; but I've learned that our own parallel path of development as parents can be at least as meaningful. In raising our kids, we as the adults get beautiful opportunities to grow into our own maturity, into our own hope, will, and wisdom. We do that by returning to these five principles that also lead to resilience: *Relationships*, *Regulation*, *Reflection*, *Rules*, and *Repair*. Through all our doubts, and even our difficult moments as parents, through times when we might feel isolated or insufficient, we ourselves can use these principles and the practices I'll outline in this book to become more confident, more grounded, and more integrated—to embody the sense of being good humans like we want our kids to grow into.

In this book, I'll teach you a lot of specific practices that will make your life easier when dealing with everything from infant sleep issues to tween screentime drama, but you'll notice the principles remain pretty constant. That's because the strategies that work for navigating toddlerhood are the same ones you'll need to draw on when your kids are teens. These principles and practices will help you maintain and return to a calm sense of confidence—a place of regulation from which you'll be able to make intentional choices. These practices include both *Regulation* and *Reflection*, also known as mindfulness, through which you'll develop the habit of grounding into the space *between* extremes.

## Visualize Yourself Grounded

As a little girl, I adored the weeping willow tree on our street. In the neighborhood park, we played under a giant oak, creating whole worlds of make-believe and magic. I loved wisteria vines, too. They seemed to climb into trees and weep like the willows but in pale purple blooms—cue the music from *Les Miserables* and you'll know what kind of kid I was.

I lived in the suburbs and then in the city, so most of the trees I came into contact with were human-planted beauties that lived mostly solitary lives of a few decades. It wasn't until later in life that I discovered the marvel of natural forests. The California redwoods awed me with their old-growth magnificence. In ancient forests, all these tree species can live for hundreds if not thousands of years, spending their first few decades sheltered under the care of their mothers. University of British Columbia ecologist Suzanne Simard has established that trees are truly social beings who through their *relationships* help each other out, sharing food and warning each other about pests and other threats via mycorrhizal fungi networks that live in their roots. Simard calls the biggest, oldest trees in the forest the "mother trees," and she's found that they recognize their own kin and favor them, sending them more carbon below ground.

Creating a shady, sheltered environment where saplings can grow slowly helps ensure their long-term well-being by giving them plenty of time to strengthen their cells before they get tall. Sometimes, when I'm in need of grounding in the middle of a hectic day of family or work life, I take a breath and imagine myself a mother tree—a weeping willow, or a broad oak, or a giant redwood in an ancient forest, thousands of years old.

I inhale and exhale in tandem with other living things. I have sturdy roots, but I'm not so rigid that I'm going to snap. I can sway, flexible in the wind, and yet I stand steady. I'm able to shelter and feed my saplings as they grow as strong and resilient as I can support them to become.

This is a book about raising humans, not trees, but as we move from the world of forest ecology and delve ever more deeply into my field of developmental psychology and the science of parenting, I invite you to imagine yourself a mother tree. Stay with me here. Try visualizing your strong and sturdy roots that keep you firmly grounded. Notice in this visualization that you can still sway. You're not so rigid that you're going to crack when the winds pick up. You'll live in your community, helping your neighbors and sharing food and news and—of course—you'll favor your own children in many ways like trees do.

Science can seem heady at times, but it's earthy, too. It's steady—like an old tree. Developmental psychology feels that way to me, too. It honestly boggles my mind that we don't learn about developmental psychology as a part of high school. It's completely illuminating!

Some of the old "expert" philosophies and practices have been debunked, of course. I'm not sure how the advice to start potty training babies *at birth* ended up in a 1932 US government pamphlet for new moms, but we clearly now know that's ridiculous. In a 1962 book,

Dr. Walter Sackett recommended giving babies black coffee starting at six months old! Obviously, I don't recommend that one, either.

More recently, in the 1980s and 1990s, Dr. William Sears, a pediatrician, and coauthor Martha Sears, a registered nurse, took one of the most important words in developmental science—*attachment*—and applied it to *their parenting approach*, and they named it "attachment parenting." This confused millions of readers, suggesting that a few particular parenting practices were a method to *obtain* secure attachment. This isn't even remotely true, and potentially made a lot of mothers feel like failures. Attachment parenting, which is the Searses' *philosophy*, has nothing to do with the formation of a secure attachment relationship, a well-researched concept that is predictive of future physical, mental, and developmental health (and a buffer for the impact of toxic stress).

All this is to say that we have to be willing to reject expert advice. We have to take every study in the context in which it was done and not blindly generalize it to every family out there. But as I continued to study developmental psychology, I found it fascinating that, despite the fact we often say the new science disputes the old or we've discovered some revolutionary new insight, much of what the twentieth-century OG psychologists theorized *has* been held up with scientific evidence. More recently, neuroscience has affirmed much of the older wisdom from the developmental sciences on resilience. Neuroscience has also found that mindfulness, visualization, and meditation—practices once considered unscientific—should be in *all* our developmental and parenting tool kits. When we breathe in, we inhale the air the trees have exhaled. When we breathe out, we exhale the carbon dioxide for the trees to send to their young. The most fundamental parenting practice is something we've been doing in tandem with the trees since our ancestors came down from their branches and started walking around with two feet on the ground.

So, breathe. Doing the best we can *more often than not* might not seem like a super-high bar for parenting, but I'm delighted to report what the scientific research has clearly shown: if we've got the essential information and we apply it more often than we don't, *that's good enough.*

Think about good parenting as a 75 percent principle. You're going to learn a lot in this book, and then I'll invite you to actively throw out about

25 percent of my advice, because it won't work for *your* family—or maybe you just don't like it. Even within what works for your family, if you're the parent you want to be 75 percent of the time (and that's probably still a high bar!), that's amazing. In our academic and work life, most of us don't aim for Cs, but I'm here to tell you that if you can implement 75 percent of the research-backed, practical guidance, you're golden.

Lehigh University researcher and attachment expert Susan S. Woodhouse studied racially and ethnically diverse low-income moms and their babies, and she found that when the primary caregiver was responsive about half the time, that built a strong-enough sense of attachment to protect their kids from the psychological risks associated with life stresses. They needed to respond only about just over 50 percent of the time to reap these benefits.

## Inhabit the Space Between

These days I get media requests whenever a new study or parenting influencer comes out saying this or that, whether about pacifiers, or screen time, or behavior modification. Often, I can't tell the journalists what they want to hear. I won't say that an extra hour in front of the television will ruin a kid's life, any more than I'd say giving them a cup of coffee is a good idea. Extremes make for clickable headlines. Extremes promise safety because they feel so certain. But it's a false sense of safety. The science is clear: humans don't thrive at extremes.

Here are the nonnegotiables in parenting I feel pretty confident all psychologists agree on:

+ Take care of the mental health of the primary caregiver.
+ Do not engage in physical or emotional abuse.
+ Do not neglect a child.
+ Commit to habits of consistent sleep, movement, and nourishment.
+ Establish clear **Rules** that enable emotional and physical safety.
+ Be sensitive (which we will define) to your child's needs (which are not the same thing as their "wants").

## Remember That Good Enough Is Good Enough

As with the beginning of all important projects, I invite you to get started by setting an intention—in this case, an intention for your own growth as a parent. Put your hand on your heart, take a deep breath, and say, "*More often than not*, I'm the parent [or mother or caregiver or father or mama or papa or zaza] I want to be." When setting an intention, it's also super helpful to name the barrier you expect to encounter (such as "I have a short temper when I'm tired"), and then come up with a plan to handle that barrier when it arises (like, "I will take a moment to breathe before I speak or act.")

The fact that you're here, reading this book, means you're engaged and are open to growth, and that's tremendous.

You're doing great.

# PART ONE

# THE FOREST THROUGH THE TREES

*Getting at What Matters*

CHAPTER 1

# Clearing Away the Noise

*Beginning from a Place of BALANCE*

*Before you speak ask yourself if what you are going to say is true,
is kind, is necessary, is helpful. If the answer is no, maybe what
you are about to say should be left unsaid.*

—BERNARD MELTZER

Eleanor wanted the day to go perfectly. Her daughter, Camille, had practiced for her part in the school play for months. Eleanor planned everything from the meals they would share before the play to the flowers she would give her daughter afterward. Everything was set to go as painlessly as possible, but onstage, Camille froze and forgot her lines. That night, she cried into the perfect flowers. When Eleanor called me, she was devastated, feeling like the whole experience had been a failure. But I had another take. I asked Eleanor to consider the fact that this had been a great parenting success. Camille was able to cry with her mother—Eleanor was a safe person, and Camille was having an appropriate response to her disappointment.

*We would all love for our children to lead easy lives with little pain, lots of laughter, and meaningful contributions—but that's not possible every day.* Real life brings with it inevitable challenges. We don't need to make childhood feel like adulthood right out of the gate, but we can help our kids ease into the realities of living in an imperfect world.

Part of the anxiety of parenting is knowing there's so much in this world we can't control. (Breathe that in and then exhale: *There's so much I can't control.*) But here's the heartening part: We *can* control our behavior as parents *more often than not,* and the science shows us

3

that our parenting is the single greatest environmental influence on our children's well-being. (Breathe that in and then exhale: *There's so much I can control.*)

I don't say this to freak you out. When I learned that parents had such a relatively powerful impact on their kids, I was in grad school and not yet pregnant, and I thought, *Duh.* When I had my first baby, I thought, *This is so overwhelming. How am I going to pull this off?*

As I've grown into motherhood, I've come to see this profound impact as empowering. As parents, we're significantly more influential than screen time, our children's peers, or which schools they attend. If we focus on what we can control—ourselves—that's something manageable. As you do the regulation exercises in this book, you'll get better and better at it all, but there will always be room for mistakes and repair.

## Understanding Regulation

Kristin came to our session ashamed and upset. She'd grown up in a household where she learned to equate masculinity with violence, and she'd made a vow not to pass that on to her boys. She didn't allow rough-housing, for one thing, and she didn't allow raised voices. When her four-year-old yelled something at his brother, panic shot through her body. She pounced on her son, screaming, "We don't yell!" Now, she cried to our parent group: "I can't believe I tried to teach my son non-aggression with more yelling!"

It makes sense that Kristin had a stress response triggered by her past. But that *unproductive* stress response—when we aren't able to self-regulate or are getting false alarms about the dangers at hand—can end up causing us to act and parent from a place of fear and panic. Often, when we feel guilty about how we handled a parenting situation, the root of the problem is our own inability to self-regulate in the heat of the moment. I reminded her that the occasional panic reaction in an otherwise loving household isn't going to hurt our kids. What would help her in the future would be if she could find another way to respond to that panic feeling in her body.

Self-regulation—and within that emotional regulation—is the human ability to respond to our experiences in ways that are socially acceptable and sufficiently flexible, but to also control or delay our reactions as needed.

My favorite way to think about self-regulation comes to us from psychologist Rollo May. In *The Courage to Create*, May wrote: "Human freedom involves our capacity to pause between stimulus and response and, in that pause, to choose the one response toward which we wish to throw our weight. The capacity to create ourselves, based upon this freedom, is inseparable from consciousness or self-awareness."

Whenever we talk about self-regulation, we're talking about activating that pause between stimulus and response *where we can create ourselves*, where we can be intentional and do the work of raising ourselves into the good parents we want to be. Being able to activate that pause *more often than not* creates a kind of freedom that allows us to walk through the world without worrying that we're going to lose our cool every time someone bumps our elbow on the subway or borrows our favorite toy. Even for adults, self-regulation usually remains a work in progress—one that's tested and strengthened in new ways by being around children. Kristin needed to remember that her reaction was understandable—*and completely forgivable*.

Children aren't born with a fully developed capacity for self-regulation; they learn it as their brains develop. A primary way we all learn self-regulation is through a process called co-regulation, which we'll more deeply explore later and that involves various types of responses, like a warm presence, an acknowledgment of distress, and a calming tone of voice, as well as modeling our own process of calming ourselves down.

When I think about how self-regulation works in a practical sense, I think about my new home alarm system.

I know only New Yorkers feel safer in New York than anywhere else, and since I'm a New Yorker, when I lived in the city, I didn't have an alarm system. Then I moved to California and into a house with my girls— and I didn't feel quite so safe. *Who would hear us scream for help if we didn't live in an apartment building?* I decided I needed an alarm system.

When I walk in the door, there's a slow beeping sound that serves as a warning signal. If there were a burglar, the alarm would go off and the police would come. When I come home, the warning signal reminds me to punch in my passcode. Then the system is disarmed and all is well. I think of that beeping sound as the metaphor for my stress response. When I feel the panic shooting through my body in reaction to a relatively nonthreatening stimulus, I need to have the passcode of self-regulation. I need to hear the beeping sound and realize when there's no burglar. I'm not being chased. My kids aren't being threatened. There's nothing bad happening. It's just me coming home with some takeout. So, I punch in my passcode and disarm the system.

The trick to developing a self-regulation muscle as a person, and especially as a parent, is to figure out your own personal passcode. Over time, you'll get better and better at recognizing the signs that your body is about to start sounding the alarm, and you'll have that much more warning time to punch in the passcode. The signs might include things like racing thoughts, difficulty focusing, fast heartbeat, dry mouth, butterflies or nausea, cold hands, quick breath, or a need to pee.

Everyone is different. When your kids do something that sets off that panic response in you, or if they're going through a dysregulated time when they're upset or freaking out about something, the alarm needs to be disabled before anything else can happen. Instead of meeting them where they are in the freak-out, or responding to yelling with more yelling, punch in your passcode. This will put you back into a state of balance and make you available as the loving, adult parent the situation calls for.

What's extraordinary about co-regulation is that your child can literally borrow from your nervous system to help calm down or learn about a limit in a receptive state. This habit alone—of finding your passcode and learning to punch it in to get yourself into a regulated mode fairly quickly—will not only improve your parenting, allowing you to be the parent you want to be more often than not, but it will also have the biggest influence on your children's ability to self-regulate in the future. It may not pay off right away. Parenting is a long game. But it will ultimately pay off.

When you find your passcode, you have a system in place so that you know what to do when you start to feel your nervous system bubbling up with anxiety. For most human beings, a passcode is as simple as taking a slow and deep breath. Or two. Or three. You can't set off that alarm while breathing. The lungs send the message to the brain through the vagus nerve: *I can be a compassionate witness here.* If it helps you to have an image, picture yourself inhaling the air a tree has exhaled. Then pucker your lips, like you're blowing out a candle, to exhale. If words help, think of a phrase: "I'm not being chased by a bear" or "All feelings are welcome, all behaviors are not." Choose a phrase that reminds you to take a breath—because you actually can. You have time. You can disarm your system before it sets off the main alarm. If you loathe mantras, instead make a habit of splashing cold water on your face—or stick your hands in a glass with ice if you don't want to mess up your makeup. Exposure to cold can actually dampen the threat response.

## How to Stay Grounded in the Here and Now

If you notice that your stress response often activates based on experiences from your past, your passcode might include a quick practice to remind yourself that you're in the here and now.

**Glance around.** Look at the room or space where you are and notice five colors you see.

**Breathe in through your nose.** Breathing in through the nose allows the air to reach the lower lobes of your lungs, stimulating the parasympathetic system, which is in charge of restoration, relaxation, and rejuvenation, as opposed to breathing in through the mouth, which can actually exacerbate panic and even cause hyperventilation.

**As you notice the colors, name them.** Say to yourself, **Blue**, then exhale through your mouth and say to yourself, **Orange**, and so on. It might feel goofy at first, but it's better than unleashing on your four-year-old, who has no idea about the intergenerational tempers you're responding to. You'll get used to these practices as your self-regulation increases and your roots grow stronger.

Whatever passcode works for you, you can use it daily and train yourself to remain regulated, no matter what's going on for your child. Words and breath may not be your thing, though. Maybe you want to put one hand on your heart and the other hand on your belly. This parental practice, even more powerfully than banning expressions of aggression, impacts the way children develop into adults who can self-regulate—because they'll have the experience of watching you, their caregiver, and co-regulating with you from infancy, across their childhood years, and even into adulthood. *Who doesn't want a parent they can call at any stage in life and borrow a calm sense of clarity?* That's what parental development will do for you: turn you into someone more grounded.

Of course, sometimes you won't be able to call on your passcode before you react. But here's the amazing truth of being a parent: we get multiple opportunities every day to disarm that stress system. At the end of the day, you just want to say to yourself, "For the most part, I'm able to self-regulate. For the most part, I'm able to co-regulate. More often than not, I can remember my passcode. And when I can't, that's another opportunity to show myself some self-compassion, because just like my kids and everybody else, I'm a human."

## The Parenting Passcode: BALANCE

If you already have your own passcode that works, keep using it. But I also invite you to borrow mine. It's BALANCE, the tool that will allow you to create the space to look, listen, and be sensitively attuned without reactivity. Again and again in this book, we'll come back to the seven steps of BALANCE, because they hold the answer to virtually every parenting conundrum you'll encounter. You might not believe it right now, but these seven, science-backed steps are applicable to virtually every scenario. Stay with me. I promise to make you a believer by the end of this book.

This is what it all comes down to:

**B**reathe. Inhale deeply through your nose, and exhale. Yes, there's rich neuroscience behind the power of the breath; and no, you can't skip this step. Take the breath.

**A**cknowledge. Ask yourself, "What is this moment bringing up for me?" For example, are you running late and feeling afraid you'll look like you can't handle your life? Are you responding to some long-ago circumstance that's more about your own history than the present moment? No judgment here. You can just *reflect* for a moment.

**L**et it go. You can unpack any baggage later, on your own timeline. When you let go of the past and future this moment is bringing up, you can focus on the present.

**A**ssess. Take stock of the present moment. Gauge your own and your child's state of mind—calm, curious, frantic, distraught?

**N**otice. Observe what's going on in your own body and what's going on in your child's body. What are the bodies present here and now trying to tell you?

**C**onnect. Let your child know verbally or with your body that you see them and care about their feelings.

**E**ngage. Now that you're in balance, you can decide which response you wish to throw your weight behind. If your child is yelling, you won't yell at them to stop yelling; you'll say it calmly, with authority. No matter what the parenting dilemma, your self-regulation is going to help you identify and respond in the space between permissiveness and tyranny.

Still don't know exactly what to do? Don't worry. You'll get there. When you get into the habit of responding from a regulated, balanced place, the clarity will follow.

These seven steps work on mechanisms in our brain-bodies so we can better manage scenarios from the toddler tantrum to the tween who just trashed the house while making a horror film that somehow involved massive quantities of green slime. Over time, you'll build the emotional muscle memory that makes a calm and balanced response feel like second nature *more often than not.* Just like we accept that the practice of working out builds physical muscles, practicing this mental workout will pay off in emotional agility and health. You'll translate the whole process to fit your personality, your child's temperament, and your own beliefs and values.

---

## Give Yourself Permission to be BAD

When I don't feel like I have time to go through all seven steps, I have a shortcut. I get that panicked feeling that warns me I'm dys-regulated, and I remind myself that it's good to be a bad mom. To be a BAD mom, I

1. Breathe
2. Assess
3. Deal

I remind myself, "All feelings are welcome, all behaviors are not." That's the shortcut. But when you can, practice all seven steps. Pretty soon they'll come so quickly, it will almost feel automatic.

---

## Eight Ways to Engage Your Parasympathetic Nervous System

The concept might sound fancy, but it's surprisingly simple to activate.

1. Breathe
2. Cold-water immersion, even just running cold water on your hands
3. Laugh
4. Have a good cry, complete with deep belly breaths
5. Spend time in nature
6. Play with a pet
7. Have a twenty-second hug with a loved one
8. Give yourself a butterfly hug: wrap your arms around

yourself and squeeze your arms, moving them up and down opposite hand to arm, using a tapping motion

## Co-Regulation

*I've learned that people will forget what you said, people will forget what you did, but people will never forget how you made them feel.*

—MAYA ANGELOU

One of the reasons taking care of ourselves helps our children so much is that co-regulation lies at the heart of all human relationships. In the parent-child relationship, it's key. Co-regulation in parenting refers to the presence of a calm and connected caregiver who can enable a child to regain balance when they're upset or afraid. It's often said that no one can make you feel a certain way. That's kind of untrue, though. Anyone who has been in a room when someone walks in very upset knows that everyone's nervous system responds. This is because humans are interdependent—or "intraconnected," as psychiatrist and professor of neurobiology Dr. Dan Siegel puts it. We co-regulate. So, when someone is upset, our nervous system responds and we're challenged not to get upset right along with them.

It's okay to acknowledge that someone might ignite a feeling in you. A goal of being a grown-up is to also have self-regulation, so you can respond with intention rather than getting swept up in this other person's emotional upset.

With our kids, we hope to co-regulate calm rather than upset, but it works the same way. When our baby is upset, we pick them up and make soothing sounds, for example. According to polyvagal theory, developed by neuroscientist and psychologist Dr. Stephen Porges, the reciprocal sending and receiving of signals of *safety*—not just the signals of the absence of danger—is what truly forges a connection between two nervous systems, each nourishing and regulating the other.

Through polyvagal theory, Porges describes how feeling secure begins deep within every person's autonomic nervous system. When safety is detected, our nervous system works to calm us. Interacting with a person whom you trust deeply creates that safe environment.

With our kids, who are still learning self-regulation, we can use these concepts of co-regulation and polyvagal theory, and we can lean into that interdependence and lend our little ones our own calm. Just rocking a baby and whispering "I'm here" activates co-regulation and helps that baby's nervous system recover from any upset or activation. Likewise, as our children get older, we can bring calm by regulating our own nervous system and responding with calm when their own system may be going into unnecessary fight-or-flight response.

## Survive and Become Wise

The human brain typically develops from back to front, also described as developing from the bottom up. First we learn to survive, and then we learn to be wise. We're all born with a well-developed back brain— or "survival brain"—that includes the brain stem and the limbic region. Our survival brain is responsible for basic functions like breathing and blinking, as well as for innate reactions to perceived threats—namely, fight, flight, or freeze. A key player in the back part of the brain is the amygdala. When the amygdala senses danger, it sounds the alarm and activates the hypothalamus-pituitary-adrenal axis to release adrenaline and cortisol to respond to the threat. The problem is that the amygdala acts on emotions and instincts and, especially early on, can have trouble distinguishing between real danger and false alarms without input from the wise part of the brain.

The front part of the brain, or the cerebral cortex, includes the prefrontal cortex—the wise, measured aspect of the brain—or the "sage brain." This is the part of the brain where complex mental processing like rational decision-making, control over emotions and body, self-understanding, empathy, and morality takes place. It's not that emotions don't play an equally key role, it's just that they give information in concert with reason to determine what we need—in fact, that is where the wisdom comes in. The front part of the brain doesn't fully develop until a person is somewhere between eighteen years old and their late twenties, with the largest periods of growth during the first few years of life and another big jump in adolescence.

During a perceived threat, the amygdala is flooded with alarm signals, and the front part of the brain's input is limited because we just don't need our inner sage when we're running from that bear. Through practice, however, one can strengthen the communication between the back part of the brain and the front part so we can better manage the strong reactions of the amygdala. This is called "brain integration," and it happens when the front and back of the brain work together, developing increased neural connections so that information flows quickly back and forth. Without this connection, humans of all ages can become overwhelmed with emotion and react, for example, with tantrums and meltdowns.

That's where we come in with co-regulation. By sharing our sense of calm with our kids, we slowly teach them how to regulate on their own when they sense a possible threat. By holding your baby and exuding your own calm, or remaining undisturbed when your toddler can't find their special lovey, you're sending the clear message: *If Mom isn't freaked out, there probably isn't a bear chasing us.* Eventually, this will allow your child to pause and consider various responses on their own and, with intention, select the choices that promise the best outcomes.

So, what stops us from acting out our every feeling? It's regulation—that often-fleeting pause between stimulus and response in which we can pull ourselves together, preferably *more often than not.* As parents, we're challenged daily to keep our behaviors in check, and we're charged with guiding our children to learn this important skill set, too.

When we can handle our children's emotional experiences without making them about our own feelings, we give them space to feel psychologically safe in sharing them. It can be burdensome to worry that when you share your feelings with your grown-up, that they're going to break down alongside you. Can you hear what your child is going through, try to make sense of it, and support them? In doing so, you support their growing sense of regulation as they mature into the confidence that all feelings are welcome, all behaviors are not, and with practice and cognitive development we can all keep our act together *more often than not.*

As with so much in parenting, it begins with us. Kids are wired to be attuned to our emotional states. Whether we like it or not, they absorb everything they can to understand themselves and the world around them. If you're feeling anxious, then acknowledge your feelings of anxiety. If you're feeling grumpy, acknowledge you might be irritable. It's okay to say so out loud—that way, you give your child the opportunity to understand that those are your feelings and not necessarily their feelings. Kids will often assume they've caused your feelings, so it's extra important that you say explicitly that's not the case.

Instead of saying, "You're exhausting me," try saying something like, "I didn't get much sleep last night, so you might notice that I'm acting extra grumpy."

Children can handle our feelings—our whole range of feelings— as long as they understand that we know how to handle our feelings, that they don't need to help us manage our feelings, and that regardless of our mental states we always love them and are able to also take care of them. They need to know that we know how to take care of them, and we also know how to take care of ourselves. They also need to know that we accept the whole range of feelings, and once we name them and accept them, we can move forward to the next steps.

This doesn't mean you're going to share all your worries with your child. It means you're going to pay attention to your own feelings and experiences, so you don't inadvertently project them onto your kids. You can try narrating what's going on for you as you shift into the present by saying something like, "I'm so annoyed right now it's challenging for me to focus on what I'm doing. Let me take a deep breath and see if I can get myself back to being able to pay attention to what I'm doing here."

So, if you have feelings ranging from sadness to anger, it's okay to share those with your children. In fact, it's better for your kids to know you have those feelings and that you know what you're going to do than for them to just notice that something's wrong and have to wonder.

## Commit to "Sensitive Caregiving"

Kids are incredibly attuned to our emotional states. They understand tension and feel it in their nervous system. If we're pretending to be cheerful, that's not really going to help our kids. But we *can* always take a breath and summon the best mood that's authentically available to us at any moment, and show up for our unique kids. In doing so, we can begin our practice of sensitive caregiving.

Sensitive Caregiving is an essential aspect of positive parenting that influences executive function development and secure attachment. The scientific concept of sensitive caregiving has been around for decades, originally defined by developmental psychologist Mary Ainsworth as the ability to appropriately detect and respond to a child's implicit behavioral signals. So when I say "commit to sensitive caregiving," I'm talking specifically about something rooted in decades of science and that shouldn't be confused with what it may sound like—the idea that a child's every want and feeling should stop the world. In fact, part of being a sensitive caregiver is knowing when and how to respond appropriately given your child and the circumstances, even when that means holding a boundary and experiencing your child's discomfort.

Sensitive caregiving, by definition, is never going to be one-size-fits-all. Sensitive caregiving means we're able to notice and respond to a unique child's signals in a way that fits with that child's needs. The definition sounds almost simple: an adult caregiver takes into consideration the individual temperament and needs of their unique baby or child, notices the child's signals, and responds appropriately. It's reciprocal and it's relational. But sensitive caregiving isn't something that comes naturally to many of us—often because it wasn't wired into us by our own caregivers.

We can, from the moment we meet our new person, or as soon as we're able, begin to get to know and accept them. What delights them? When do they get distressed? Do they like a lot of activity and bright colors? Do they feel safer when they get space and quiet time? When babies and children babble, gesture, or cry out, and their adult responds appropriately with words, eye contact, or a hug, that builds and strengthens neural connections in their growing brains that support the development of communication and social skills. Developmental psychologists call this process "serve and return"—because they see it as a back and forth, like tennis or Ping-Pong—and the science shows us that these interactions shape brain architecture. When we as parents and caregivers are sensitive and responsive to a child's signals, we provide an environment rich in serve-and-return experiences.

We'll take a deep dive into temperament in Chapter 6, but for now I want to assure you that sensitive caregiving isn't about following a particular script; it changes over time as children grow through their developmental stages. If a three-month-old is crying and inconsolable, a sensitive caregiver would go to that child, pick them up, check to see if they're wet, and check to see if they're hungry. If a typically developing four-year-old is hungry or wet, or too hot or too cold, they should be able to communicate that and address at least some of it for themselves, so at that point the sensitive caregiver could guide the preschooler to get their needs met without fixing everything for them just because they're making noise.

If you're gearing up to do a puzzle with your nine-month-old because their older brother liked puzzles, but this baby is pointing to the book, sensitive caregiving means that you'll shift to the book. The sensitive caregiver says, "Oh, you notice the book. Let's go see—what is this book?" So, we're talking about being responsive to both the intellectual and emotional needs in an age- and temperament-appropriate way. These small moments when you're playing with a puzzle or reading a book might seem inconsequential, but they're letting the child know that who they are and what they need are things they're able to communicate to this very important caregiver in their lives, and that the caregiver is able to respond *more often than not.*

Your response doesn't always have to be yes. If it's 2:00 a.m. and your five-year-old wakes you up demanding a book, a sensitive caregiver responds appropriately, which is to send the message, "No. It's time to rest."

## How and Why Kids Watch Us

*As children develop, their brains "mirror" their parents' brains.*
*In other words, the parent's own growth and development,*
*or lack of those, impact the child's brain. As parents become*
*more aware and emotionally healthy, their children reap the*
*rewards and move toward health as well.*

—DANIEL J. SIEGEL, MD

It's natural to want our kids to be able to regulate themselves and act the ways we want them to from, well, birth, but because they've just arrived and their brains aren't fully formed, they need to learn how to do these things. The primary way they learn is by watching us. They watch us lose our temper or they watch us get into balance and respond sensitively to them and the other people around us. This can feel like a lot of pressure, but let's face it: learning to be a good human would take a lifetime if we didn't have any examples. That's why children watch and imitate.

One of the best-known experiments in the history of psychology involved a slightly creepy-looking life-size clown doll named Bobo. With this doll, Stanford psychologist Dr. Albert Bandura and his colleagues exposed kids to two different models: an aggressive adult who used verbal insults and went so far as to beat the clown doll with a mallet, and a nonaggressive adult who played nicely with some Tinkertoys. The children were then shown a series of fun games they were allowed to play with for only a couple of minutes, intentionally building up their frustration levels, and then they were left alone with the clown and secretly observed the children imitating the behaviors they had witnessed in the adult models. Interestingly, when children in the experiments were told that the adults faced consequences for their aggressive behaviors, they were less likely to imitate them.

Even when the children saw the bad behavior and only heard that the adult faced consequences, they were able to turn away from the negative example. But when bad behaviors go without mention, the lessons really start to get coded into our children's brains. Believe it or not, prior to those experiments, a lot of people never thought about the impact that modeled behaviors were having on kids.

We can use Bandura's social learning theory to demonstrate and model behaviors we want to see, too. You can start by getting intentional about walking your talk—and honest about when you realize you haven't hit the mark. Kids learn as much from your ability to say, "I didn't react the way I wanted to, and I wish I had done something different," as your ability to get it right the first time around. We all have feelings. We all perform behaviors. And the more we're able to pause and reflect between the feeling and the acting out, the more we're able to conduct ourselves intentionally.

When I remind the parents I work with that *all feelings are welcome, all behaviors are not,* it is to reinforce the importance of separating their emotions and their behaviors. It's okay for our kids to *feel* angry with their sibling, but it's not okay to *hit* their sibling. It's okay *feel* frustrated with a toy that isn't working, but it's not okay to *smash* that toy against the wall. It's okay not to care for onions, but it's not okay to tell grandma she's a lousy cook. When we separate feelings from behaviors, we can begin to separate shame from expectations. We get to feel however we feel, and that's separate from how we act and how we're expected to act.

It's tempting at times to say "You should feel grateful" or "You love your brother" when really what someone feels is not up to us—but how they *act* on that feeling we do have some say about. That is where expectations come in. You get to *feel* however you feel, but you do not get to *behave* however you want to behave. This is how we can "discipline" our kids without worrying about shaming them about the feelings they are having.

## The Benefits of Not Fixing Everything

A lot of people define mental health as having positive emotions—feeling good, feeling happy, feeling calm, or feeling relaxed. But emotions, even positive ones, come and go. Psychologist and author Lisa Damour says that's a problematic definition because we could all start the day feeling good, but anything can come up that can start to ruin your day and you won't feel happy and you won't feel calm and you won't feel relaxed. That doesn't mean your mental health is up for grabs. Mental health is not about feeling good or calm or relaxed, it's about having feelings that make sense in the moment that match their context. And most importantly, handling those feelings well, handling them effectively, and handling them in a way that brings relief and does no harm.

Being a happy person doesn't mean you'll be happy all the time. Being mentally healthy doesn't mean you'll be happy all the time. Children need to experience uncomfortable feelings and get really good at recognizing they can survive that discomfort, that it is only temporary.

It's so natural to want to make things easier for our children. We love them and we want them to feel the easier feelings. I know that fixing things comes from such a loving place, but fixing and avoiding can send a message that we don't believe our kids have the capacity to take on the challenges of life. If we want our children to believe in themselves, we have to believe in them, too. Every time we fix something that they could have fixed for themselves, every time we make it so that they don't experience a challenge—even if it's difficult to watch because you love your child and you don't want them to go through any difficult emotional experiences or push themselves—when you fix it or make it easier, you're essentially saying to them, "I don't think you can handle this." When you step back, however, you're letting them know, "I trust you've got this. It might take a couple of tries, it might take a while, and it might be uncomfortable in the process, but I believe in you!"

Kids don't need their feelings fixed; they just need to know that we love them through the whole range of feelings that they have, so that as they grow they can also grow their ability to handle those feelings well, handle them effectively, and handle them in a way that brings relief and does no harm.

## Micro-Meditations

### Mindfulness You Have Time For

1.  Even if you can't carve out twenty minutes to meditate, start making a practice of taking a deep breath every time you walk through a doorway or every time you shift from one activity to the next. See if you can commit to a one-minute-a-day practice.

2.  Set a timer for one minute and just count your thoughts. Don't judge the thoughts' quality or content; just notice each thought and let it pass, like it's a billboard on a highway. Just information. Most of it, nothing to do with the present.

3.  Put your hand on your heart and say: "*More often than not,* I'm the parent I want to be."

4.  Count your steps as you walk. Try taking three steps per inhale, three steps per exhale. You don't have to empty your mind to meditate. Just the act of counting your steps will give you the moment you need.

5.  If you're feeling like you need a release, try doing a lion's breath. Inhale long and then open your mouth wide and stick out your tongue and make a roaring sound!

## REGULATION EXERCISE

*Breath Meditation*

A powerful way to build your self-regulation and disarm hyperreactivity is through a consistent practice of meditation—and I'm not talking about something that's going to be just another pipe dream on your to-do list. Pairing this practice with your passcode of BALANCE is going to build your self-regulation muscles so that more and more often, you'll be able to access that space between stimulus and response, and you'll anchor yourself in the freedom to act with intention.

Most meditation practices taught in the United States come to us from Buddhist traditions, but mindfulness is ancient and cross-cultural. I like to think of mindfulness as *heartfulness*, too. (In many Eastern languages, including Sanskrit, the words for *heart* and *mind* are synonymous.) Neuroscience research over the past two decades has confirmed what monks, mystics, and prayerful grandmothers have known for millennia: mindfulness meditation benefits our cognitive domains, including attention, memory, executive function, and cognitive flexibility. It might seem like a cruel irony that just when you most need support with all this mental agility, you literally don't have time to meditate; but the kind of mindfulness I'm talking about—and the kind I practice— doesn't require a special room or some crazy amount of alone time when no one's going to bother you.

If you have time to breathe, you have time to breathe intentionally. And that's a legit meditation practice.

The specific amount of time is up to you. Virtually all smartphones have timers on them. You can download a mindfulness app if you're like me and you prefer your alarm to sound like you're in a monastery rather than hiding in your laundry closet.

1.  Sit down or lie down—whatever is most comfortable for you. Some people like to sit with their feet firmly on the ground. Some people like to have a lot of pillows under their hips. Whatever works for you or feels practical will

serve the meditation, but direct some consciousness to your posture. Just notice it.

2. Pause and take a deep breath, noticing how it feels in your body as you inhale through your nose. Pucker your lips a little bit as you exhale through your mouth—almost like you're blowing out a candle very gently, not wanting to spill the melted wax.

3. As you keep breathing, introduce a count, inhaling with a silent count to four, holding for a silent count to six, and exhaling through your mouth with a silent count to eight.

4. Remind yourself that your breath and this count are your anchors.

This practice will reset your nervous system. If your attention drifts to *Why am I doing this?* or *Is this really doing anything for me?* know those are great questions. Remind yourself that there's rich science behind the practice. This practice is going to make you the parent and person you want to be. And then go back to the breath.

As you move through this book and try different mindfulness exercises, and start or restart your daily meditation practice, you may discover that the breath is not the best anchor for you. We start with the breath because that's what works for most humans, but if focusing on your breath seems to increase your anxiety, you've got other options. If that's the case for you, another anchor—like looking at your toes or a spot on the wall or visualizing a color—may become your preferred go-to.

# Five Parenting Practices and Five Teachable Skills to Set Up Your Child for Resilience

## *The Ordinary Magic of Raising Kids Who Can Weather Life's Storms*

*I've learned that you can tell a lot about a person
by the way he/she handles these three things: a rainy day,
lost luggage, and tangled Christmas tree lights.*

—MAYA ANGELOU

How many times have you heard someone say, "Children are resilient"? While children do bounce back, and that sentence might serve us when we're panicked at tough times, the truth is that resilience depends on a host of factors, and it can be harmful to keep repeating the word as though children are solely responsible for "being" resilient.

Any seed that sprouts has a chance at survival, but trees that thrive for hundreds of years are shaded, with roots in relation to other trees in the forest. Likewise, human resilience is a process that requires support systems that extend beyond the individual.

Ann S. Masten, a professor at the Institute of Child Development at the University of Minnesota and one of the world's preeminent researchers on resilience, defines the construct broadly as "the capacity of a system to adapt successfully to disturbances that threaten the viability, function, or development of the system." She has found that resilience arises from "ordinary magic" and relies on a host of factors, including attachment relationships, caregiver mental health, social relationships, self-regulation, and problem-solving skills. She notes that "resilience is made of ordinary rather than extraordinary processes."

We can't always control our kids' or our family's *exposure* to adversity, but we can do our best to dress for the weather. We can't control each individual family member's *sensitivity* to hard times—that's about their own temperament and developmental stage—but we can do a lot to bolster their *adaptive capacity*. And that makes all the difference in this equation.

I've identified five parenting practices and five teachable skills that can bolster this equation in our children's favor and set them up for life-long resilience. I call these principles and teachable skills the Five *Rs* and the Five GAMES.

## Understanding Executive Function

Executive function is a major set of skills that involves the conscious self-control of thoughts, actions, and emotions. It's an overarching aspect of brain development that has a huge impact on how we become who we are.

Typically acquired beginning in childhood, executive function continues to develop through our life spans. While some kids have an easier time developing these skills than others, executive function is cultivated in the context of **Relationships** with caregivers. Relationship is the first of the five principles of parenting, but as we'll learn throughout this book, each of the principles works to bolster executive function. By using these principles, you'll help your child's neural pathways grow.

Most adults use executive skills without even thinking about them as we go about our daily lives. We know where the produce is located in the store, but we usually don't flip out when they've moved the tortilla chips. We simply ask someone who works there, and we're able to follow their instructions to get our hands on what we want. Kids aren't born with any of this. One way to help kids develop executive function—before they throw a fit in the grocery store—is to walk them, out loud, through the steps of resolving everyday challenges. You might say, "Let's go get the tortilla chips. Oh, my goodness, this feels frustrating; the chips used to be right here. I wonder where they went. Do you think someone who works here might know where they've moved them?" This acknowledges and normalizes the processes we all go through, usually silently or even unconsciously, as we engage our brain's executive function.

Parents can also engage in what researchers call "goal-directed problem solving" appropriate to the child's developmental level (which we will delve into in Chapter 13 when we talk more about autonomy). With goal-directed problem solving, we practice all aspects of executive function—and specifically the core skills of inhibitory control, working memory, and cognitive flexibility.

Inhibitory control includes things like giving a thoughtful response rather than an impulsive one, resisting temptation, resisting distraction, and staying focused. Maybe your child has a strong inclination to grab another child's toy. Inhibitory control will be the skill that stops them from acting on that inclination.

Working memory is another executive function, and it entails the ability to hold information and work with it. Examples include translating instructions into action plans, considering alternatives, thinking about what you might do in the future, or reflecting on what you've done in the past.

A third core executive function is cognitive flexibility—being able to think outside the box, look at something from different perspectives, and update your thinking or planning with new information. For example, maybe you don't agree with someone on most anything, but you can find commonalities in your taste in music. So cognitive flexibility is about reframing, seeing things in different ways.

Executive functions have been referred to as the mental tool kit for success because they're so critical for almost anything we want to do in life, from the really big stuff to getting chores done. When you ask a young child to wet a rag to wash a counter or take a handful of strawberries from a container and transfer them to a bowl, you're helping them develop that ability to focus and concentrate.

## The Five *R*s

The Five Rs of **Relationships, Reflection, Regulation, Rules,** and **Repair** lead to the sixth R, Resilience. These are parenting practices that we can build on every day. They are as follows:

## Relationships

The single most powerful external influence on your child's capacity to bounce back from tough experiences is the presence of a nurturing *relationship* with at least one loving, supportive, stable adult. We know from research that relationships *build* resilience. It's on us as the adults to make sure we provide connection and community for the kids in the world so they have a chance to grow the skills of resilience with the support of the adults around them.

## Reflection

We know that *reflection*—particularly *self-reflection*—is by nature contemplative, so I'm going to ask you to stay with me here. As parents, particularly if our kids are still young, most of us don't feel we have time for much contemplative meditation, but if we let go of the image of the lone meditating monk with nothing to do all day but look at his cave wall, we can make room for mindfulness and micro-meditation in the spaces *between* even the busy moments of our daily lives. If you have time to breathe, you have time to breathe intentionally, and that intentional breath resets your nervous system. In that space between the moments, you can pause to think about your own experiences and how they may impact your perspective.

Developmental psychologist Stephanie Carlson notes that reflection invokes and supports agency, and therefore autonomy: "With agency, one can reflect on the self," she says. "Reflection occurs when we interrupt a reflexive response by pausing and adopting a wide-angle lens on the situation. Reflection thus provides a kind of psychological distance, the space between stimulus and response, in which to notice one's options. Without agency, children will behave reflexively, exhibiting poor Executive Function skills, whereas with agency, they will reflect on their options for responding, engage Executive Function skills, and be more likely to act in accordance with their goals."

There's nothing like parenting to bring up issues from your own childhood, and in these moments of reflection you can find opportunities to break old cycles that you may not want to repeat. Reflection in parenting also means you have time—even just in those moments between the moments—to reflect on what your child needs right now. When we reflect with our children, we observe, consider, and go over what has happened, and with that reflection we're able to respond accordingly and teach them how it's done. Reflection in the context of goal-directed problem-solving allows us to promote our own and our children's executive function skills.

### Regulation

This means we're able to stay intentional, not letting our emotions and our behavior react into fight-or-flight unnecessarily. With children, we get multiple opportunities every day to keep calm or to shift into other appropriate emotional responses, and to *co-regulate* with them. This act of co-regulation certainly helps our kids learn *self-regulation*, but it does at least as much also to tone and strengthen our own regulation muscles. Whether or not our kids ever learn not to throw a fit in the bookstore (spoiler alert: they likely will!), we ourselves can use the daily practice of parenting to—breath by breath—move away from our "bad influence" self and into our "wise grandma" self. And remember, we all lose our cool sometimes! What we're aiming for is intentional regulation *more often than not*.

### Rules

These encompass both boundaries and limits, and go hand in hand with sensitive caregiving, regulation, and modeling of the behaviors we want to see in our children. *Boundaries* are the rules one has for oneself, as well as things that happen interpersonally—or between people. *Limits* are rules that refer to unacceptable behaviors. Kids need both boundaries and limits to feel safe. As parents, it's our job to establish those rules, and then to hold them in an authoritative way.

### Repair

This refers to both the spontaneous and intentional processes humans use to mend their relationships with others and within themselves. This isn't about fixing mistakes that never should have happened. Repair is the space in which we grow, so mis-attunement is a necessary part of healthy development. If we ignore our baby for a few minutes while we answer texts, they might get anxious, causing a mini rupture in our relationship, but when we recenter them, the repair begins without our having to do anything else.

Repairing ruptures as soon as we become aware of them is important, but making repairs isn't rocket science: repairs are made by being warm, empathic, loving, curious, and playful. A more conscious effort might be something as simple as saying, "Oops, I thought you wanted help reaching that spoon and you wanted to do it yourself, I'm sorry." With a teen, a repair might be something like watching a favorite TV show together after a tough day and sharing a laugh.

As our children grow up, we have many opportunities for repair; some of those moments will feel simple and some will take more introspection, forgiveness, and work. Relationships can withstand all kinds of ruptures and mistakes, and the science shows that the healthiest relationships can grow stronger after discord. This is because the breaking and restoring of confidence in our connections is a huge part of the way humans learn to trust in the safety of the world. It's like those microruptures that make muscles stronger during exercise. Ruptures don't break the connection; rather, they enable our kids to feel the strength of that connection even more now that it has been tested and healed.

## The Research on Resilience

Sometimes when people talk about human resilience, they're talking about adapting in the face of major adversity or trauma. The science emerged after World War II, during which time so many children were victimized, orphaned, and displaced. In *War and Children*, one of the first volumes written in the aftermath, psychologists Anna Freud and Dorothy Burlingham noted that children rarely showed "traumatic shock" when a parent was present during the adverse event, and that caregivers' responses were important for children's responses. Freud and Burlingham directed the Hampstead War Nurseries, providing British children, many of whom had lost their homes to German bombs, with residential care and comparative safety. While the staff did their best to protect the vulnerable children, they soon discovered that children's separation from their families could be scarier than the Blitz. Freud and Burlingham observed, "The war acquires comparatively little significance for children so long as it only threatens their lives, disturbs their material comfort, or cuts their food. It becomes enormously significant the moment it breaks up family life and uproots the first emotional attachments of the child with the family group."

Freud and Burlingham's findings have been replicated again and again. This is why even the American Psychological Association and the American Academy of Pediatrics, both nonpartisan organizations, came out against child separation at the US–Mexico border in 2018. All early childhood experts agreed that this separation caused unnecessary trauma by disrupting the first principle of parenting: the safe **Relationship** that leads to resilience.

## The Resilience GAMES

Beyond having a parent with us to help us through hard times, human adaptive capacity is made up of a constellation of inborn and environmental factors—the environmental ones being the Five *Rs*—that enable us to make positive adjustments after setbacks, adversity, or big traumas. And it's never too late to build on those factors. Whether you've got a senior in high school or a toddler, there's room for growth and strengthening by engaging the Five *Rs*.

This is also when you activate the skills I remember with the acronym GAMES. I always love an acronym, and interestingly, many traditional childhood games are designed to activate the underlying traits of resilience, so I think of these skills in terms of GAMES:

**G**ratitude
**A**utonomy
**M**otivation
**E**mpathy
**S**elf-regulation

Now, let's look more deeply at what these each mean.

### G Is for Gratitude

Mike, a single dad in one of my groups, had thrown a big birthday party for his daughter, complete with her favorite taco bar and red velvet cupcakes. He'd let a bunch of kids sleep over and didn't complain when their giggling kept him up half the night. The next day she came in, being a fresh tween about something, and threw her backpack down.

Mike was indignant. "You have no right to talk to me that way," he said, filled with righteous anger. "You just had the night of your life. Why aren't you happy?"

Alas, children and tweens are meant to be self-absorbed. No matter what we do to raise grateful children, it doesn't mean they're going to say "I appreciate you" when we want them to. Sometimes, special events just raise the bar for what our kids expect every day. That doesn't mean we shouldn't celebrate, and even indulge our kids sometimes, but those moments don't tend to be the ones we're going to get a heartfelt "thank you" for. You can let go of that fantasy; and by letting go of it, you'll be noticeably less incensed when you don't hear it.

Accept that tweens often live in the moment. When Mike's daughter giggled with her friends, maybe that was her way of expressing her happiness and appreciation in the moment, even though it wasn't a formal "thank you" card to her dad. It's perfectly normal that the next day she's back to her old mildly snarky ways. Remember, *long game*.

Instilling gratitude, like so much of parenting, is all about playing the long game.

As with virtually all traits associated with resilience, gratitude springs from *relationships*. We develop a sense of appreciation over time through interactions with other humans. Robert Emmons, a professor of psychology at the University of California at Davis and a leading researcher on youth and gratitude, writes that gratefulness is a "relationship-strengthening emotion because it requires us to see how we've been supported and affirmed by other people."

As parents, we can manage our expectations so we won't get frustrated or start spiraling into feeling ungrateful about our ungrateful children, but we can also support them as they develop the gratitude muscle. Try answering these two questions for yourself:

+ What is your greatest wish?
+ What would you do for the person who granted you this wish?

Notice if your answer to the second question could be categorized as verbal, such as, "I'd say thank you"; or it is more reciprocal or concrete, like, "I'd buy them an electric sports car"; or it is more relational, like, "I'd remain a loyal friend to that person or do whatever they asked of me if I could."

Cross-cultural studies spanning more than eight decades and four continents have analyzed children's responses to that second question and have noted that kids tend to evolve from mostly verbal expressions of appreciation to more reciprocal, and ultimately to more relational modes of gratitude as they get older. Toddlers typically begin to say "thank you" around age two, but those early verbal expressions are more about manners and the way kids learn to make the adults in their lives happy. There's nothing wrong with good manners—I'm a big fan of good manners!—but that deeper sense of gratitude psychologists associate with everything from better health and happiness, to better grades and lower stress levels at college, seems to emerge when kids are around seven years old. Gratitude remains a work in progress throughout childhood and adolescence.

Fairly simple practices, like keeping a weekly gratitude journal and counting one's blessings, increases the actual experience of gratitude in adults, as well as children. Maintaining a gratitude journal for as little as three weeks can result in better sleep and more energy.

## Promoting Gratitude

You guessed it: it starts with us. Try checking in with yourself, mornings and evenings. In the morning, say to yourself, "I'll say thank you to someone today." "I'll show appreciation to someone today." "When someone helps me today, I'll feel a sense of thankfulness." "I'll notice three people or things I feel lucky to have in my life today." Then, in the evenings, circle back by asking yourself, "Did I say thank you to someone today?" "Did I show appreciation to someone today?" "When someone helped me, did I feel a sense of thankfulness today?" "Did I notice three people or things I feel lucky to have in my life today?" It's okay if the answers are no—this is just an exercise to check in, without judgment. What we focus on grows.

**Promoting gratitude with infants:** Because gratitude isn't a thing in infancy, we begin by *modeling* gratitude. Name three things that give you delight about your baby.

**Promoting gratitude with toddlers:** Start going on gratitude walks and sharing what you're thankful for. You might say, "I'm so glad this flower is blooming." If your toddler expresses delight in a puddle, name the feeling: "You're feeling *grateful* for this fun puddle."

**Promoting gratitude with preschoolers:** Start doing a "rose, bud, and thorn" practice at the dinner table or wherever your family gathers. A team exercise born in the Design Thinking community, "rose, bud, and thorn" has become a popular way for families to connect.

In the exercise, each family member shares one thing they're grateful for that happened that day (that's the rose), one thing they didn't like so much (that's the thorn), and one thing they're looking forward to (that's the bud). One of the parents I work with likes to add a feather—something that made them laugh. This practice can help children and adults hunt for the good stuff without denying that, sure, there are going to be thorns in life, too. We're allowed to be grateful even as we feel the whole range of emotions that humans experience.

**Promoting gratitude with elementary-age kids:** When kids are in elementary school, add a family gratitude journal to the mix. One to three times a week, have each family member note what they're grateful for. Start an allowance jar and have kids divide their money among give, save, and spend. Giving bolsters the giver's, as well as the receiver's, sense of gratefulness.

**Promoting gratitude with adolescents:** Continue having family conversations about gratitude, whether it's with any of the strategies just mentioned, or other regular expressions of gratitude you experience in your daily life. Have tweens choose a local community-service project and commit to giving back.

## Q & A Session

**Question:** I took my seventh-grade daughter to the Grand Canyon and all she could talk about was how excited she was to go home, because she knew her grandmother had sent her new clothes for the holidays. I told her she was being ungrateful and that she didn't deserve the trip. We fought the whole plane ride home. Is she going to be a selfish ingrate all her life?

**Answer:** You're not alone. And no, a middle-schooler being a middle-schooler on vacation doesn't predict her future attitude of gratitude. So many family vacations bring up these dynamics and feelings. If you've planned a once-in-a-lifetime vacation and your child says their favorite thing about the day was ice cream, or if they're just excited to get home, the impulse is to yell, "I just spent all this time and money and we had this amazing day; how can you not be happy?" The truth is that kids don't yet know that life is short and experiences like going to the Grand Canyon with their mother are precious. They're not supposed to know that yet. Next time, try saying something like, "Listen, I love you (**Relationships**). I know you're excited about your new clothes. Here is where I'm coming from: I planned this trip. It wasn't easy to get off work and pay for it all. This is very special to me. I get why you don't value it the way I do, but I'm asking you to table the discussion about your new clothes until we leave and bring your attention back to where we are" (**Rules**).

### A Is for Autonomy

Sonja came to me stressed out and bone-tired, with too much on her plate. A single mother of three, she got up at 5 a.m. to start making her kids' breakfasts and lunches, and she didn't stop providing for them until the last kid's homework was done and checked, late in the evening.

Sonja was a good mother by anyone's standards, but one of the first things we did was to sit down and look at *what the kids could be doing for themselves*, without her support. Sonja realized that part of her drive to do so much for her three-, seven-, and ten-year-olds came from a feeling of guilt that they didn't have a second parent. Like all of us, Sonja loved her kids and wanted them to feel cared for, but the science shows us that when we do everything for our children, we actually remove their opportunity to become self-sufficient.

It may seem obvious that a child's sense that they're able to use their own skills, thoughts, feelings, and actions to get along in the world builds resilience, but today's kids are less autonomous than ever before. When a kid can carry a twig, let them carry that twig. Let children do for themselves what they can do for themselves. Provide support so that they don't fall down too hard, but don't give so much support that they don't have the chance to practice standing up on their own.

Guide and encourage kids to do things they can *almost* do. Russian psychologist Lev Vygotsky first theorized that kids learn best in a "zone of proximal development," the just-right zone where children best learn new things, defined as the space between what a child can do without assistance and what they can do with adult guidance or in collaboration with more advanced peers.

## Help Kids Build on Skills They Already Have

Let kids do for themselves what they can already do, guide and encourage kids to do things they can almost do, and teach and model things they can't yet do. If your preschooler can independently do a twelve-piece puzzle, let them do it themself. Guide and encourage them to a twenty-four-piece puzzle with your presence. Make a point of telling and showing them that you trust them.

To teach and model something your child can't yet do for themself, try these steps:

1.  Show, don't just tell, your child how to do the task—this means that you do the task while giving a verbal narration as you do it.

2.  Do the task together.

3.  Let your child show you how they do it.

4.  Pass the torch of ownership of that task to your child.

Of course, there will be things kids truly *can't* do for themselves, whether the holdup is developmental or cultural. Sending a six-year-old to the grocery store to do the family shopping, for example, would be jumping the gun in most communities. So, teach and model what children can't yet do for themselves. When your child says, "I can't do it," gently remind them, "you can't do it *yet*."

## Supporting Autonomy

**Supporting autonomy with infants:** When babies are engaged in tummy play, activate that zone of proximal development by putting a toy *almost* out of reach.

**Supporting autonomy with toddlers:** When toddlers get dressed, encourage them to stretch their skills. You might help them get their head through the shirt, but let them get their arms in by themselves. When you're reading to them, let them turn the page. When they're sad, acknowledge their feelings and remind them that you're confident they can get through it.

**Supporting autonomy with elementary-age kids:** School-age kids can start packing their own lunch. Remember, as with any new task, no matter how old the kids are when they start doing it, it's ideal to walk them through that zone of proximal development the first time or first few times. Show your child how to do the task, do the task together, let your child show you how they do it, and finally tell your child they've got it.

**Supporting autonomy with adolescents:** When tweens have multistep projects for school or work, help them develop a plan. You don't need to set the plan, but you can sit down with them and ask, "What is your plan to break this down? What are the steps you need to take?" Then you can talk them through it. As kids get older, you can just say, "Show me your plan." When they get even older you can say, "I noticed you had a plan. I see that you have this under control." Or, "I see that you're struggling—What would help you to get back on track?"

### M Is for Motivation

When and why do you do your best? Parents come to me all the time, concerned that their kids aren't motivated in school or don't want to do extracurricular activities that they do seem to enjoy most of the time. Here's what I tell them: It's natural for human motivation to ebb and flow between intrinsic and extrinsic motivations. And let's face it— some days we just have to get through our tasks.

I love my job. I get to teach child development, interview brilliant people, and guide and problem-solve with great parents every day. Still, sometimes I'd rather binge-watch *Fleabag*. Sometimes I'm intrinsically motivated. (I got to interview Professor Alan Sroufe again today, and I literally jumped out of bed when I opened my eyes.) Other times I need to engage in extrinsic motivation. I might want to go to the beach, but I tell myself, *Aliza, finish this chapter today, and as a reward, we'll go to the beach in the morning.*

We all wish our kids approached every single task in front of them with intrinsic motivation that just mystically bursts forth from their little heart, but the truth is that if our children are going to grow into successful adults, they're going to have to learn to balance intrinsic and extrinsic motivations, and they'll even do well to learn how to turn those on and off at will.

Motivational behavior is regulated by chemicals in our brains, by our environments, by the motivation levels in the people we hang out with, by the resources we have access to, and by the way we feel when we wake up each morning to face the day. Dr. Angela Duckworth, professor of psychology at the University of Pennsylvania, defines *grit* as living life like it's a marathon, not a sprint. Looking at commonalities among high performers in various fields, Duckworth notes that it comes down to passion and perseverance. She emphasizes the importance of intrinsic motivation, noting, "It's really about being motivated from interest and from values, to search for truth and curiosity. So that's my recommendation for people who would like to be a little grittier: Understand that you're motivated by external and internal factors. I really think the things that come from inside you are the ones that keep you at something consistently for a long time."

Motivation is, of course, key in whether children develop into the kinds of adults who can meet their goals, but some aspects of instilling motivation may seem counterintuitive. When we look at achievement motivation, most people tend to put in the effort to study or prepare for two different reasons: mastery of the material or performance.

If you study hard in geometry, for example, either you want to get better at geometry or you want a good grade—or some combination of those two things. A 2011 study by psychology professors Kou Murayama and Andrew J. Elliot asked participants to engage in a problem-solving task. Some of the participants were told that the goal was to develop their cognitive ability; others were told the goal was to show they could do it better than the other people in the study. Researchers then gave the participants a surprise memory test. The second group—those whose goal was to perform competitively—showed better memory on the immediate test. But when all the participants' memories were assessed again a week later, it was the ones who'd aimed to get smarter who managed to retain more. So, yes, cramming works in the short term, but we need a deeper motivation if we want to master something in the long term.

When looking at performance motivation, researchers break it down further and look at what they call performance-approach goals like, "My goal is to do better than the rest of these suckers," and performance-avoidance goals where it's more like, "I just don't want to do worse than my best friend." Research suggests that the performance-approach mindset has more of an impact than the performance-avoidance mode, but overall competition ignites a pretty complicated set of internal responses, and it doesn't bring a consistent motivational benefit.

What does impact motivation is what's called a "growth mindset." More than thirty years ago, psychologist Carol Dweck and her colleagues got interested in middle-school students' attitudes about failure. They noticed that some students rebounded, while others seemed devastated by even small setbacks. After studying the behavior of thousands of children, Dr. Dweck coined the terms "fixed mindset" and "growth mindset" to describe the underlying beliefs people have about learning and intelligence. When students believe they can get smarter, they understand that effort is what pushes them closer to their goal. Just understanding this, kids put in extra time and effort, and that leads to higher achievement.

Imagining a future in which we've met our goals also impacts motivation. In a recent study, researchers at the University of Minnesota gave preschoolers three marbles and showed them three games they could play with the marbles. They reminded the kids not to use up all their marbles for the first game, because then they wouldn't have any marbles left for the second game. Eighty percent of the four-year-olds in the study didn't have the self-control to save any marbles.

Then researchers did something else through pretend play. They offered the kids storyboards with little felt representations of themselves, their parents, the marbles, and the marble games, and invited the children to imagine their future selves. What would it feel like to have saved the marbles? The kids who were able to imagine a future of happily saved marbles made it happen. They saved their marbles.

Researchers also tried a negative version of the same future-self pretend play. They asked the kids to imagine how they would feel if they didn't save their marbles. Would they be sad? The kids who were able to reflect on the negative outcome of not saving their marbles saved more marbles than the kids given no future-reflection exercise, but they didn't save as many marbles as the kids who had made a positive association with all this marble saving.

When we reflect and think, *I don't like how that feels when I don't have any marbles,* we're more likely to save our marbles. But not as likely as the kids who imagined the positive version. In both cases, the children reflected on the fact that they had a choice in the matter and some agency to create their own futures.

---

### Props Can Help with Future Reflection

You can adapt future reflection pretend play for kids of any age (see page 38). Use dolls or storyboards to help little kids imagine their future selves after having shared their toys with a friend. Use drawing to help school-age kids imagine a future in which they've engaged with their schoolwork. Show tweens how you yourself use visualizations of the future to make choices.

---

## Supporting Motivation

**Supporting motivation with infants:** When you're interacting with your baby, notice what they pay attention to and follow their lead. This supports internal motivation by allowing children to find the things they're interested in, rather than the things their parents or others might want them to be interested in. Pay attention to your baby's eyes. What they're looking at is what they're attending to.

**Supporting motivation with toddlers:** Play is intrinsically motivating, presenting opportunities for new experiences and requiring active engagement. Play alongside your child. Notice when they make that block tower and how they engage with the task of trying not to let it fall down. You can say something like "Look at you; you are figuring out that having more blocks on the bottom of the tower than on the top is helping it stay up!" What other motivating factors do you notice in your child's play?

**Supporting motivation with preschoolers:** Using the framework of imagination and pretend play, you can create your own opportunities to practice and model positive associations with motivation. You can say, "I'm feeling pretty cozy inside right now, but I know I always feel better after a walk, so I'm going to push myself to get up!" Use puppets or other pretend-play toys to play with kids and help them envision their future selves having a fun time with their baby brother instead of clocking him with the wooden train.

**Supporting motivation with elementary-age kids:** Show children how to set achievable goals and how to break big tasks into smaller, more manageable steps. For example, if your child has a science project due at the end of the month, help them identify steps such as coming up with an idea, doing research, developing a testable question, designing and conducting the experiment, examining the results, and communicating their experiment results in a teachable way that works for the assignment. When kids feel overwhelmed, that can train their neurotransmitters to motivate *away* from wanting to work hard, because they can feel like their efforts are futile. When kids can see their progress in a more step-by-step way, that builds the drive to keep on achieving.

**Supporting motivation with early adolescents:** During the tween years, a child's motivation system can become increasingly influenced by peers and the reward of social acceptance, as well as exploratory learning. Support kids with guardrails and limits. When it comes to schoolwork and other responsibilities, remember that sometimes our kids just aren't going to be feeling the work they have to do. Instead of insisting that the only good motivation is intrinsic motivation, normalize strategies for just getting through things sometimes. Show and teach your child to set a timer for twenty minutes and to reward themselves with five-minute breaks in between.

### E Is for Empathy

> *Compassion is not a relationship between the healer and the wounded. It's a relationship between equals.*

—PEMA CHÖDRÖN, *THE PLACES THAT SCARE YOU*

Harvard University recently named empathy as the top employability factor. In a world where many of our children will grow up to do jobs that haven't even been invented yet, empathy is a timeless skill we can bank on. Can an employee step into their client's shoes? Can they anticipate what their coworkers might need? Your child's future employer can probably teach them to program a robot when the time comes, but empathy is becoming a prerequisite skill for most jobs.

Here's the best part: empathy is teachable. Young kids are naturally self-centered. You'll see the building blocks of empathy in babies, but don't expect a child to be able to imagine what's going on for another person before about age four. From there, empathy remains a work in progress.

Before you tell your little one, "Eat your spinach! Some kids don't have enough food to eat," know that kids can't be shamed into becoming compassionate. The science shows us that shame actually *reduces* empathy. Telling a kid "You're a bad person" can crumble their sense of themselves, without doing anything to increase their empathy. In fact, empathy—including self-empathy or inner empathy—is the *antidote* to shame. Saying something more like "You're a kind person, but that behavior feels unkind" is a way to emphasize that space between who we are and what we do, and a way to encourage **Reflection** and **Regulation**.

Parents who take the time to point out to kids how good they make other people feel when they're kind and caring allow their kids to begin to *see* themselves as kind and caring—and from that foundation, kids begin to build their own internal moral identities and compasses. So, it's even more impactful to catch our kids being good and saying something like, "When you shared your sand toys with your friend, you were so kind and thoughtful. I bet that made him feel really good."

One beautiful concept in developmental psychology that fascinates me is called "theory of mind." It's a cognitive shift that starts around age four and keeps developing throughout life, if we let it. Simply put, it's what allows us to understand that the mental states of other people are different from our own.

We call it *theory* of mind because none of us can actually know what another person is thinking or feeling, but starting at around age four or five, we typically begin making guesses based on what we do know and can observe. This leap is huge! Watching it develop in our children can even shift fraught interactions into moments of fascination.

There are precursors to this big shift in consciousness that you can watch along the way. When your doctor asks you if your infant is pointing at ten months or twelve months, the reason they're asking is that pointing is a precursor to understanding the perspective of another. By age two, kids may pretend to talk on the phone or pretend to make dinner. They're experimenting with what it's like to be in someone else's shoes.

The next core component tends to emerge in toddlerhood, when kids start to understand intention—and they start to understand that people are motivated by desires. They're focused on themselves at first, but they do start to understand that if they're hungry, they can reach for food or point to food or say, "I'm hungry."

After these precursors of pointing, imitation, and beginning to grasp the concept of intention, the real shift happens. In a famous study that established a typical timeline for theory of mind, an experimenter sat with a child while their mom walked away for a moment, and then they showed the child a crayon box—very recognizable. The experimenter said, "What do you think is inside this box?" The three-year-old said "crayons" because they recognized the box. The experimenter opened the box, and inside there were indeed crayons. "That's right." Then the experimenter showed the child another box of crayons and said, "Let me show you what's inside this box," and it was paper clips.

Now, when the mother started to come back, the experimenter

asked the child, "What do you think she's gonna think is inside this box?" The three-year-old said "paper clips," because a three-year-old doesn't have theory of mind and can't fathom that the knowledge she has is different from the knowledge her mother has. She really thinks, *Well, I know there are paper clips in there, so my mom will know.*

What's so cool is that when the experiment was performed with kids who were four or five years old, when they asked what they thought their mothers would say was inside the box, the four- and five-year-olds said, "crayons." They understood that even though there were paper clips in that crayon box, their mother wouldn't know that. These older kids understood theory of mind.

The exact age attached to theory of mind, like all of child-development research, will vary from child to child, but just understanding that theory of mind is something we all *develop*—not something we're born with—can help us support our kids when they feel confused about other people's behaviors.

So, as you're reading your bedtime books or helping your child understand food preferences, or why they might not be invited to a birthday party, or why somebody might want to play a different game from them, think about theory of mind and how incredibly beautiful it is to watch this development unfold—and to help it along, whether through pretend play, through joint attention (which is just two people paying attention to the same thing, like looking at a page of a book together or watching the rain together), or through talking and communicating about other people's mental states.

As adults, we can start to notice how much theory of mind comes into play in our own daily interactions. We can catch ourselves when we make assumptions about other people's perspectives, including our children's as they grow into their own young people. This can help us in all our relationships and interactions. If we can model a sophisticated capacity for theory of mind, our kids can learn to embody that maturity, too, and develop confidence in the fact that we don't expect them to think just like we do.

### Promoting Empathy

**It starts with you:** Sometimes responding with compassion just means holding a hand and offering a connection, without saying anything at all. Let your kids see you treating others with compassion. Let them experience being treated with compassion by you. Let them see you treat yourself with compassion. Engage your child in a pretend-play scenario in which stuffed animals treat each other with empathy. You can also try doing a "metta meditation." During a traditional metta meditation, you silently recite positive phrases aimed at bolstering friendliness toward yourself and others. Here's a traditional Buddhist metta meditation.

You can start with "I" as the focus, then shift to "you" and picture your child as the person you are saying the "you" to, then try it saying "all beings." With your children, you can do it out loud:

> May I/you/all beings be filled with loving kindness.
> May I/you/all beings be safe from inner and outer dangers.
> May I/you/all beings be well in body and mind.
> May I/you/all beings be at ease and happy.
> May I/you/all beings be safe.
> May I/you/all beings be peaceful.
> May I/you/all beings be healthy.
> May I/you/all beings live with ease.
> May I/you/all beings be free.

**Promoting empathy with infants:** In shifting our focus to our children, we want to be sure we're considering through a developmental lens what they have the capacity to understand. For infants, that means showing them empathy—they are just the receivers at this point. Soothe your baby. Let them experience empathy.

**Promoting empathy with toddlers:** Label your young child's feelings. This is the first step toward emotional fluency. Are they cold, hungry, tired, frustrated? Helping them acknowledge and label feelings can help your child develop perspective-taking skills as they grow.

**Promoting empathy with preschoolers:** Play pretend. Trying on what it's like to be someone else is one of the best ways to develop perspective-taking skills. Encourage your child to play-pretend whenever you can. When explaining to your toddler what you expect of them, you can make a role-playing theater game of how they might do things differently next time, more in alignment with the *Rules* and expectations. Play-pretending with role-playing also activates theory of mind and your child's growing ability to understand that others have beliefs, desires, plans, hopes, information, and intentions that may differ from our own. So, while we can't expect a baby to give a hoot about how others feel, because they can't even conceptualize that others have feelings different from their own, as theory of mind grows through the preschool years, empathy can start to turn on, too. Read with your kids. Point out, wonder aloud, and notice what the characters are experiencing.

**Promoting empathy with elementary-age kids:** Invite your child to think about how someone else feels while empathizing with their own desires. You can say something like, "Did you notice how excited your friend was when you invited them ice skating?" Or, "I know Grandma is looking forward to your call, so let's reach out to her before we go swimming." Invite your child to notice other children's pain, too, saying something like, "It must have really hurt Billy's feelings when those other children called him names; I wonder what we could do to remind him that we care about him."

**Promoting empathy with adolescents:** Hold a weekly family meeting to go over what everyone's needs are for the week.

Encourage reading literary fiction—it helps the reader imagine what it would be like to stand in someone else's shoes.

### S Is for Self-Regulation

Self-regulation gives humans the ability to make choices about how we're going to respond in any given situation. It's what is taking place in that pause between stimulus and response that we talked about in "The Parenting Passcode" section of Chapter 1. We use memory, inhibitory control, and cognitive flexibility to filter distractions and resist impulses that don't align with our values. As parents, self-regulation gives us the ability to make choices about how to respond to our kids. It's that moment when we can punch in our passcode, get in BALANCE, and be the person we want to be. It doesn't mean we're always going to be cool or that we're never going to raise our voice, and it doesn't mean we're always going to have the right answer; but it does mean that we'll be able to formulate our answers with intention, making decisions with our hearts and brains instead of letting our panicked nervous systems make the decisions for us.

My colleague Dr. Phil Zelazo describes self-regulation as that capacity for "conscious goal-directed problem solving." Others talk about regulation as learning to control emotions and stay appropriately steady under stress. Instead of reacting to a playground bully with fear or more bullying, self-regulation allows us to take a step back and consider what might shift the dynamic. This regulation happens on three levels— the emotional, the cognitive, and the behavioral.

Self-regulation is an executive-function–based skill housed in the prefrontal cortex, and it helps us manage our responses to things so we can meet our goals without getting in our own way. Not all stress is negative, and not all reactivity to stress is negative, but toxic stress can hijack the development of self-regulation. When we're stressed out, we're more likely to get swept away and make mistakes. So, self-regulation is both more challenging and more important when we're at our wits' end.

The human prefrontal cortex is not fully developed until sometime between the ages of eighteen and thirty, so it's important to remember that even when your kids are not particularly stressed out, their prefrontal cortex is still a work in progress.

Now, here's the amazing news: traditional children's games and activities you're probably already doing with your kids—or they're already doing at school—are *all* about building self-regulation. Basically, any activity in which your brain wants to do one thing and you have to train your body to do another is going to build self-regulation. Games build resilience because they help us practice intentional movements when we ask our bodies to work in tandem with our minds.

## Twelve Activities to Build Self-Regulation

With a nod to the Harvard Center on the Developing Child, here are activities that build self-regulation:

1. Board games
2. Simon Says
3. Double Dutch
4. Hokey-pokey
5. Choreographed dance parties
6. Chess
7. Singing in rounds
8. Bingo
9. Memory games
10. Martial arts
11. Musical chairs
12. Rub-your-belly, pat-your-head

It's an amazing bonus that this can happen while simply having fun with our kids, letting them learn a game, or getting exercise. Play opens us up to learning in a way that fear never can. So, let's do the hokey-pokey. The science tells us that, in fact, *that's what it's all about.*

REGULATION EXERCISE

## Teaching Kids to Meditate

There's rich science supporting the fact that mindfulness practices can help kids build self-control, attentiveness, empathy, and respect for family members and classmates—all while reducing stress. School-based mindfulness programs have been shown to help children balance their emotions and reduce bullying. Still, fewer than 2 percent of American kids meditate. Taking the time to teach breath and mindfulness practices to our children will put them in the ninety-eighth percentile! Kids tend to be very much in their bodies, so begin teaching them concrete exercises.

**Balloon in the belly:** Ask your child to picture a giant balloon. To help them picture it vividly, ask "What color is your balloon?" Tell your child or children what color you picture your own balloon. Lead them as you inhale slowly and deeply through your noses, imagining the balloons in your bellies inflating. You can have them stretch out their arms as they see themselves as a giant balloon getting bigger and bigger. When your balloons are completely full, have everyone hold their breath for a moment and then pop the balloon by pointing a finger to each other's bellies and deflate, maybe even falling down as you let all the air out.

**Smell the flower, blow out the candle:** Use your index finger to represent both the flower and the candle. Breathe in through your nose as you "smell the flower" and breathe out through puckered lips as you "blow out the candle."

**Hot cocoa with marshmallows:** Pretend you're sipping hot cocoa with marshmallows on top. Blow just softly enough to gently move the marshmallows without splashing the cocoa.

**Stuffie on your belly:** Put a beloved stuffed animal on your belly and have your child do the same. Watch your bellies go up as you breathe, "helping" the stuffed animal meditate.

**Belly to belly:** Hug and breathe together, belly to belly, for as long as your little one thinks that's fun.

**Eat pretend dessert:** For older kids or kids who are super wiggly, silently pretend you're both eating dessert. Eat the pretend dessert slowly, savoring each bite.

Doing these exercises may feel a little silly at first, but the science shows just how worthwhile these exercises can be.

## CHAPTER 3

# What Makes a Good Human?

## Getting at What Really Matters to You

*We should never separate our values from the ways
in which we encourage our children to become effective
family members, friends, collaborators, and citizens.*

—MADELINE LEVINE, PhD

A generation ago, a few very vocal men with strong opinions co-opted the phrase "family values" and created a campaign to convince the world that kids could thrive in only one type of household. As far as they were concerned, it was the traditional midcentury nuclear family with a stay-at-home mom and a working dad—or bust.

They were wrong, of course. Science tells us that families can blossom in all kinds of circumstances. The question isn't whether your family structure looks exactly like mine, or if you follow a particular religion, or whether your mother-in-law indulges the kids with extra sprinkles on their ice cream on Saturdays. The question is: What do you think makes for a good human? That is, what are your unique family values, and how can you parent in alignment with those values more often than not? Decades of psychological literature and contemporary neuroscience have established that's good enough.

Whenever you have a parenting question, you can take a breath and ask yourself: What do I value? What does this family value? Am I parenting in alignment with my values? That's easier said than done, perhaps, but it gets a lot easier when we sit down and define those values. Getting clear about our own unique family values also makes us less susceptible to passing political campaigns and social-media obsessions that can make us all feel like we'll never quite measure up.

## What Does *Your* Family Value?

We all have values, whether we've articulated them or not. We all bring our individual histories, dreams, and priorities to our parenting. When we don't define our values, however, we and our children are much more susceptible to peer pressure, social-media influence, and the extremes of group thinking. With clear values, we can make decisions with more confidence and clarity.

Defining values as a family also serves to remind us that we don't necessarily have to keep up with the neighbors or do the things they do; we can simply assume they're working within their own value systems and different values are part of what make our communities diverse.

While each family member might have their own individual values as well, it's important as a unit to feel like you're all on the same page. If your child was bullying another child at school, for example, an established core family value of empathy will help you explain to your child why bullying isn't acceptable. So, the first step is to become conscious of your values so you can start living with more intention and integrity. Living with integrity means that you're an integrated person—that, *more often than not*, your actions are aligned with your core values. Your outside and your inside make sense, they are integrated. Family values can evolve and change over time, of course, so we're not talking about setting anything in stone. We're just talking about creating guidelines that make sense to us in a world full of noisy and often conflicting opinions.

Fiona Mendoza came to me, concerned that her son was picking up racial biases at his new school. As we got to talking, I said, "It sounds to me like you really value social justice." Fiona shrugged. "Doesn't everyone?" In fact, not everyone would put that at the top of their value lists; some might prioritize general kindness, academic achievement, or teamwork building.

Spend a couple of days thinking about your parenting values and start writing them down. Ask your spouse or parenting partner to do the same. Do you admire hard work above all else? Kindness? Intelligence? (There are truly no wrong answers here, and that's the reason there is no one-size-fits-all in parenting!)

For some, focusing on three to five values will feel straightforward, but if the exercise sparks a lot of ideas, go with it. Make a long list. Fill a whole page in your journal, if you can. Think about a big choice you made in your life and what drove you to make that choice. Those motivations likely included your values. Think also about three people you admire. What do you appreciate about them? How do you want your children to describe you when they're talking about you to their great-grandchildren? Think about what makes you feel most authentically yourself. Maybe you're in your zone when you're immersed in natural beauty—even if you don't get into the forest very often; if so, jot down "nature." When you think about your goals—your real goals, not your for-other-people goals, your own deep goals—what values align with them?

Once you've brainstormed your values, read over your list and see if you notice any themes. Can you combine any of your values into broader concepts? Do any of your words or phrases represent stepping stones to an even more fundamental ideal? Maybe you've listed military service because you deeply value citizenship or courage. If you've listed college, ask yourself whether you see it as a path to self-sufficiency, as reflective of a love of learning, as simply a networking tool, or just because it's what everyone else in your family has done. Maybe when you mentioned money, you can see that on a deeper level you value comfort or ease. If so, name those underlying values.

Try to distill what's most important to you in three to five key words or phrases. If you're a single mom with an infant, these are your family values. If you've got more than one person over the age of five in your family, it's time for some discussion. Ask your spouse or parenting partner to do the exercise, too. Compare your notes.

A great activity in this regard is to ask your kids to list what five things they would guess each of their parents holds most dear. If you've decided you value honesty, safety, manners, and empathy and your kids think you value money, good grades, and compliance, take that in—without any judgment. This is information. Maybe good grades *do* belong on your list. Or maybe you've just gotten into the habit of sweating the small things that you don't fundamentally care about.

Ask your children to list their own core values. A kindergartener might say they value ice cream—and maybe you can help them broaden that to "yumminess" or even "delight." Older kids might surprise you with their self-reflection.

When everyone in the family has identified their core values and narrowed those down to three to five key words or phrases, have a meeting to compare notes. Where do your core values overlap? Where do you differ? Write each word or phrase from each family member's list on a separate square of paper and start shuffling. See if you can group these values into themes. As you develop your deck of shared values, remember: each of you get to keep your own values, too.

Here's what Fiona's family came up with for their individual values:

**FIONA:** Arts, education, social justice, humor, and financial freedom

**JAIME:** Creativity, competency, fun, happiness, and humility

**SIERRA:** Compassion, respect, honesty, patience, and wonder

**RICKY:** Legos, video games, sharing, science museum, and knock-knock jokes

With these individual lists at hand, they sat down over pizza—a shared value of its own—and debated and discussed, and looked words up in the dictionary, and compromised and moved the cards around until they had distilled all those values into five key guiding principles for their family. Notice that a few of the words came directly from one person's list and others were umbrella concepts they came up with by combining ideas.

| *Individual Values* | *Family Values* |
| --- | --- |
| Social justice, sharing, respect | RESPECT |
| Humor, knock-knock jokes, fun, happiness, Legos, video games | JOY |

| *Individual Values* | *Family Values* |
|---|---|
| Education, competency | LEARNING |
| Humility, compassion, honesty, patience | EMPATHY |
| Arts, creativity, science museum, wonder | WONDER |

With these family values established, it became much easier for Fiona to talk with her son about bias in the context of respect and empathy.

Post your values on the refrigerator, or somewhere else you all can be reminded of them often. For example: Fiona's family at its core believes in respect, joy, learning, empathy, and wonder. As the kids get older and as you as parents grow and change, revisit your family values and allow them to evolve.

### Teaching Values Is a Long Game

Younger children may not be able to take part in the family-values exercise, but you can trust that you're teaching them your values from day one. Teaching children values doesn't happen in a lecture setting. Rather, we model our values for our kids and talk about all the opportunities life gives us to live our values every day. By doing this *more often than not*, we're engaging in the work of raising great humans.

Here's how to instill values:

1.  Define the value for yourself. If kindness is on your list of values, consider the behaviors that define being kind. What does it feel like inside when you exhibit kindness? Spend a few moments exploring each of your core family values.

2.  Support perspective-taking skills. Activities like reading books about people who are different from you and puppet-play require you to look at issues and events from

someone else's point of view. This helps children develop the ability to act with kindness, generosity, and other core values. These skills take time to develop, but as parents we can support them in everyday ways. What would Mr. Frog Puppet think about that?

3.  Have conversations about everything and anything. Your children are listening and learning your values, thoughts, and feelings—even if you're struggling to communicate them. Behaving in alignment with your values *more often than not*, and having conversations about anything and everything as your children grow up, is the slow and steady path to imparting your values.

4.  Normalize the mistakes. We all forget our own values sometimes. We snap at a friend because we're tired. We cut in line because we momentarily think we're the only person with someplace to go. We lose our mind over a disappointing grade when we've been bragging that we don't care about external validation. When you do something that goes against a core value, get in the habit of noticing it, verbalizing it, and making a **Repair** if you have the opportunity. Even if a do-over isn't practical, you can say, "Gosh, that wasn't very kind of me, and I value kindness. I'm going to try to breathe before I blurt next time." **Repair** doesn't necessarily have to be an apology. Sometimes **Repair** is simply a touch of the hand, a shared laugh, or a gesture of reconnection.

All this said, you don't have to become a *Saturday Night Live* skit of "teachable moments." It's 100 percent possible to be yourself, teach your children your values, and do both without a script. In fact, *please* do both without a script!

## REFLECTION EXERCISE

*What Really Matters to Me?*

Make yourself comfortable and set your timer or mindfulness app for two or five or twenty minutes—whatever amount of time you have. Inhale through your nose for a four count, hold the breath for a six count, and exhale through your mouth, lips slightly puckered, for an eight count. Ask yourself: What really matters to me in my parenting? Allow any answer to bubble up from your body. Notice this answer.

Inhale for another four count, hold the breath for a six count, and exhale, lips slightly puckered, for an eight count. Ask yourself again: What really matters to me? Continue breathing and asking yourself this question until your timer dings or gongs, or does whatever it does. No judgments on the answers that come up. Just notice.

## CHAPTER 4

# Raising Good Parents

*Meet Your Parenting Archetypes*

> *Do you want to model for your child the idea that when*
> *they have kids the rest of their life is over? Is that what you*
> *want your kids to take away from what it's like to be a parent?*

—ROBERT WALDINGER, MD

So much of the expectation of parenting is that we'll shape our children—and to a certain extent we do, by virtue of being their first teacher and most powerful environmental influence. But parent development is at least as important as child development. Even when we think our job is raising good humans, what we're really doing is raising good parents. And parent support sets the stage for mindful parenting.

We become parents when our children come into our lives. Our needs and our way of being in our families and in our larger communities change right along with our kids as they grow. There's a huge motivation for change during the early transition to parenthood, but the parents' development doesn't stop there. As our children grow, the experience of parenting brings with it countless opportunities to get to know ourselves better and to thrive in ways we may never have dreamed of.

*To become a better parent is to become a better person.*

I'd love for everyone to have the motivation to love themselves and practice self-care with or without kids, but there's nothing wrong with using the motivation of parenthood to work on ourselves.

## A Parent's Hierarchy of Needs

Psychologist Abraham Maslow came up with a human "hierarchy of needs" back in the 1940s; the idea is that we need to tend to basic needs before we can build on them. At the bottom of the needs hierarchy and working our way up are physiological needs, then safety, then belonging and love, then social needs or esteem, and finally self-actualization and transcendence.

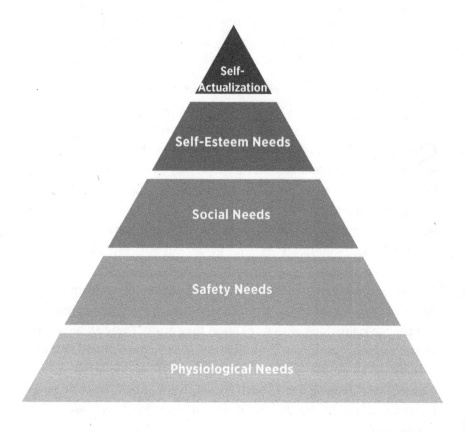

I find it helpful to adapt this theory to focus on a parent's needs, as follows.

**Physiological Needs:** At the base of a parent's hierarchy of needs are our basic survival needs. We need food, water, air, shelter, clothing, heat, and sleep.

**Safety Needs:** When our physiological needs are taken care of, safety takes precedence. Do you feel safe from violence at home? Do you feel safe in your job or secure in your other sources of income? Do you feel stable in your physical and emotional health? We all go through ups and downs in terms of feeling and being safe, but the need is pretty basic and it's okay to prioritize it over other needs.

**Love and Social Belonging Needs:** Parenting can change our relationships, and sometimes even make us feel isolated from old friends, coworkers, or family. Studies show that when parents go through financial stress, depression rates go up—and it's not just because basic needs aren't being met. This stress strains all our relationships, including parent-child relationships. When we're stressed out about providing for our kids, we work more and miss out on our relationships. Of course, those basic needs are fundamental, but we also need to find ways to prioritize our relationships and sense of connectedness and belonging. This is also why, as a society, we need to support parents!

**Self-Esteem Needs:** Feeling inner respect and self-esteem, as well as the respect and esteem of others, may not be as primal as our needs for food, basic safety, and relationships. Because parenting means doing something brand-new as adults, our inevitable mistakes can take a toll on our sense of competence and by extension, our confidence. As parents, we're often focused on helping our kids see themselves as competent and capable learners, but we need to remember to prioritize our own dignity and self-respect, too.

Can you do some small thing each day to underline your own competence as a human and a parenting-learner? Notice when you get better at being patient and take a moment to pat yourself on the back. If you have a partner or even another parent-friend, make a deal with each other to notice when the other one is doing something well.

**Self-Actualization:** At the top of the parenting hierarchy of needs comes self-actualization. We all have to make choices that make sense for our families, and sometimes that's going to mean putting off those flamenco lessons, not surfing as much, or renegotiating our career ambitions. But as we make these compromises, we have to find a balance so that we don't fall into the martyr-mom role. It's like Jung says: "The greatest burden a child must bear is the unlived life of its parents." Oversacrificing our dreams for our children doesn't ultimately do them any favors.

## Who's Caring for the Caregiver?

*If we value our children, we must cherish their parents.*

—JOHN BOWLBY

In their 2019 report *Vibrant and Healthy Kids*, the National Academy of Sciences made the research clear: if we want children to do well, we have to make sure their caregivers are doing well.

This starts with you. How are *you* doing?

---

### Give Yourself a "Love Hormone" Boost

Put your hand on your heart. This is a scientifically established hack for boosting oxytocin, or the "love hormone." While oxytocin is released in a major way during labor, breastfeeding, and sex, the science shows us that we can also activate it with a simple caring touch, even if that touch comes from ourselves. So, remind yourself silently: "*More often than not*, I'm the parent I want to be." Breathe and ask yourself, "Who's parenting me?" It's okay to acknowledge it when you feel like the answer is *no one*. But see if you can add . . . *yet*.

---

The science tells us that it's not a luxury to take care of the primary caregiver—it's a necessity. We're not talking about spa days here, although a massage and facial can be amazing. We're talking about connections. Spending an hour a week with people you can be yourself around, and who can comfort you when you're feeling overwhelmed, can make a world of difference.

Psychologist and professor emerita Dr. Suniya Luthar, who spent decades studying resilience and maternal well-being, identified the "big four" pillars of support we all need: satisfaction with friendships, feeling unconditionally loved, feeling comforted when we're distressed, and having a sense of authenticity in our relationships. (Partner satisfaction had some associations with personal well-being in Luther's research, but interestingly, being married in itself had a negligible impact.)

Let's look at Luther's four pillars of support caregivers need from our relationships and our communities:

**Friendships:** It's not even the quality of our friendships that is super important; it's the frequency of being with people who make us feel like grown-ups and who can remind us that we have our own thoughts and lives, and that we can connect with others. Can you buddy up with some other caregivers and make a weekly date for coffee and conversation while your kids entertain each other? How about a book group? Is there someone you can schedule a regular lunchtime walk with? Regular contact with other people is an essential form of community building, and you don't need to live in the same town as your best friend to reap the benefits.

**Acceptance:** Just like our kids, parents need to experience unconditional acceptance. Do you have people in your life who accept you as you are? Do you accept yourself—physically, personally, professionally? I know it can be complicated, but not feeling accepted can wear on any parent. If you don't feel accepted by the people you spend your time around, try making a list of three contexts where you might find more acceptance. Pick the one that seems most attainable and write down three steps you might take to cultivate this accepting community, group, or individual relationship. Take one step toward that this week.

**Comfort:** Do you feel confident that someone will be there for you when you're stressed out? If not, it's okay to acknowledge that as an unmet need and start strategizing how you might build some relationships of comfort into your life. These comforts can be small and attainable. Which barista makes the best chai latte in your neighborhood? Is there an exercise class that gives you comfort? Prioritize the people or activities that give you comfort when you're feeling stressed.

**Authenticity:** Can you be yourself with people in your family, community, or workplace? It's not always safe and practical to wave our fabulous freak flags, but if you're hiding who you really are, that can take a toll. Prioritize finding at least a few contexts where you feel safe being yourself. Try starting a parent group that meets in person or remotely. Make time for old friends who get you for who you are—even if they aren't parents.

### Prenatal Toxic Stress and Postpartum Depression

Prenatal toxic stress is a huge risk factor for postpartum depression, but we're all susceptible to it to some degree, and it's nothing to be ashamed of. Between 10 and 20 percent of mothers in the general population, and up to 40 percent of those living in poverty or in adverse situations like chronic abuse or violence, suffer from postpartum depression. When pregnant women and new parents experience toxic stress–which can be defined as unrelenting stress, anxiety, and depression–it affects them, as well as their child in utero and any infant at home. If you have any thoughts of harming yourself or your baby, contact your doctor or midwife right away, or go to the emergency room. What you are going through is common, likely has a physical hormonal component, and can be treated.

A common questionnaire to screen for postpartum depression is called the Edinburgh Postpartum Depression Scale. Parents are asked to review their experience just during the past week and to consider whether they've been able to laugh or look forward to things (1) with a sense of joy as much as they always could, (2) a little bit less than usual, (3) definitely less than they used to, or (4) not at all. The scale also asks us to consider if parents are blaming themselves for things that go wrong; feeling anxious, scared, or panicky for no good reason; are having difficult coping; are feeling so sad they have trouble sleeping; are feeling sad or miserable most of the time; feel so sad that they have been crying; or are having thoughts of harming themselves.

Noticing big challenges or changes in more than three of these areas, or moderate challenges or changes in five or more, suggests that the parent may be dealing with minor or major depression. If this is your case, ask your healthcare provider for a formal screening.

If you're experiencing symptoms of postpartum depression, or having thoughts of harming yourself, you're not alone. Contact your healthcare provider. This professional will be able to connect you with the necessary resources to get through this very common and difficult time.

## Tending to Mom Brain—Not What You Think

We joke about it. Forget to put the onions in the onion soup? Mom brain. Spaced out during a morning meeting? Mom brain. It's true enough that interrupted sleep coupled with the sometimes overwhelming demands of mothering can make you forget the small stuff, but recent scientific research shows that the transition to parenthood—for biological as well as nonbiological parents and for caregivers of all genders—is actually associated with brain growth.

When I was finishing school and writing my dissertation with a new baby in the house—okay, occasionally leaving her in her crib while I wrote about attachment—I noticed I had fewer resources to remember things like where my keys were, but I could attend with laser focus to the things that were important to me.

Developmental psychologists have long understood that the first few years of a baby's life are a time of tremendous neuroplasticity—when little humans are particularly open to new experiences and input. It's the reason a baby can adapt to any culture they're born into, learn Chinese, Arabic, or sign language, and figure out how to deal in whatever historical context they find themselves. Neuron and synapse formation and differentiation start in the prenatal stage and continue at high speed through the first few years of life. By the time a kid is six years old, 90 percent of that brain is grown.

The second period of major neuroplasticity in a human's life comes during adolescence. The prefrontal cortex—the part of the brain responsible for decision-making and, you know, not trying to take a selfie with a rabid squirrel—isn't fully formed until sometime between a kid's eighteenth and thirtieth birthdays. This means that your high-schooler who's able on the one hand to rebuild your entire computer system and, on the other hand, decides it's an excellent idea to take Grandma's speedboat for a joy ride, probably isn't a sociopath. She's just going through a natural neural reconstruction period, and she needs a lot of sleep and maybe it's time to discreetly hide the speedboat keys.

Recent brain-imaging research led by Pilyoung Kim and Sarah Enos Watamura, at the University of Denver, identified a third predictable neural growth spurt. It comes with our transition to parenting—and it's not just for biological parents. The act of caregiving itself signals the brain to shift into a third period of immense neuroplasticity. No matter your gender or your relationship with the child in your care, you're shifting into this powerful new phase of potential brain development.

As your reward circuit is being activated by increased levels of oxytocin and dopamine, sensitizing you to focus on infant-related cues, your midbrain literally grows in size. Neuroplasticity and neural changes in the social information circuit of the brain enhance your empathy as well as your ability to self-monitor and self-reflect in support of sensitive caregiving.

Finally, increased activation in the emotion regulation circuit supports your growing ability to handle stress and self-regulate even under stressful circumstances. Comparing images from two to four weeks postpartum and three to four months postpartum, researchers Pilyoung Kim, James F. Leckman, Xin Wang, and James E. Swain noted that increased gray matter in the midbrain of both men and women was associated with positive perceptions of the new baby. So, there's an awesome love-expansion synergy clicking on.

Anything you can do to increase your support system, decrease unnecessary outside stress, and generally give yourself as much breathing room as possible during your transition to parenthood, the more you'll be able to take advantage of this exciting neural opportunity.

### Seven Ways to Engage Your Mom Brain

The following are some suggestions for exploring and utilizing your expanded mom brain.

1. **Delight in your new family member:** Marvel at that baby's toes, their tiny face. Every new human contains a universe. Every time you take a moment to delight, you're building the connections that boost both your baby's brain and your brain.

2. **See the magic in your older kids:** As kids grow, remember that you can consciously reignite that sense of wonder in their unique universe when you need a brain boost. Breathe in through your nose and out through your mouth. Intentionally notice something magical about your child or tween.

3.  **Get comfortable saying no:** If a task is neither enriching to you nor necessary for your family's survival, empower yourself to say no. You don't have to meet up with a work pal who stresses you out, just because she asks you to let her "pick your brain." When you say no to one thing, remind yourself of the space that this no opens up for you—a yes to giving your brain an opportunity to clear out some of the clutter.

4.  **Sleep when your child sleeps:** It's an old adage—much easier said than done, and sometimes infuriatingly unrealistic to hear—but it's also a concept you can expand to fit your actual life. Wherever possible, get in that extra sleep. And not just when your kids are infants. Just like we need to sleep when the baby sleeps, we need to sleep when the school-age kids sleep and sleep when the tweens sleep.

5.  **Chill when your child chills:** If you can't nap when the baby or toddler sleeps, at least lie down and relax on the couch, staying off the phone (unless it's a real point of connection and relaxation for you). As the kids get older, continue to prioritize your own down time. Read when the kids are doing sports. Watch TV when the teenagers are watching TV. When you notice yourself needing a break, resist the cultural script that has caregivers telling themselves they can't stop. If your child wants to take martial arts, instead of using that time to frantically do errands, see if you can find a park nearby where you can do mindful exercise while your child does mindful exercise. Then take your child with you on the errands.

6.  **Delegate:** If you have a spouse, parenting partner, or visitor, have them feed the baby on the night or morning shift, so you can get some much-needed rest. If you're breastfeeding, pump an extra bottle so you can get those additional couple of hours of sleep. As your children grow,

keep finding ways to delegate. Delegating gives others purpose. It's generous. Have the elementary-age kids get themselves dressed. Have the middle-schoolers make their own breakfasts—and yours, too, while they're at it. If you really struggle with delegating and saying no, remind yourself of what you're saying yes to in that moment— saying yes to something or someone else, including your own self-care, is something you can feel good about. Your brain will thank you.

7. **Get to know your brain and what it needs:** Our brains don't ever stop changing. If you're exhausted or stressed, your brain might feel slow. When you're learning new skills, that might make it temporarily harder to access other skills. If you're a caregiver approaching perimeno- pause, know that new changes are happening in your brain. While this can be frustrating, you can also take it as a new opportunity to have compassion for your children's self-regulatory challenges, to practice radical self-compassion, and to keep breathing.

    Remember: in through the nose, out through the mouth. You can say: "I'm getting to know my brain." At different times, your brain may have different needs. You may need to make lists if you're going through a forgetful time. You may need to talk to your doctor if brain changes are getting in the way of your functioning.

## Don't Believe the Myth of the "Parent Gut"

Often people will tell new parents "Trust your instincts" or "Go with your gut," and that's fantastic when it takes the pressure off. But our gut isn't always available or clear. Please don't ever think you're lacking if becoming a parent didn't give you an instant "mom gut" that knows what to do all the time.

The voices that tell us we'll always be able to intuit what's right for our kids can be toxic. It's great to tell parents "You've got this," because we do "got this" to some extent, but it's developmentally appropriate for you *not* to know what to do when you're trying something new—like parenting. And if you were raised in the context of unhealthy attachments, or trauma or screaming or abuse, or any cycle you intend to break, your instincts may lead you to a confused place; your nervous system has been wired to respond in ways that don't serve you.

Experience is the way we develop our "gut" instincts, and we all lack experience when we first become parents.

There's nothing wrong with you. You just need to give yourself the information and support to rewire your nervous system. If you had a traumatic childhood, what feels like instinct may actually represent a trauma response. Even if your background is more the garden variety not-quite-what-you-want-to-repeat, most of us need to build and bolster healthy instincts as we continue to grow up as adults. We can become more conscious of what's behind some of our impulses, discover the underlying reasons for some of the subpersonalities we're ashamed of, and develop practices that help align our actions with our ever-evolving values.

---

### Practice Self-Compassion

Start speaking to yourself the way you hope your child will speak to themselves. When you practice self-compassion and compassion for others, it will help your kids use that same voice.

Next time you catch yourself berating yourself, try a new perspective. Say, "Today, I did the best I could and even if it wasn't what I had hoped for, I have a new chance tomorrow." Or say, "I wonder what is going on for me that this was so challenging? What do I need to better support me?"

---

### Reparenting Ourselves

To parent with intention, each of us has to come to terms with the way we grew up. Some of the parents I work with find renewed empathy for their own parents when they have kids of their own, but for many of us it's more complicated than that. Think about body image, for example. For our kids' sake, if for nothing else, a beach body needs to be whatever body we bring to the beach. Having kids who you hope will grow up comfortable in their skin, knowing that bodies are tools rather than objects, is a great motivator to put on that bathing suit and hit the sand, pushing through whatever messages you may have gotten about what a beach body *should* look like.

Many of us hope to redraw our parenting blueprints in some way. Psychologist Dr. Richard Schwartz developed one framework for thinking about how our past impacts our present; he calls it the Internal Family Systems model. It's getting a lot of attention right now, so let's try to understand this model.

Basically, this model sees each of us as having subpersonalities, or "families," in our heads, just like in the movie *Inside Out*. These subpersonalities are informed by all our experiences, including the wounded parts of ourselves and painful emotions like anger and shame.

Our subpersonalities are often in conflict with each other and with our *core self*—the balanced, confident, compassionate "best self" that all of us have at our center. If we behave in a way we're not proud of, that doesn't mean we're bad people, or "bad parents"; it just means that in a moment of stress or dysregulation, one of our subpersonalities who isn't a good babysitter took over.

When one internal voice says "Go for it!" and another says "Why even try?" that is not to say that we've got a split personality; it's that we're experiencing normal parts of ourselves that have evolved to take on specific roles in our decision-making process. According to Schwartz, our internal voices can be categorized loosely in three groups. The first group is our *internal managers*, whose role it is to keep us organized and safe. On good days, they do just that. But when they get out of hand, they can push us toward perfectionism or even keep us from doing cool things out of fear of risk-taking.

The next group of internal voices is our *internal exiles*, typically the parts of ourselves that have experienced trauma. Just like anybody who doesn't get enough attention, they tend to scream louder. When we try to silence these parts of ourselves without acknowledging their existence and their hurt, they can become extreme, overriding our internal managers.

The third group of internal voices is the *internal firefighters*. You can be pretty sure your firefighters aren't just springing into action when needed but, rather, are getting out of hand when you notice yourself putting out emotional fires at any cost—often even starting "backfires" with addictive, unhealthy, or unhelpful behavior.

Recognizing and accepting these parts of ourselves and the realities of our histories are key to healing and being able to parent from a place of balance—of being the best version of ourselves *more often than not.*

## Make Friends with Your Inner Multitudes

Just as it's important to remember that all feelings are welcome (and all behaviors are not), the Internal Family Systems model encourages us to remind our inner voices that all *parts* are welcome, even when all behaviors are not.

We can make friends with even the most shameful-seeming parts of ourselves. A helpful exercise here is to sit down with some time, some calm, and a notebook. This is not so much a goal-oriented exercise as one in which you build your **Reflection** muscles. Remember: **Reflection** isn't self-indulgent; it's one of the Five Rs.

Let's say you've read some new research on yelling, and you've decided that you want to break that cycle in your own family. That's your manager making that decision. But let's say yelling is wired into your experience of how authorities in your family communicated with you. In making the decision not to yell, that decision essentially exiles your inner yeller. The key here is not to approach any of these parts of yourself as "bad" or even "irresponsible" but, rather, as a neutral part of yourself whose feelings and survival skills are welcome but whose go-to behaviors might not be welcome anymore.

The Internal Family Systems model tells us that all these inner voices are normal, and that we can make huge steps toward healing and integration by acknowledging them, accepting them, and even having conversations with them. This way, you're not approaching the particular internal voice as bad. You can picture the exiled part of yourself believing that yelling is the only way to get the results you're looking for. This part of you isn't bad; it may simply have learned through trauma that violence is a reasonable way to communicate disappointment. Alternatively, if you're focusing on shopping behavior, remember that this part of you isn't bad, or even irresponsible; it's just a firefighter trying to save you from another emotional hardship.

### Explore Your Inner Parts

Here's a process to experiment with if you're interested in working with one or more of your internal parts, as embodied in the Internal Family Systems model. Pick one of the parts and walk through these steps, talking to that part as if it were a whole person:

1. Say—out loud if you can—"If you overwhelm me, I'm not going to be able to help you." This reminds these parts of yourself that if they keep overriding your internal managers, you're going to continue to have a hard time integrating them.

2. Say the following, as a request: "Please just sit here with me without trying to take over. When you're ready, let me know who you are, what you're trying to protect us from, what your positive intent is, or what you're afraid of, and I'll write that down." This lets your inner yeller or inner shopping maven know that you're willing to accept them, and they don't have to act out so much to get your attention. For instance, maybe your inner yeller is afraid that there is shame associated with children who don't quickly comply. Maybe your inner shopper hopes that new business shoes will make you feel more in charge.

3.  Make note of all the parts you have noticed during this exercise and what, if anything, they had to say to you. If you tend to be a visual thinker, you may even find it helpful to draw little pictures of an internal manager, an internal exile, and an internal firefighter. Write little captions to let each of them express what they're afraid of, how they feel about you as a whole, or what they need to feel safe. (If this feels too goofy, don't do it! Definitely not required.)

Make notes about what you notice when you acknowledge and even converse with these inner parts of yourself. You don't have to "do" anything with these notes, but notice as you return to them from time to time whether your internal parts are resorting to fewer drastic act-outs as you begin to engage with them and show your acceptance and your willingness to work with them in more loving and *regulated* ways.

## Meet Your Parenting Archetypes

A similar way of reflecting on the multitudes we contain comes to us from the Swiss psychiatrist Carl Jung. He conceptualized the personality as consisting of our persona, our shadow, our anima/animus, and our true self. If we adapt his thinking to focus on ourselves as parents, we might view our personal archetypes as being a parenting persona, a parenting shadow (which mirrors the Internal Family Systems model of the internal exile), a parenting anima/animus, and our parenting "true selves" (which aligns with the Internal Family Systems model of core self).

It's not always safe or practical to let our weird "true selves" shine in a public context that may or may not accept a mother who likes to sing songs from *Hamilton* at the top of her lungs while dancing on the see-saw, but the more integrated we can become as parents, the healthier we're going to feel emotionally, and the more available we're going to be to ourselves, our children, and the other important people in our lives. But let's consider the other archetypes.

**Parenting persona:** Our parenting persona is the parent we are out in the world. Are you stricter or more lax when you're in public with your kids? Do you show the neighbors a perfectly put together family at the same time you feel like a chaotic mess on the inside? Do you ham up imperfections that aren't even real, just so no one will feel intimidated? No judgment. Just reflect.

**Parenting shadow:** Our parenting shadow represents the parts of ourselves we're ashamed of but can't seem to shake. Were you raised being told that children should be seen and not heard? Do you have a fear of carbs that you don't want to pass down to your kids? When your brain goes to your shadow parent, try putting your hand on your heart and sending a silent message to yourself that says, *I accept the part of myself that feels this way.* You don't have to act on your shadow urges in order to accept them as part of who you are.

**Parenting anima and animus:** Most of us bring our personal ideas, cultural norms, and family experience of gender roles to our parenting. What would you bring to your parenting if you identified as another gender? Is there anything you'd like to do with your kids that you feel aren't your cultural or gender role? What would happen if you did them anyway? Again, no judgments or criticisms here—just reflect.

## Q & A Session

Now, imagine what it would look like to integrate all your parenting personalities. How often do you honor your persona, your shadow, and your anima/animus as accepted parts of the whole of who you are? Consider setting an intention to accept all of who you are.

**Question:** I grew up in a household that was really cold, and to this day I'm just not a hugger. I don't want to pass on that standoffishness to my kids. Is there any way for me to change at this point in my life?

**Answer:** If you wish you'd had more physical connection, but in your body you don't feel like an affectionate person because it just wasn't how you were raised, you can build that by starting to do different things with your body that are a little uncomfortable. Take a dance lesson (**Reflection**). You don't have to force yourself to become an instant hugger, but practice being a little bit out of your comfort zone (**Regulation**). As you get more comfortable in those uncomfortable body spaces, you can also slowly stretch yourself to demonstrate your warmth with more physicality.

## Let's Be Done with the Martyr Archetype

*The greatest burden a child must bear*
*is the unlived life of its parents.*

—CARL JUNG

As a parent, you're never doing something wrong if you genuinely love showing up for your child. There's tremendous value in supporting your kids and cheering them on when they're doing something they love. It's certainly a great pleasure of mine! But it's so important to find the balance between being supportive of our kids and holding onto the things that give our own lives meaning, purpose, and joy. When a sacrifice isn't serving the parents or the children, even though it may feel like it is, we're shifting into the martyr archetype.

When you're always at every practice and every game, or doing every carpool, it's okay to check in with yourself with a sense of curiosity: Is this really serving me or my child? Does this make me feel like I'm winning at parenting?

Ask yourself: Am I sacrificing because I've got my heart set on becoming that "perfect" parent? Am I acting based on what everyone else seems to agree is worthwhile, or because I think it's worthwhile? Is there room for my own needs amid the responsibilities I have to my family? Have I deferred my interests and my own nonparenting life in order to nail parenting? Do I worry that my poor kid is feeling neglected if I don't attend every tournament, or will miss out if I don't get us to every social activity? Am I trying so hard to do the opposite of what my parents did that I'm heading into extreme parenting territory? Do I worry that choosing to do something that fills my own tank makes me selfish?

Contemporary parents have become uniquely focused on every whim, need, and event in their children's lives. It can be confusing when experts (including myself) highlight the power of being a sensitive parent—and it can be easy to sometimes confuse that sensitivity of care with doing everything we can to make sure our children never feel disappointed in us. But it can be helpful to reframe this and think about the ways our children see us sacrificing our own needs or time. Does one parent do it more than the other? Is this what we want to model for our children?

Once, when one of my daughters made a misstep at school, she asked if I was going to lose my job because she wasn't "perfect." My brain nearly exploded. My *child* felt pressure to be perfect because she viewed my job to be about being perfect at raising a perfect kid. Oh, boy. Her observation helped me shift my thinking. Consider how much pressure our kids might feel to be the center of our universe! To feel all their successes and failures are so important to us—that *our* sense of self is tied to *their* performance?

Now, I try to check in with myself about all these things when I make decisions in my day-to-day life. I actively think about how I can model for my daughters what it is to be a friend, a citizen, part of a family, and part of a community. When I'm satisfied with my own life, I can be present for my girls in a different way. I show them that although they are always my most important priority, they're not my *only* priority. I show them that they can work hard at practice without me as an audience, that they can feel good about themselves because they're proud of the work they did, and that they get to tell me all about it when we come together. And sure—do I need to check in regularly to be certain that I'm making choices that honor when it really does matter for me to show up? Yes.

We need to nurture ourselves in order to be the parents we want our kids to have. We need to do the things we love. We model for our families what it means to spend our time in ways that feel good. We help our children gain new skills, independence, and understanding of the many aspects of our lives that really matter. But we also need to make mistakes, forgive ourselves, and make another try. If we only have today, we have to make the most of it.

---

## Good Morning, I Love You

Psychology professor Shauna Shapiro encourages a practice of greeting ourselves each day with, "Good morning [insert your own name], I love you."

Surely that's how we hope our children will feel about themselves, so let's all start modeling it ourselves–and if our kids catch us doing it, all the better. Practicing this statement over and over wires it into your consciousness. Put your hand on your heart and say it with me: "Good morning [or afternoon or evening], I love you."

---

## Q & A Session

**Question:** It's always at bedtime when my son wants to tell me everything that happened at school and every little detail of some movie he watched. I want to be there for the connection, but sometimes I'm just so tired. And it's bedtime!

**Answer:** On the nights when you have the energy, go ahead and snuggle and listen to all the tales of the day (***Relationship***). On the nights when you are exhausted, it's okay to tell him it's time to cuddle and just tell you one thing that happened at school and that you look forward to hearing the rest in the morning. Being connected to your child doesn't mean you have to listen to the entire day's reenactment. Let's face it, it's often when we do push ourselves past the point of exhaustion that we end up snapping at our kids and feeling our worst. And while that's not the end of the world, getting in the habit of gently winding things down before you get frustrated is key (**Regulation**).

## REFLECTION EXERCISE

### Dream up Your Own Unicorn Space

Most parents I talk to wouldn't hesitate to give their kids a space to explore their interests—whether they want to learn how to bake cakes or try their hand at pottery—but too often when I ask parents about their own space for projects for creative growth, they look at me blankly.

*Unicorn Space* author Eve Rodsky suggests that each of us create space in our lives for pleasure, dreams, and meaningful activities that bring us joy and purpose. I find this idea especially beneficial to parents. We don't hesitate to create unicorn spaces for our children, but we need our own unicorn spaces, too. It's so easy to put our own needs last, to forgo even taking time for ourselves. Sometimes this is out of guilt; other times it's about thinking we just don't have the energy or it's just downright impractical. But self-care is an imperative for being effective parents. As Eve Rodsky reminds us, "A unicorn space is mythical. It doesn't exist until we reclaim it. It's a practice of curiosity, connection with others, and completion."

Do you have a unicorn space for yourself? If not, imagine what one might look like. What brings you joy? What are you curious about? When you're burned out, you feel depleted, you feel disconnected and ineffective. But when you find respite from this burnout, you feel more hopeful and sense more integration between what you long for and how you live your life.

I remember being asked what my hobbies were when my girls were quite young. I was so pissed! I was like, "What? Now, on top of everything else, I'm expected to also have a hobby?" So, this isn't about a hobby. Hobbies sounds so voluntary and extra. No, this is about making sure there is a good fit between the life you live and who you are on the inside.

So, sit someplace comfortable and take a few mindful breaths. Close your eyes. Envision what your own unicorn space would look like. If you feel inspired after this exercise, jot down a few action steps you might take to carve out that space to honor your own curiosity and pleasure.

## CHAPTER 5

# Foundations for Strong Relationships

## *Setting the Stage for Secure Attachment*

*There is no development without relationships.*

—JACK SHONKOFF, MD

The first of the five Rs, **Relationships** begin with our primary attachment relationship. All kids need an attachment relationship with at least one caregiver that leads them to believe this person—despite their human limitations and the inevitable ruptures and **Repairs** any relationship will go through—can provide a safe and predictable base for meeting their needs.

As we become increasingly sensitive caregivers with practice—and with "serve and return," the process talked about in Chapter 1—we also notice and adjust our behavior and our children's environments to improve what psychologists call "goodness of fit," which basically means that we accept our children for who they are and we meet them where they are, *more often than not*. So, let's talk about these basics.

## Demystifying Secure Attachment

*Life is best organized as a series of
daring ventures from a secure base.*

—JOHN BOWLBY

The next thing kids need after nutrition and sleep is an attachment Relationship with at least one caring adult who they feel like they can count on *more often than not.* The science behind this is beautiful and consistent, but there's a lot of misinformation out there, so I want to spend some time going over the misunderstandings and then delving into the real science.

The most important points to remember are these: Attachment is a **Relationship**. It's dynamic and it can be **Repaired**. And it doesn't depend on specific procedural practices. Babies throughout history, in all kinds of contexts, have developed secure attachment relationships, and your baby or child can, too.

### Secure Attachment Doesn't Depend on "Attachment Parenting"

Although the word *attachment* is often used as shorthand for the attachment relationship, it's important to remember that the term in developmental psychology does refer to the unique and dynamic **Relationship** between two people. And in this field, relationships aren't considered optional—they're the first of my Five Rs that lead to Resilience.

Secure attachment isn't about baby wearing or breastfeeding; it's about a child's deep and abiding confidence in their parent's availability and responsiveness. So, it's not co-sleeping that matters for attachment but, rather, the fact that a baby is sleeping well and having quality interactions when they are awake. It's not the skin-to-skin contact—though it's always nice to allow time for that with your newborn, if it suits you—but, rather, the caregiver's attunement to the relationship.

"Attachment parenting" (see Chapter 1 regarding this theory) has never been scientifically linked to the development of a secure attachment. Many of Dr. Sears's recommendations may be fine for you and your baby, even positive. But the rigidity of his approach and its champions leaves many parents feeling lost and isolated. For example, Dr. Sears has suggested that babies must have constant physical attachment. Unfortunately, this has created a generation of parents worried that putting a baby down to take a shower was harmful. He has said nothing about reading baby's cues or seeing when and how they like to be held, or when physical contact may not be ideal. He also has spoken fervently about the need for breastfeeding, scarring mothers who could not or did not breastfeed, making them feel worthless. Sears's work was filtered through a lens that left parents feeling like being a martyr was part of parenting, rather than acknowledging that a parent's mental health is inextricably linked to an infant's health and development. And he neglected to notice that attachment is a dynamic process, changing as the child grows, leaving parents with no way to end the cycle of co-sleeping or other physical attachments. In truth, it's just not related to those procedural things. At worst, spending time stressing over these details can undermine a parent's developing a strong connection to their child.

Don't get me wrong—I have some clients who practice "attachment parenting," and it's fine when it works for them. But many mothers come to me terrified that they're doing something awful by letting their kids sleep in another room. The science says this is nonsense: "attachment parenting" doesn't make you a better parent. Remember: It doesn't matter how kids sleep; it matters *that* they sleep. It doesn't matter *what* diverse nutrition children get to eat, it matters *that* they get that diverse nutrition. It doesn't matter what gender the primary caregiver is or how or if they are biologically related to their child; it matters that *more often than not* the caregiver is emotionally responsive and attuned to their particular child.

The primary caregiver needs to be sensitive enough to notice and respond to their child's unique cues and in doing so, meet the child where they are; over time, that improves the goodness of fit in the relationship. *That's good enough.* Your child will develop both confidence that their needs will get met and coping skills to get through the times when not every cue gets a response—because you're human. And it takes a human to raise a good human.

### The Real Science of Attachment

So, let's talk about *real* attachment theory. Back in the 1930s, London psychiatrist John Bowlby noticed that the kids he worked with who had emotional problems seemed to lack parental affection. Bowlby—himself raised by a nanny and nursemaids in England (which underlines the truth that psychological research is often "me search")—started to see mothers as the emotional anchors for their children, and he theorized that kids needed a warm, intimate influence to develop stability amid the normal and inevitable storms of life.

According to Bowlby, healthy babies formed a "small hierarchy of attachments"—that is, the number of people they were attached to had to be limited for the baby to learn relevant emotional cues, but not so limited that the baby felt there wasn't any backup when mom went out to play darts with her mates.

In the 1950s and 1960s, American Canadian developmental psychologist Mary Ainsworth expanded on Bowlby's theories, working first in Uganda, studying babies' responses to her (the first white person they'd ever seen), and later in Baltimore. She began defining the relationship patterns between toddlers and their mothers based on how children responded to separations and, more important, to reunions. Babies with secure attachments played and explored freely from the "secure base" of their mothers' presence. When the mothers left, some of the toddlers got angsty. Either way, when the mothers returned, the babies lit up, sometimes recognizing their moms from a distance and sometimes reaching to be picked up. Research around the world since has affirmed what Ainsworth found: about 65 percent of babies do have a secure-enough attachment relationship to their primary caregivers—not exclusively mothers—to use them as their secure base from which to explore the world.

Inspired by both Mary Ainsworth and the peace movement in the San Francisco Bay Area in the late 1960s—when Janis Joplin recordings blared from VW bus windows and the word *love* first started making its way into academic papers—a young developmental psychologist named Alan Sroufe got interested in attachment relationships. With a team at the University of Minnesota Institute of Child Development, Professor Sroufe launched what would become the longest-running study of human psychological development ever conducted. In the study, clinicians met with children periodically—from infancy through their childhoods and teen years, into their adulthoods, and even through their transitions to parenthood—and established the basic tenets of how the way we are parented and the ways we experience security impact us and, when ruptured, how they can be **Repaired**.

Here's the upshot: caregivers who foster secure attachment relationships are attuned to their own feelings and from there can be attuned to their babies. They're loving, responsive, tender, and emotionally available *more often than not*. They pay attention and adjust their behavior when their baby is shutting their eyes from overstimulation. They notice and care when their toddler feels anxious. They step back and let their little ones experience a bit of distress as they slowly stretch their tolerance for everything not going right. They make **Repairs** when there is rupture. Their children grow confident in their caregiver's ability to handle their feelings—from glee to terror.

As you develop a secure attachment relationship with your child, you're also introducing them to co-regulation. You can soothe them with your own calm, even as you hold the boundaries they're counting on you to hold. You're right there with them, but you're going to be the adult when things that need adulting come up. You can be their ocean and rock them to sleep. Even when your kids are adults, there are times when they're going to need you, and you can be there. *More often than not* is all we're looking for.

### Kinds of Attachment

The secure attachment relationship is ideal, because it's one that allows children to comfortably explore their environment. When children trust that if they encounter a threat, they can return to the parent for safety, that means they view their parent as a secure base. In contrast, an insecure attachment relationship is evident when kids seem afraid to explore. They may worry whether their parents will be there when they return, which in developmental psychology we call "insecure ambivalent." Or they may be able to explore but may not view their parent as a source of comfort when they're faced with a threat or perceived threat, and that's known as "insecure avoidant." A final classification known as "disorganized attachment" refers to children who have conflicted and inconsistent responses—usually because the parent's behaviors may be erratic or confusing. This type of reaction is often seen with chronically maltreated children.

While I think it's important for parents to know all this, it's also important to remember that the majority of children *are* in securely attached relationships. All this said, some children simply are more careful by temperament and, beautifully, even an insecure attachment isn't a one-and-done curse. Remember: one of the Five *R*s that lead to resilience is **Repair**. Even if parents haven't been that secure base until now, owing to anything from absence to addictions, they can work on showing up emotionally when they are there physically, and healing their own barriers to stability so that they can offer that secure base to their kids. In doing so, they activate **Repair**.

### Attachment Is Dynamic—And It Can Be Repaired

A lot of parents these days have determined that attachment is important, and they are terrified that one wrong move will break the bond forever. They come to me all the time, deeply worried and vulnerable and ashamed, convinced that they've somehow ruined their baby or child. One mom was going back to work after maternity leave and, desperate to get some sleep, she had let her baby cry it out; now, she was terrified she'd left a permanent scar. Another parent couldn't breastfeed. One mother confessed to saying something horrible to her toddler when she felt overwhelmed. Another was worried after she had told her tween son that he smelled and needed a shower.

I assured them—and I'm here to assure you—that most kids do form secure attachment despite their parents' diverse work and sleep schedules, and despite their parents' very human stress responses. The science tells us that if a caregiver is responsive to a baby's needs *more often than not*, that's good enough for secure attachment. But even if something does get misaligned in the attachment process, that bond can be **Repaired**. In fact, passing interruptions in a caregiver's availability or responsiveness will activate a reparative process in the **Relationship**, and the child's confidence in their caregiver will be on the mend without needing any particular intervention. That break-

and-mend pattern, known as "rupture and repair," is part of the way healthy kids grow and thrive. Remember that **Repair** is one of the Five *R*s that lead to resilience—and that's not just for babies but also for all humans throughout their childhoods and their adult lives.

Dr. Edward Tronick, a professor of psychology at the University of Massachusetts, and one of the most influential scientists in child development, did the now-famous "still face" experiment back in the 1970s, when most psychologists still saw babies as blank slates waiting to be filled in by their parents, and when most researchers were focused on kids' cognitive development. Tronick was interested in looking at the *social* connections between babies and their caregivers. He and his colleagues asked mothers to interact normally with their babies and then to stop abruptly, go into another room for a quick break, and return in a neutral, disengaged mode. The mothers were then instructed to leave the room for a second brief break, and then to return normally. (You can watch the experiment on YouTube.)

In the first step of the experiment, the mothers and babies were delightfully connected, obviously involved in a complex social interaction. The next step was honestly kind of heartbreaking as the babies wilt at their mothers' disengagement. Those first two parts of the experiment dramatically showed the social and emotional connectivity between parents and babies. But the third phase, when the caregiver returns, was even more inspiring. Almost instantly, the babies in the experiment began a reparative process with their mothers and reengaged. This was **Repair** in action.

Does that "still face" stress out a baby when he's not sure what it means? Absolutely. But the back and forth—this disconnecting and reconnecting through the normal messiness of daily life—is part of the way we build lasting, secure relationships with the people around us. Similarly, it's an important process as children develop their sense of secure attachment to others.

---

**Q & A Session**

**Question:** I often text with friends when I'm with my child. Is this messing with their sense of attachment?

**Answer:** No; as long as you're somewhat engaged with your child, they'll likely be fine. In later research, Ed Tronick established that most parents, even when they're with their children, are only super-engaged about 30 percent of the time (*Repair*). Part of what helps our children build trust in the fact that we will be there for them when they need us is their learning to wait for our attention. (*Relationship*). Little by little, they will develop optimism about the future, even when we're on the phone or otherwise not right there with them emotionally. Here's one thing you can practice: see if you can balance responding to friends enough to feel connected to them, but not so much that your child feels less relevant than your phone (*Reflection, Rules*).

## Good Enough Is Good Enough

In order for the relationship to be a secure one, your child needs to know that they have a parent they can trust, who is relatively predictable, and with whom they feel safe. Time is not a factor; quality is. Maybe you don't get home for bedtime. Maybe you have to leave some mornings before your child wakes up. Research consistently shows that being emotionally present when you're physically present allows for higher-quality interactions, and those interactions give you the most bang for your buck.

So, own your availability. If you won't be home in time to put your child to bed, tell them. If you don't live with your child, be realistic about how often you'll see them. Let your child know when and how they can reach you. Be available when you say you'll be available, and be honest when you can't. Building trust with your child means that they can believe you: you say what you mean and mean what you say.

When you *are* with your child, commit to putting away your phone for reasonable periods of time. Give your attention to your child and the activity you're doing together. Develop new and meaningful traditions—like breakfast or dinner on Saturdays or trips to the park on your visitation day. Children form important memories around rituals or traditions that add to their sense of belonging and self-esteem.

## Retrofitting Attachment

During the pandemic, I moved from New York to California—earthquake country. Love the weather, but the thought of the ground beneath me giving way without warning was off-putting, to say the least. I still haven't been through a noticeable earthquake, but I did have my house inspected, and it turned out not to be as resilient as the newer homes being built, so I had it retrofitted to ensure it wouldn't fall down. It's such a safe feeling knowing that our home is sturdy. I made an investment to ensure that while it might shake and sway, it's probably not going to collapse.

Attachment can be retrofitted in the exact same way. If the secure base isn't there from early on, or if things have gotten shaky because of life's quakes, you can retrofit.

My client's spouse was deployed when their first daughter was born. The mother was worried that when her husband came home from the deployment, it would be a disaster because he was going be so excited to see the baby but he would be a stranger to their daughter, and that she might have a bad reaction.

This mom made a booklet for their baby that she read nearly every day from the time their baby was about nine months old. It was one of those books you can make online, and it had different pictures of him, and pictures of the parents together. By the time he came home from deployment and met his daughter, she ran up to him and hugged him. He was like Elmo—a familiar character in this child's comforting stories. Whether you're the absent parent or the parent who stays home, you can do some version of this to remind your child of your love and the presence-of-heart from afar.

Professor Alan Sroufe, mentioned earlier in this chapter, who became one of the premier development psychologists in the world, got interested in attachment because he lacked it as a child. When I interviewed him for my podcast, he reminded listeners that all children's development tends to progress with periods of equilibrium and periods of disruption. Sometimes things are going swimmingly, and sometimes they aren't. He talked about two cases that have really stayed with him.

One boy started out very positively—securely attached—and then all kinds of challenging things happened in his life. His parents had an acrimonious divorce, his father and siblings moved away, and then his mother died. Just a heartbreaking series of events. Predictably, he went through some tough years in adolescence, but as a young adult he met someone to love, and he was able to rebuild his sense of trust that other people could be there for him. He became one of the best dads Professor Sroufe had ever seen—and Sroufe has seen a lot of dads.

What that man got early on was a strong foundation, so that when he fell in love he was able to take the opportunity to learn to be more open to his feelings, because he was in a safe relationship again like he had been early on. In a contrasting case, a baby girl's family was in turmoil from the start—with abuse, chaos in the house, addiction in the family, and an understandably insecure attachment. In elementary school, she and her mom both got therapy, and the girl was able to build an island of safety in her life. She fell apart again as a teenager but rebuilt over time. She had trouble trusting, she felt very vulnerable, but she was able to reach back to that island of positivity in her childhood and build on that. Even when a lot has gone wrong in our lives, Professor Sroufe reminds us that we all have "these islands of positivity and support" in our histories—"and we can build on those."

## RELATIONSHIP EXERCISE

### Meeting Yourself Where You Are

Attachment relationships thrive in the context of presence, so anything we can do to practice being present with ourselves is going to help us become more and more natural at clicking into presence in our relationships. Set your timer for five or ten minutes. Sit somewhere comfortable and allow yourself to relax. Allow yourself to look around where you are. Look for the colors around you in the room, the light and the darkness. Take in your environment.

Notice five things you see in the room. For example, "I'm noticing the chair. I'm noticing that there's light coming in the window. I'm noticing the stack of books in the corner. I'm noticing my cat looks kind of feral. I'm noticing that I need a pedicure."

Allow your eyes to close. Let your shoulders relax and your arms and hands rest. Think of yourself arriving with a sense of dignity and alertness, a sense of presence and relaxation. And just notice the sounds. Listen and notice. For example, "I'm hearing the air-conditioning. I hear the little footsteps of my dog." Maybe you hear a car going by. So, just notice five sounds.

Now you've noticed five things that you saw. You're noticing five sounds that you heard, and then you take a pause and a breath and you start to notice: "Is there something that I can taste or smell or anything I can think of that brings to mind a taste or smell?" "Does the room smell like spit up?" Can you imagine the taste of chocolate ice cream?

Touch the chair you're sitting on or the floor or the steering wheel in front of you, because the only five minutes you have is when you're waiting to pick up kid number three from preschool. Notice the texture of that steering wheel. Go through each of your senses, breathing through what you notice.

Now, take a pause and notice the state of your heart. Is there curiosity? Is there exhaustion? Is there sadness? Is there excitement? Is there tenderness? You're doing this with the intention of noticing. You're not making any judgments. Just feel your body. Now open your eyes, arriving exactly present where you are.

———————

This is exactly the place from which you can be the parent you want to be *more often than not*. This is exactly the place from which you can raise good humans.

## CHAPTER 6

# Parent the Kid You Have

*Temperament, Parenting Styles, and
Making the Best of "Goodness of Fit"*

> *You are a shepherd. You don't design the sheep.... Shepherds are
> powerful people. They pick the pastures in which the sheep will
> graze and develop and grow. They determine whether they are
> appropriately nourished. They determine whether they are
> protected from harm. The environment is important, but it does
> not design the sheep. No shepherd is going to turn a sheep into
> a dog. Ain't gonna happen. And yet, that is what we see parents
> trying to do all the time. Step back and see yourself as the shepherd.*
>
> —RUSSELL BARKLEY, PhD

When I was a little girl, I dreamed of becoming a ballerina. I didn't end up having the body for a professional career, but I envisioned someday having a daughter on that stage, accepting her tiara and bouquet of pink roses. We all come to parenting with dreams and ideas about what kind of a kid we'll get.

*Maybe he'll have a natural talent for jazz saxophone.*

*Maybe she'll win a Nobel Prize in chemistry.*

*Maybe they will get really tall and powerful and become a star volleyball player.*

Sometimes these imaginings match who our kids are, and sometimes they don't. Just like some days you have a favorite kid. We have to let go of our shame around these things.

The antidote to shame is empathy for yourself. You can say, "You know what? It's totally reasonable that I was a ballerina and I dreamt of having a ballerina. I'm not going to be hard on myself, but I'm not going to take it out on my kid, either. I'm not going to try to turn her into someone she's not." That's very different from saying, "I was dreaming of having a ballerina and I feel so bad about being disappointed that I won't even acknowledge it to myself."

Just as we're teaching our children that all their feelings are welcome even though all behaviors are not, we can lend that empathy and compassion to ourselves as well. When we have empathy for ourselves, we can look to our kids to show us who they are and what they're interested in. By appreciating a whole range of ways of being in the world, we can help them feel valued for exactly who they are.

And who are they? It all begins with temperament, and that shows up very early.

## Temperament

You're not going to make a social butterfly out of a hermit crab.

Don't believe in the importance of temperament? Try having more than one kid. My firstborn flutters around every room she finds herself in, introducing herself with a friendly bounce. My second, a classic introvert, thinks before she speaks and chooses her interpersonal connections carefully. Both have been in essentially the same environment, with the same parents, and both of them have wonderful skills, unique ways of seeing the world, and separate personalities. Parenting matters, but *deep* aspects of temperament don't change.

When we talk about kids' temperaments, we're talking about genetically based individual differences in how people move through the world. Twentieth- and twenty-first-century science tells us that temperament remains relatively consistent across situations and over time. It can be influenced by our environment and parental responses, but at a basic level, we each are who we are.

Psychologist Dr. Alexander Thomas and psychiatrist Dr. Stella Chess researched child temperament across several decades, from the mid-1950s through the late 1970s, and they found that far from being a blank slate—the theory that had dominated Western philosophy and psychology since ancient Greece—every baby is unique in how they respond to their environment. Every parent is unique, too, and our basic compatibility with our children can make our relationships easier or more challenging. But we can all become good-enough parents to the children we have.

### Each of Us Is Separate and Unique

When we understand our children as separate entities from ourselves—people with their own unique temperaments different from our own—we're better equipped to respond with sensitivity and appropriate boundaries.

Drs. Thomas and Chess defined three general types of children: easy, slow-to-warm, and difficult. Easy children are generally happy and active from birth, and they adjust pretty effortlessly to new situations and environments. Slow-to-warm children are mellow and less active, and they are more cautious when adjusting to new situations. Difficult children—or what many of us prefer to call "spirited children" these days—have irregular habits, tend to have a hard time adjusting to new situations, and can often get pretty intense. Okay, as much as we want to call them "spirited," they can be pretty difficult for their caregivers.

Jerome Kagan, a Harvard psychology professor considered a pioneer in developmental psychology, did another long-term study that started with the videotaped reactions of babies and toddlers to unfamiliar objects, people, and situations. He then correlated those reactions to interviews with them later in life. The highly reactive, fearful, or inhibited babies tended to become shy adults. The low-reactive, uninhibited babies tended to become bold and sociable.

Basically, Kagan's research indicated that introversion or extraversion show up very early and stay with us. Our influence as parents is real, but we're not going to make a class clown out of a bashful type, and we're not likely to make a hermit out of a social butterfly. It just can't be done, and it can be harmful to give our kids the message that who they are on this very basic level—something they themselves didn't choose—is wrong or disappointing in some way.

Over the last couple of decades, researchers have also come to see an individual human's sensitivity level as fairly steady. In their 2005 paper, "Biological Sensitivity to Context," Bruce J. Ellis, of the University of Arizona, and W. Thomas Boyce, of the University of California, borrowed two Swedish idioms to name a new concept in genetics and child development: *orkidebarn*, meaning "orchid child"; and *maskrosbarn*, or "dandelion child." As Ellis and Boyce explained in their paper, dandelion children seem to have the capacity to survive—even thrive—in whatever circumstances they encounter. They're psychologically resilient, and at least some of that is genetic.

Orchid children, in contrast, are highly sensitive to their environments, especially to the quality of parenting they get. Genes linked to particular enzymes or brain chemical receptors in orchid children, if combined with family stress or maltreatment, can lead to a bunch of behavioral problems and even to mood disorders. If neglected and left to fend for themselves in crowds that don't support their sensitivity, an orchid child promptly withers. But if they're nurtured, they not only survive but also can truly flourish, doing better than their dandelion peers and becoming "a flower of unusual delicacy and beauty."

In 2018, researchers at Stony Brook University in New York State and Queen Mary's University in London asked hundreds of young adults a series of questions, including things like "Are you easily overwhelmed by strong sensory input?" "Do other people's moods affect you?" and "Are you deeply moved by arts or music?" They found that about 30 percent of respondents could be classified as dandelions, about 30 percent as orchids, and the remaining 40 percent fell somewhere in between. In keeping with the flower metaphor, they called the people in the middle tulips—less fragile than orchids but more sensitive than dandelions. This established that the dandelion-orchid categories might be better envisioned as a spectrum.

Still, it's our orchids that we need to be particularly delicate with. Boyce advises parents of orchid children to use the letters of that word to remember six parenting strategies that conveniently spell out ORCHID:

**O**wn: Let your child discover their *own* true self.

**R**outines: Establish predictable *routines* in the household and family life. Routine is especially important, Boyce advises. "Orchid children seem to thrive on having things like dinner every night in the same place at the same time with the same people, having certain kinds of rituals that the family goes through week to week, month to month," he says. "This kind of routine and sameness of life from day to day, week to week, seems to be something that is helpful to kids with these great susceptibilities."

**C**ompassion: Express your *compassion* often.

**H**uman: Recognize the *human differences* among your children.

**I**maginative: Be sure your orchid child has time and space for *imaginative* play.

**D**anger: And finally, because orchid children do tend to be fearful, help them confront *danger* in small, manageable ways so that, little by little as they grow up, they can stretch their capacity for facing their fears.

> *When a flower doesn't bloom, you fix the environment*
> *in which it grows, not the flower.*
>
> —ALEXANDER DEN HEIJER

Quiz: Is Your Child an Orchid, a Tulip, or a Dandelion?

Circle all of the following that apply:

1. Your child seems to prefer routines. If you usually have a muffin waiting for them at home after school, stopping for pizza instead causes some stress.

2. Your child loves a surprise party.

3. Your child prefers to sit in a corner reading, even when other kids are present.

4. Your child loves to roughhouse with others.

5. Your child seems to respond to a gentle correction but feels overwhelmed when they think they're being punished.

6. Your child doesn't respond to the gentle correction and seems to need a super-firm limit.

7. Your child seems to thrive only with a lot of positive reinforcement.

8. Your child barrels ahead with projects that interest them.

9. Your child has a strong reaction to loud or irritating noises.

10. Your child doesn't seem to mind any particular noises.

11. When your child's clothes get wet or sandy, they want to change right away.

12. Your child seems to have an attitude like, "What's a handful of gravel in my underpants when there's a swing to jump on?"

13. Your child seems to do better trying new tasks when no one is watching them.

14. Your child doesn't seem to notice whether or not they're being observed.

15. Your child has a hard time accepting that their book is not where it was yesterday.

16. Your child doesn't seem to notice if a toy has been moved.

17. Your child pulls at their clothes when the fabric is scratchy.

18. Your child doesn't seem to care what their clothes are made of.

19. Your child notices and empathizes with the pain of other people and pets without being prompted.

20. Your child needs reminders to think about how other people are feeling.

Results

**Mostly odd:** Your child may be an orchid—a highly sensitive being. They're pretty unique! Only about one in five kids is considered highly sensitive.

**Mostly even:** Your child sounds like a dandelion. They root and thrive well in a number of different environments and sometimes have to be reminded that not everyone is comfortable in their rough-and-tumble happy place.

**About the same odds as evens:** Your child is likely a tulip—sensitive in some regards and fairly hearty in others.

The good news is that we *can* all live together, finding common ground. The key is to tap into our empathy and celebrate our differences. If you've got a dandelion on your hands, instead of thinking, *My child is heartless, she ignores other people's feelings and doesn't even seem to notice her own sometimes*, remember that the science shows us that resilience is a superpower, and empathy can be learned. If you've been graced with an orchid, instead of thinking, *My child is so delicate; he'll never make it in this harsh world unless I toughen him up*, remember that the science encourages us to treat our orchids with all the more sensitive caregiving. In their own time, given the care they need, they will blossom into something exquisite. The science also reminds us that resilience can be reinforced and developed. Remember the Five *R*s that lead to resilience don't include yelling "Toughen up, kid!" but, rather: *Relationships, Reflection, Regulation, Rules*, and *Repair*.

### Communication that Affirms Their Style

In our group, Simone said, "All of your kids tell you everything. One of my kids talks to me, but the other one doesn't talk to me about anything."

We asked, "Well, what does she like? What's her way of communicating?"

Simone replied, "She's a reader and she loves reading and writing."

I suggested that Simone could write her daughter a letter and see if the two of them could start exchanging letters.

Simone had to adapt her own personality to each daughter's way of communicating. There's no rule that says a close **Relationship** has to be built strictly on verbal communication. So, Simone started a correspondence with one of her daughters. Once she did, she and this quieter daughter started sharing thoughts, and that was how Simone learned so many of the things her daughter was experiencing. They never had to say a word. Simone reminded her daughter that they could talk any time, but they also never needed to—these were private letters.

The answer to how best to communicate with a child is going to be different for different families, but the process of coming to the answer is the same thing. Like taking a breath, you figure out how you feel about it. You think about what your child is actually needing right now.

### You've Got a Temperament, Too

*Roaring like a tiger turns some children into pianists*
*who debut at Carnegie Hall but only crushes others. Coddling*
*gives some the excuse to fail and others the chance to succeed.*

—AYELET WALDMAN

Are you an introvert or an extrovert, or a little bit of each depending on the context? Are you easygoing or more spirited? Do you see yourself as an orchid, a tulip, or a dandelion? Are you fearful each time your child reaches a new milestone? Does your family see you as a bull in a china shop? We're all unique, but our **Relationships** can require more **Reflection** when there's a mismatch between our kids' temperaments and our own. The sense that we're not a good fit is one of the most common sources of parent-child distress—and it can lead to reactive behavior problems in children.

Go through the questions on pages 95–96 and apply them to yourself, instead of your child. Are you a dandelion parenting a tulip? That might create an opportunity for you to stretch your own sensitivity. Are you an orchid parenting a dandelion? That might mean you've got to practice increasing your own tolerance for loud noises and rough-and-tumble behavior. Maybe you yourself were an orchid child who didn't get the sensitive caregiving you needed to bloom, and you're determined to do better with your own orchid child. Fear not: there still room for all of us to bloom.

Not being a temperamentally natural fit doesn't doom your relationship with your child—not by a long shot. The key is to try to find the right balance that satisfies both you and your child, and that helps keep the family in harmony as much as possible.

For example, resist the urge to scream "You're just like your father!" or whatever it is you're thinking in the heat of the moment. Breathe in through your nose. Breathe out through your mouth. Remember your parenting passcode.

---

### Reframe Your Parenting Worries

**Instead of asking**, "Why is my child behaving this way?"
*Ask yourself*, "What is my child's behavior trying to communicate about her needs?"

**Instead of asking**, "How can I fix this about my child?"
*Ask yourself*, "What is hard for me about my child's experience?"

**Instead of asking**, "How can I help my kid become successful?"
*Ask yourself*, "What does my kid do well?"

**Instead of asking**, "Why is my child interested in that?"
*Ask yourself*, "What about this interest is difficult for me?"

**Instead of asking**, "How do I make sure my kid gets into Harvard?"
*Ask yourself*, "How can I raise a child with purpose?"

**Instead of asking**, "How can I make my child happy?"
*Ask yourself*, "How can I raise a person who has emotional agility, range, and purpose?"

---

### *Use a Co-Parent or Friend to Balance Your Strengths*

Nirmala came to me to discuss her fear of playgrounds. "I'm in a constant state of terror that my child is going to fall and hurt himself. I don't want to sit there and watch. I just can't, but I know my anxiety is not good for him."

"You're right," I said gently. "He doesn't need to take on your fear and anxiety. So, what to do? Is there some other way he can enjoy the playground that doesn't involve you?"

By my giving Nirmala permission to have her own feelings, she was quickly able to come up with a solution, realizing that her co-parent could take over playground duty and one day, maybe she would not be so afraid. In the meantime, she let her child play fear-free with Dad.

If you have a co-parent—whether that's a spouse, partner, or ex—you can balance each other's strengths. Successful co-parents make up for what the other parent lacks in attending to the needs of their children. For example, maybe physical activity is your thing, while your spouse gets anxious on the playground. Lean in and get playing with your children during "your time." If your child's other parent is not very affectionate, you can take extra steps to provide hugs and kisses.

## Goldilocks and the Three Parenting Styles

In one of the mom-groups I've been with for over a decade, Mariah and Mandy represent two extremes of the parenting continuum. Mariah is a perfectionist, Type A overachiever who's taken her academic and career success as a lawyer and put them to work, as she's the first to acknowledge, in her approach to parenting. She comes to the group anxious and eager to lay down the foundation for her two children to be better, stronger, faster, and mentally healthy. She's not sure why her children have started hiding their report cards.

In contrast, Mandy is the classic laid-back, free-to-be-you-and-me parent who's reluctant to assert any structure or limits for fear of shaming her kids until they push her too far and then she loses it unpredictably. Her children are closely connected to Mandy, but kind of wild and quite anxious. Mandy comes to the parenting group with anecdotes that leave her bewildered as to why, when she is so attuned to her kids, they do things that are defiant and seem fraught with self-doubt. Research shows that this is likely because of a lack of limits and boundaries, which causes kids to feel insecure about whether their parent is ready to be the grown-up when it's necessary.

Over the years in my working with Mariah and Mandy, and hundreds of other parents, I've learned that we can all learn to self-regulate and become authoritative, behaving from a place of balance *more often than not*. And remember: in parenting, all we need to aim for is *more often than not*.

We all share traits and characteristics of both Mariah and Mandy. Some days, we all just want to give in and let the kids do their thing. Other days, we need for them to be on task. Neither of these positions is wrong. There's no one right way to parent, and over time we're all going to have a too-chaotic day and a too-rigid day. We're all—myself included—doing the best we can. We're all acting from a deep love for our kids.

The science holds that when we're (*more often than not*) permissive, giving in when our child is staging a high-pitched fit or bargaining with them every time we need them to do something, they actually tend to grow up a bit more anxious, wondering, *Who's bottom-lining my physical and emotional safety around here?* Children need their parents to protect them from too much chaos.

When we're authoritarian, arguing with our kids, over controlling, or handing down punishments with no explanation beyond "because I said so," there's too much rigidity. Many kids just react to authoritarianism by learning to get covert, to lie to their parents, and to live in a state of fear rather than openness and growth. Even if you had authoritarian parents, and you believe this fear-based parenting approach got you straight As and no dumb partying mistakes, that's unlikely the story for your sibling, if you had one. Only certain temperaments can thrive under this kind of over-control.

The impacts of parenting styles have been studied across cultures, and at first glance it may seem like there have been different findings, but it's more likely that the cultural differences are in parents' and researchers' interpretations and presentations of parenting styles. For example, in Spain, researchers found that parents of permissive kids had more positive outcomes; but when they got into it, the way the Spanish were interpreting "permissive" was what US researchers would call "sensitive with boundaries," aka authoritative.

In the 1960s, developmental psychologist Dr. Diana Baumrind did a bunch of research with preschool-aged kids and their parents, and she defined three different parenting styles that, like the dandelion-tulip-orchid kid types, I like to think of more as a continuum: On one end of the continuum there's the permissive parent who is low on demands and expectations and high on sensitivity. On the other end of the continuum, there's the authoritarian parent who is high on demands and expectations and low on sensitivity. Somewhere in the middle, there's the authoritative parent—high on limits and boundaries *and* high on sensitivity. Developmental psychologist Dr. Stephanie Carlson calls this position "Goldilocks parenting"—the optimal balance. And the research has remained steady: Goldilocks parenting is associated with the most integrated child developmental outcomes—and more evidence that a middle-of-the-road approach gets better results than the rigid or extreme approaches.

## Quiz: What's Your Go-To Parenting Approach?

Answer each of the following questions:

1. Suppose you find your five-year-old drawing a map of the universe on the wall and you're not actually into impromptu murals. You . . .

   a. Confiscate the crayons and put the kid in an hour-long time-out.

   b. Say, "We don't draw on the walls; it damages them. Here is paper to draw on instead." You help them clean it off, and help them get set up with some appropriate art supplies.

   c. Figure you'll repaint when you move—kids will be kids.

2. If parents provide food, love, and shelter, kids pretty much raise themselves.

   a. Strongly disagree
   b. Disagree
   c. Agree

3. Your child is playing on their soccer team and gets benched. You . . .

   a. Force your child to practice daily for an extra hour so it never happens again.
   b. Ask them what they might do to improve their likelihood of getting more playing time and help them determine the effort they're willing to put in on the side and follow through.
   c. Berate the coach for being unfair and take your child for ice cream midgame (why waste your time cheering on others and feeling rejected?)

4. Your nine-year-old picks out a zany outfit that includes their older sister's discarded high heels and shorts. You . . .

   a. Remind them that they're not old enough to pick out their own clothes and make them change into the mom-approved blue slacks and blue sweater.
   b. Acknowledge their cutting-edge fashion sense and direct them to adjust the outfit for safety and warmth.
   c. Figure they'll learn when they fall trying to walk in the heels and freeze in the shorts.

5. Someone says, "I grew up with a 'spare the rod, spoil the child' philosophy. I turned out fine, and that's the way I'm going to raise my kids."

   a. Agree

   b. Disagree

   c. There's no such thing as "spoiling."

6. Your son is struggling working on an age-appropriate puzzle. You ...

   a. Guide his hand for him to get it in the right spot.

   b. Gently move a useful puzzle piece a bit closer to his view so he can come up with where it goes on his own (and feel so much more accomplished when he does it).

   c. Watch as he puts the puzzle piece wherever he feels like even though he knows where it goes.

7. Your thirteen-year-old daughter calls you when she's drunk, asking you to pick her up, which just about gives you a panic attack, given the history of alcoholism in your family and, *Hello, she is only THIRTEEN*. You ...

   a. Call the police, have her arrested, and upon her release, ground her for another month.

   b. Go pick her up, express that you're glad she told you the truth and say you will never make her regret that, but you'll figure out the appropriate consequences once she's sobered up and you've both gotten a good night's sleep.

   c. Pick her up, get her home, and don't mention it again. What's important is that she trusted you enough to call!

Results

**Mostly As:** A bit too authoritarian. Breathe in and breathe out. Tell yourself, *It's okay to let things go sometimes.* Your challenge is to be sure you're being sensitive to who your child is, rather than deciding how it's going to be and expecting everyone else to meet you at that standard. The antidotes to authoritarianism are empathy and connection.

**Mostly Bs:** Ding, ding! Authoritative for the win! You're in the flow.

**Mostly Cs:** A bit too permissive. Breathe in and breathe out. Tell yourself, *I'm the grown-up now. It's my job to say no sometimes.* The antidotes to permissiveness are boundaries, limits, routine, and structure.

### Reflection: Are You Acting Controlling or Coercive?

This is a more nuanced feature of some authoritarian parents. Control can be psychological or emotional, and it can creep up on the best of us. For a big family event recently, my daughter wanted to wear gold shoes. I thought in this case, her dress would surely look better with silver shoes. No disrespect to gold—love gold shoes. I said, "Of course, honey, this is your decision." Then I went and found a few pairs of silver shoes I was willing to buy her. I showed her the shoes and said to pick one, emphasizing again that it was her choice. She said, "Well, it isn't really my choice, because my choice was gold and these are all silver." She was right.

I had a strong opinion about the color, and I was paying for the shoes; the problem was that I was using my awesome parenting voice of "choice," and there was no choice. It was a way of being coercive and controlling without acknowledging it. Luckily, between not having to get it right all the time and her confidence in the safety of calling me out, it turned out fine. We got a laugh. But it was a moment when the better response would have either been to actually show her gold options *or* to say, "You know what? This event is really important to me and I'm choosing your entire outfit. I know it's controlling, and I'm giving myself a pass." This way, I'd name it and own it, and not make her question if in fact silver *was* her choice.

Here's a more disruptive example. A client described watching her child say something less than nice about her mom to her grandmother. Her grandmother elegantly teared up and said, "You hurt me when you say things about your mom. You harmed me. You have to give me a hug now and tell me how much you love your mom." This is a coercive way to convince a child they need to feel a certain way, they need to take on the adults' feelings, and they need to express their feelings of love in a particular way to fix it.

Control can also be cognitive control. Think about watching your child do that puzzle. If you use your hand to guide the child to the correct spot, that's control. It's hard for some of us to lift our control—not out of cruelty, but because we often really think we're helping because, without us, they would struggle to get the puzzle piece in the right way. None of this kind of behavior is going to hurt a child when you do it now and then, but persistent control does have associations with negative outcomes. We're all sometimes a bit controlling or a bit rigid or a bit lax, and this isn't going to damage our kids. The key is getting it right *more often than not.*

## Rules, Boundaries, and Limits Defined

*Boundaries are the distance at which*
*I can love you and me simultaneously.*

—PRENTIS HEMPHIL

So how do we learn to become, or at least make strides toward, Goldilocks parenting? If you tend toward the permissive, the answer is non-shaming boundaries and limits—no matter what your child's temperament. Boundaries are love. Limits are safety.

***Rules*** encompass both boundaries and limits, and go hand in hand with sensitive caregiving, regulation, and modeling the behaviors we want to see in our children. We're going to talk a lot about **Rules** throughout this book, because they're one of the five principles of parenting, so I want to start with some basic definitions.

**Boundaries** refer to the rules one has for oneself, as well as things that happen interpersonally—or between people.

**Limits** are rules that refer to unacceptable behaviors.

It can be confusing because a boundary isn't something we can see. There is no bright yellow caution tape. But with attunement and sensitivity, we can start to notice boundaries *more often than not*.

For example, some little ones like to be picked up and held closely. Some feel overwhelmed by it. As we learn about our children and their unique sensibilities, sensitive caregiving means that we'll pay attention to their responses and learn to show our love in a way that also gives them their space. That space is a boundary.

Boundaries change over time as children develop. A five-year-old who wipes off your kisses all of a sudden and says "Yuck" is really saying "My boundary is that sloppy wet kisses are not for me anymore, so please respect that rule." An adult might have a boundary like "I don't respond to texts after 9 p.m." Again, it's not something we can see, and in this case, it's not even something that needs to be communicated to other people; it's just a personal guideline that says: *This is the distance at which I can love and respect myself while I love and respect whoever might be texting me at this ungodly hour.*

Another example of a boundary is the boundary between adults and kids when it comes to our roles. While it might be a great point of connection and happiness to get down on the floor and play blocks with your child, they also need to know that you can get up and do your jobs as the adult and keep them safe if suddenly there's a kitchen fire. This boundary between ourselves and our children says: *We both know how to play, but as the adult I also know my role when there's an adult problem.*

Likewise, a boundary between grown-ups and kids comes up when we've got a co-parent and we want to hash out our approach to discipline or discuss adult topics. It makes children feel safe to know that adults will take care of the adult issues in the family and will generally present a united front. Here, we're using our skills of regulation to be the grown-ups and keep adult issues in adult spaces.

Boundaries do get reconfigured over time. From that first moment when a new baby's umbilical cord is cut and on through adolescence, when it's no longer cool for us to walk into their room without knocking, boundaries are the ever-changing distance that determine how we can love and respect each other, and ourselves.

Limits, as opposed to boundaries, refer to **Rules** determining what a person is not allowed to do. While limits may be interpersonal, they generally refer to behaviors that are and are not acceptable in your family or in the larger world. Examples of limits are that you won't allow a child to stay up past bedtime, that you won't allow them to destroy property, or that you won't allow them to bite their friend, all without experiencing the consequences of those behaviors—for example, in the case of the bite, the friend will feel very upset and may not want to play with them anymore, *and* you will need to place more space between their body and their friend's body because you have to help protect the other child's body.

A boundary, then, is the distance between people that allows them to feel at once safe and respected in their person. We can be sensitive to our children's boundaries, and we're in charge of setting and making clear our own boundaries. A limit, then, is any rule that doesn't involve the psychic or physical space between people. For example, *We don't bang our spoons on our plates* or *We only allow one hour of screen time per day*. We need both limits and boundaries in order to set up a safe environment, and we can talk about them together even though they are different.

Showing your child respect and letting them know you expect them to develop respectful interpersonal behavior, giving them structure, including boundaries and limits, is an expression of how much you care for them. Children need these guardrails to learn and grow, to learn what's acceptable, and to feel safe. Consistency helps them regulate their behaviors and lets them know what to expect in given situations. Boundaries and limits can be communicated by what you model, by what you allow in your home, and through conversations around reasoning, logic, and family values.

Just like it's our kid's job to push our boundaries and test our limits as parents, by trying on various behaviors, it's our job as parents to define what we will and will not allow. I go into this more in Chapter 11, but the matter of boundaries and limits comes up in virtually every aspect of parenting. Like breathing, boundaries and limits are a theme!

## The Surprising Science of Praise

No matter our child's temperament or our own parenting tendencies, most of us love to praise our kids. They *are* amazing, aren't they? Lighting up to support your child is never a bad thing. We should all light up around our kids. But helping them to build their internal motivation systems can require a little more delicacy—when possible. Resisting the urge to constantly praise is actually a part of the way we show our children that we see them for who they are. Accepting our kids and loving them unconditionally means *not* turning them into icons.

It may seem like lionizing someone by letting them know that you just think they're the most extraordinary human in the world, but if you must tell them that, remember to add "to me." After all, there might be a few other amazing kids in this big world. A lot of us imagine that more praise would drive our kids closer to us and make them feel amazing around us, but that's not what usually happens. When we pile on the praise, kids can end up retreating into themselves and feeling unseen by the people who put them on that pedestal in this well-meaning, loving way that parents sometimes do. What we want our kids to know is that we love them—flaws and all—and that we have a realistic appraisal of who they are, and that we love them unconditionally.

When we praise a kid for something they're already doing, it can actually diminish their motivation and focus it outward. There are times when we want motivation to be inward, especially for things they're already passionate about. Over time, children can actually lose confidence in their own capacity to assess themselves if their parents overpraise, and this leaves them susceptible to peer pressure and pop culture. So, instead of telling your child that everything they put on paper is a masterpiece, try simply noticing something about their work. You can say, "I like the way you used so much blue in this one." Or even just, "I notice you used several different blues."

Here are some alternatives to praise:

+ Ask your child about their process.
+ Ask them to teach you about it.
+ Ask your child how they feel about it so they can self-evaluate instead of looking for external evaluation.
+ Describe what you notice instead of taking the next step and judging it.

But let's not throw the baby out with the bathwater. There's a space between lavishing praise and withholding it. So, I'm not saying that you can't share with your child how incredible they are, but be *specific* when you're telling them things you appreciate about them. If you choose things that they value in themselves, instead of what you value, they will feel much more at ease with those compliments, rather than feeling it's not something they can live up to.

Focus your praise on effort, not outcome. Focus on the process over the completed work. It's about the amount of studying you did, not the grade. If you are attached to saying, "good job," you can keep saying that, but fill in specifically what they've done a good job with. Say, for example, "Good job tying your shoes."

The idea is that we're teaching our kids not that they're magically amazing at everything they do but, rather, that efforts lead to specific results; and when they don't, we can, as resilient humans, get through that without catastrophizing or interpreting everyday failures to mean anything about our intrinsic goodness and worth.

In Chapter 2, I talked about "growth mindset," a key component of motivation and learning. But Carol Dweck, the psychologist who defined the concept, later worried that parents and educators had gotten it a little wrong. She says, "A lot of parents or teachers say 'praise the effort, not the outcome.' I say wrong: Praise the effort that led to the outcome or learning progress; tie the praise to it. It's not just effort, but strategy . . . so support the student in finding another strategy. Effective teachers who actually have classrooms full of children with a growth mindset are always supporting children's learning strategies and showing how strategies created that success." So, when possible, *praise the strategy, not the outcome.*

## Use Disappointment as an Opportunity

It's natural to want to see our kids win, even if we realize we've sometimes got to bite our tongues when it comes to praise, but the real growth opportunity for internal motivation often comes with losing—or not getting what we want sometimes. It's a real gift to teach a young child how to handle disappointment. Kids get to see that their parents aren't worried they're feeling whatever they're feeling. We want to help them—slowly—expand their window of tolerance for discomfort and help them understand that feelings aren't as scary as they might seem at first. They'll get through their feelings.

It starts small, like not being able to stay up when your parents are having dinner with houseguests and you want to stay awake, or not getting the blue cup when you really, *really* wanted the blue cup. As parents, we can acknowledge the disappointment, but we don't have to fix the problem.

If kids don't experience small disappointments throughout their childhood, they won't be able to handle the inevitable, big disappointments that pop up over a lifetime. Think about working out. If you stretch and start with modest, attainable goals, you're less likely to injure yourself. Slowly, over time, with small, recoverable muscle ruptures and **Repairs**, you can build your endurance and do that triathlon. If you go from a year on the couch to running a 10k, you're likely to injure yourself to the point where you might have to spend another year on the couch. Likewise, the psychological concepts of positive, tolerable, and toxic stress refer to the stress response system's effects on the body.

Positive stress is a normal and healthy part of development. Meeting a new caregiver might cause a brief increase in your child's heart-rate and a wide-eyed look on their face—and this is a good thing. They're noticing that something is unfamiliar, and it's stretching their emotional muscles toward agility. Tolerable stress activates the body's alert system to an even greater degree. Think about the way your child reacts to losing a pet, or to a dangerous storm, or to falling from a play structure. If the stressful event takes place over a short period of time and there are caring adults with whom your child has existing relationships to support them, tolerable stress can even become a building block for resilience.

As the adults, we also have to keep practicing the experience of sitting comfortably—or uncomfortably—through our children's disappointment without allowing it to throw us into a tailspin. Sure, it's hard to watch our kids not get what they want. Especially if we could fix it with a snap of a finger or a bitchy phone call. We could just use a different color cup, or we could let them stay awake. We could go so far as to threaten a teacher to give them a better grade. But if we do, we're robbing our kids of the experience of knowing they can survive despite the fact they were disappointed and it was uncomfortable. Disappointment is an opportunity to practice for that one guarantee in life: that we won't always get everything we want.

If, however, we realize our children are experiencing or approaching toxic stress levels, we do have to take action. Toxic stress can occur when children live with physical or emotional abuse, a caregiver's substance abuse, or exposure to violence without enough adult support. These experiences that trigger prolonged activation of the stress response don't build resilience. Instead, they can disrupt brain development and increase risks for stress-related diseases later in life. This bad stress—what psychologists call "toxic stress"—is never something we would wish upon kids, but it's worth noting that even under those circumstances, it's possible to move kids from the experience of toxic stress to tolerable stress with the addition of a sensitive and loving caregiver. So, while we want to keep our kids away from anything that would cause them toxic stress, know that if they do experience it, your sensitive care will help activate *Repair*.

**Question:** My six-year-old has *big* feelings, never wants to name them or talk about them, and just pushes us away.

**Answer:** Sometimes we want to say something, label a feeling, show empathy with words when our kids are letting us know they're not available to have us speak to them. In those cases, show them with your body that you know how to handle their big feelings simply by taking a breath and saying something in your head like, *My child is going through a big feeling right now; feelings are part of being a person.* If they're interested in touch, you can put your hand on their arm or their leg to help calm their nervous systems (***Regulation***).

You can also put your hand on your own heart to calm yourself, and your child can co-regulate with you. Some kids will go into their rooms and self-regulate, and never want to talk about what happened. Take the message that they're not interested in naming or talking about things in the heat of the moment. When they're regulated again, there's an opportunity to use books, or if you're at the park observing other kids experiencing different kinds of feelings, label those feelings, talk about the characters in the book, or talk about stuffed animals during pretend-play (***Relationship, Repair***). In that way you can give your big-feelings kid more fluency about social-emotional language, and about feelings, but in a much less threatening way. That said, your child may not become a big talker-about-feelings, and that's one of the perfectly healthy ways to be a good human.

## Loving the Family You Have

There's more to discuss on the growth mindset in the coming chapters, but for now just remember: there's still room to bloom. Every day is a new opportunity to love the family you have. Put your hand on your heart and say, "More often than not, I'm the parent I want to be."

Our children's development is shaped by their own, unique characteristics in interaction with us as their parents and with their larger environments. If you can see them for the unique people they are, treat them and yourself with empathy, and behave in ways that will expand their and your own tolerance for disappointment, you lay the groundwork for harmony.

## REPAIR EXERCISE

### "Just Like Me"

This exercise is adapted from the teachings of American spiritual leader Ram Dass.

Sit somewhere comfortable and let yourself relax. Set your intention to center on your own compassion for your child. Bring to mind one of your children (or your partner, or one of your children's teachers, or friends for whom you could adapt this)—someone you're having a hard time feeling compassion for or someone you're just completely disappointed in. Picture your child in your mind's eye. Now, say silently to yourself:

*My child has a body and a mind, just like me.*
*My child has feelings, emotions, and thoughts, just like me.*
*My child has experienced pain and suffering, just like me.*
*My child has felt unworthy or inadequate, just like me.*
*My child has worries sometimes, just like me.*
*My child longs for connection, just like me.*
*My child is learning about life, just like me.*
*My child wants to be caring and kind to others, just like me.*
*My child wants to be content with what they have been given, just
    like me.*
*My child wants to be safe and healthy, just like me.*
*My child wants happy, just like me.*
*My child wants to be loved, just like me.*

Allow feelings of well-wishing for your child to rise up in your body. And then say:

*I wish for my child to have the strength, resources, and support to*
  *navigate this difficult moment with ease.*
*I hope to help with that strength and support.*
*I wish for my child to be set free from their current sadness.*
*I wish for my child to feel peaceful and happy.*
*I wish for my child to feel loved because this child is a fellow human*
  *being, whom I love, just like me.*

You can adapt this exercise for a partner, co-parent, or one of your child's friends or teachers you've been wanting to rip to shreds.

## CHAPTER 7

# Perfect Parenting Is the Enemy of Good Parenting

## The Benefits of Imperfection and Self-Compassion

*Perfectionism is not the same thing as striving to be your best or excellence. Perfectionism is the belief that if we live perfect, look perfect, and act perfect, we can minimize or avoid the pain of blame, judgment, and shame.*

—BRENÉ BROWN, PhD

Ariana had been in my parenting group for about a year when I realized how much she was struggling. An investment banker put together like a supermodel, she seemed to be on top of everything in her life. When a few of the moms in the group were looking for solutions to getting their toddlers to sleep on their own, I gave them all an assignment to create visual routine boards to walk their kids through the bedtime process. Most of the moms came back with four to six steps illustrated simply: put away toys, brush teeth, put on PJs, then story time, for example—but Ariana impressed us all with a gorgeously designed twenty-one-step spread. The other parents ooohed and aaahed, kind of ashamed of their own small efforts, but then Ariana welled up. Her beautiful board wasn't helping her kids get ready for bed. It was too complicated.

Another client came to me about his son Aiden's plummeting motivation and worsening mood. Aiden had been a high achiever in elementary school, with consistently strong test scores bordering on gifted. Now in middle school, Aiden procrastinated, sometimes even missing deadlines for big assignments that his dad knew he could handle. His dad was convinced he was on drugs, but when Aiden agreed to a urine test, it came back negative.

A third client, Natasha, described herself as "an immigrant who came from nothing." A florist and a loving mother, she saw herself as someone who knew firsthand how tough it can be to get ahead in this world. She wanted to make sure her kids capitalized on all the advantages she'd worked so hard to achieve. She knew the statistics about Ivy League admissions, and she came to me for advice on convincing her daughter to drop out of a board-game club she adored because it was interfering with Natasha's hopes that her daughter would earn an above-4.0 GPA.

Ariana, Aiden, and Natasha were all suffering from unhealthy levels of perfectionism. They were all operating from places of fear. Research affirms what many of us sense: more and more parents expect perfection—from themselves and from their kids. The ever-presence of social media since the late 2000s has accelerated this trend, to the point of its becoming dangerous. Dr. Thomas Curran, a psychologist who studies perfectionism and how it impacts mental health notes that, "Images of others at carefully selected moments of their lives has distorted our perceptions of their lifestyles and careers." In other words, if we're comparing ourselves to someone else's social-media feed, we're setting ourselves up for failures. Curran says, "We are surrounded by these images and messages all the time, and have internalized unrealistic ideals and values. It is one of the reasons why we have seen a rapid rise of socially prescribed perfectionism and a lot of its allied mental health issues, such as negative body image, anorexia, as well as malignant forms of mental health." Perfectionism is just one aspect of the cultural changes we've seen over the last couple of decades, but it's one we can be aware of and work to relieve.

The pressure to measure up can feel intense, but here's the good news: we can ease up on the perfectionism and our self-expectations *and* raise pretty amazing kids.

## The Nature of Perfectionism

I want to be clear that when I talk about perfectionism, I'm not talking about the pride we take in doing things well. I'm all for each of us striving for self-actualization and taking pride in doing the best job we can. But the perfectionism monster is the part of our striving that can't shrug off a B+, that beats us up if we don't get things right on the first try, and that may leave us so worried about messing up that we don't even try. When we're steeped in perfectionism, we can't enjoy all the things we actually do well; that one typo glares at us like an unforgiving judge, and we feel we can't really improve. Perfectionism undermines the very performance growth we're looking for. As we parent our children, we also want to raise good parents—ourselves. And perfectionism maintains the fixed mindset that is the enemy of that growth.

In 1990, researchers designed the Frost Multidimensional Perfectionism Scale. They defined perfectionism as having unrealistically high expectations, coupled with overly critical self-evaluations. The Frost Scale includes six dimensions of perfectionism:

1.  Extreme concern about making mistakes
2.  Super-high personal standards
3.  The sense that your own parents expect a lot from you (whether it's objectively true or not)
4.  The sense that your own parents are highly critical (again, it doesn't matter whether they would agree)
5.  A lot of doubt about whether you've done things "right"
6.  An excessive preference for order and organization

Notice that two of the six items here directly address parent-child relationships.

Holding ourselves to high standards and striving for achievable goals that inspire us can contribute to our sense of well-being and self-esteem. That's what psychologists call *adaptive perfectionism*. It helps us. But perfectionism becomes toxic—*maladaptive*—when we start taking things further. Maladaptive perfectionists often establish unrealistic goals for themselves and place enormous pressure on themselves to achieve them. An interesting test for yourself or your kids is to notice whether you're able to enjoy your achievements or if you keep raising the bar for yourself. Ariana's perfectionism, for example, expressed itself by taking what I had hoped would be a helpful, quick assignment and turning it into something more like a presentation she might give at her high-stakes job, where she'd become accustomed to overperforming.

Dr. Carol Dweck, the Stanford psychologist who developed the concept of the "growth mindset" is also a leading researcher in perfectionism, and she's questioned whether we should consider adaptive perfectionism as perfectionism at all; it's just conscientiousness. So, from this point on, when I use the word *perfectionist* or *perfectionism*, know that I'm talking about the maladaptive kind. And let's face it: in this social-media–drenched world, few of us can escape its toxic spray.

The relationship between perfectionism and stress is well established in the science. Perfectionist children may exhibit many different symptoms, including difficulty completing assignments, sensitivity to criticism, low self-esteem, indecision, and excessive critiques of others. Perfectionism unchecked has been associated with anxiety, depression, eating disorders, obsessive compulsive disorders, insomnia, migraines, panic disorders, and even suicide. What looks like a kid who has no motivation may indeed be a kid frozen in perfectionist tendencies. Aiden's perfectionism, for example, expressed itself as procrastination. He wasn't lazy; he was frozen in fear of not being the star student he'd been in elementary school. When you don't do something at all, you have a guarantee it won't be a failure.

## The Strength of Self-Compassion

I don't want this to become another thing for perfectionists to beat themselves up about, but it's something to be aware of and to work with. Every day is an opportunity to get better at *self-compassion*. Studies show that self-compassionate people are just as likely to have high standards for themselves as those with low levels of self-compassion—so there's no need to drop all your expectations. But self-compassion *has* been proven to increase motivation to change for the better, to lead to more effortful learning, and to encourage more resolve to avoid repeating past mistakes. In one study, people trained to feel compassionate about the difficulties of giving up smoking reduced their vice more than those trained to simply reflect upon and monitor their smoking. In academic settings, studies show that high self-compassion, rather than leading to a bunch of Ds on report cards, is linked to more adaptive motivational patterns, less procrastination, and increased confidence.

Self-compassion can be defined as directing care and understanding inward, especially when we're feeling inadequate or like we've failed at something. Researchers Kristin Neff and Christopher Germer identify the three components of self-compassion: *self-kindness*, meaning that we treat ourselves with warmth and understanding instead of self-criticism; *common humanity*, meaning that we contextualize both our positive and negative experiences as part of the shared human experience, instead of feeling isolated and alone in our ups and downs; and *mindfulness*, which, with practice, increases our ability to be realistic and nonjudgmental when we assess our experiences, as well as our children's experiences. Through mindfulness, the science shows, we can get better and better at acknowledging our feelings and emotions as they are, without fixating on them or overidentifying with them.

## Quiz: Are You a Perfectionist Parent?

For each of the following questions, give yourself a score of 0 to 5, with 0 meaning never and 5 meaning constantly.

1. Do you feel like whatever you do as a parent, it's just not good enough?
2. Do you think you hold the keys to your children's academic and professional futures?
3. Do you feel strongly about the importance of tests, competitions, and scores?
4. Do you feel like you just can't figure out this parenting thing?
5. Do you hope your child will go further with your own favorite activities than you did?
6. Do you worry you're doing irreparable harm to your kid with your everyday decisions?
7. Do you criticize yourself, or compare yourself and your children to other families?

8. Do you offer your child more suggestions for improvement than you do praise for a job well done?
9. Do you feel like you're to blame for your children's struggles or failures?
10. Do you take the lead on making sure that your children's tasks or homework get done?
11. Do you second-guess your own parenting decisions?
12. Do you connect your self-worth to your child's achievement?
13. Are you frequently disappointed in yourself?

Results

**0–15: Pragmatist.** Perfectionism is not your burden. You can skip to the next chapter.

**15–35: Flexible.** You like to keep yourself accountable, and now and again you overly stress yourself out by trying to do everything "right." Happens to the best of us.

**35–50: Idealist.** You hold yourself to high standards, but you might not be getting the results you're looking for.

**50–65: Perfectionist.** Hot zone! This much beating yourself up isn't kind or sustainable. Put your hand on your heart and remind yourself that you're good enough.

Perfectionism may come from a place of love, but it impacts from a place of fear. Self-love, forgiveness, and acceptance are the antidotes to perfectionism. Remember: most of our job as parents is to teach our little humans how to get through the ups and downs of life in all its *imperfection*. Practice "B+-ing it"—or even B--ing it. Go for 80 percent of what you imagined you could pull off. Normalize mistakes. You can start with normalizing very small mistakes if that feels more doable.

## How Do You Express Your Perfectionism?

A mom in one of my groups valued her own homemade upbringing, and so she knit all her first baby's booties, blankets, and sweaters. She even found the process of knitting kind of meditative. With that first kid. With the second baby, she committed to making sure she provided just as much homemade softness, but she admitted it wasn't as relaxing when she had so much more to do, taking her older child to preschool and catching up on work. By baby number four, she arrived at our group with her wrist in a bandage. "Knitter's wrist," she sighed. She was so invested in giving each of her children exactly the same experience that she had literally injured herself.

What's your version of giving yourself knitter's wrist? Researchers have identified several different kinds of perfectionists. Do any of these resonate? Which one resonates *today*?

### Cat-Eye Parent

When you comment on others—whether it's about their appearance, behavior, or other things—you're training your child to measure I against others rather than being intrinsically motivated. "Other-oriented" perfectionists set unrealistic standards for others that reflect a fear of their own inadequacy. If you find yourself doing the cat-eye, your challenge is to stop yourself from silently emotionally managing other people.

Think of the people in your life who made you feel really uncomfortable and judged without saying a word. Be conscious about how you pass that along. Encouraging kids to be aware of what it takes to meet their goals is one thing, but having a parent who is always judging sends the message that, in the greater world, someone is always watching and judging them, too. At the extreme, that can become dangerous messaging.

### Orangutan Mom

In the treetops, orangutans are the ultimate full-service moms. They build a new nest for their kids every single night, and literally never put the baby down while they're doing it. The human orangutan mom says, "*I* have to be perfect or my kids will fall from the treetops," and she imposes impossible standards on herself.

Researchers call this "self-oriented perfectionism." I have orangutan moms in my groups who worry they work too much, worry they were too young or too old when they had their first children, and fixate on perceived "lacks" that have everything to do with cultural norms for families and nothing to do with real-child outcomes. If you struggle to name one thing that you did well as a parent this week, take a step back and ask whether you're holding yourself to a reasonable standard. If not, consider where the guilt might be coming from, acknowledge it, and see if you can let it go. It's okay to relax into some more self-compassion and put the baby down while you build the nest.

## Ostrich Energy

There's nothing wrong with being a high achiever. But when pushed too hard, children can start to show signs of anxiety. This is another example of "self-oriented" perfectionism, when kids try so hard to do everything right the first time that they get overwhelmed. If you notice children seeming like they're freezing up or suddenly not performing— the equivalent of shifting from go-getter to head-in-the-sand—you can start paying more attention to what messages you're giving with regard to their achievements and their failures. Are you focusing on their thoughtfulness and conscientiousness—on their existence itself—or are you focusing more on their achievements or external markers of success? We can help our kids see that the world doesn't begin and end with every decision they might make.

## Show Dog Handler

"Socially prescribed" perfectionists feel that high standards have been placed on them by external sources, like their parents or their community. They're convinced that the judges will be highly critical if they disappoint them. They may be right. Studies show that socially prescribed perfectionism is on the rise with social-media use. In this competitive and often-curated world of public parenting, it's very natural—but what are our kids hearing? One client came to me with concerns about her child who had frozen at their new, prestigious school, and I pointed out that she led with the name of the school. Kids need to know that even as their parents support them in their self-actualization, our love for them simply does not rest on their achievements, how many "likes" they get on social media, or what school they attend.

———

Studies show that all these types of perfectionism are negatively associated with self-actualization. Meaning that, over time, they simply don't work.

## Becoming a Recovering Perfectionist

Perfectionist parents tend to want to recover from their perfectionism perfectly, of course, and it doesn't work that way. But here's the awesome news: our relationship to perfectionism, just like our intelligence, can grow and change.

Stanford psychology professor Carol Dweck encourages shifting into a growth mindset when it comes to perfectionism. Dweck questions whether we should even call comfortable high achievers "perfectionists" at all. If you're saying things like, "I try to do my best at everything," and that's not causing you problems, don't worry. Maybe you're a healthy striver. But if you're telling yourself things like, "I need to get everything right the first time," you do have an opportunity for growth by making room for mistakes.

Many of us may have perfectionist tendencies, but perfectionists aren't just aiming for success; they're also often operating from a place of fear and insecurity about their own abilities and self-worth. They may even be seeking external validation more than they're working from self-motivation. So, let your children see you make mistakes and then recover. Even better, let them see you discover what an opportunity a mistake can be.

---

### Shine a Light on Perfectionism to Neutralize It

A powerful antidote to perfectionism is simply flipping the light onto it. You can say, to yourself or to your kids, "Wow, we're smart and we didn't get that right. Good thing we're learning that smart people make mistakes—that's how we get smarter."

---

## Helping Your Perfectionist-Leaning Kids

Carol Dweck has studied the effects of praise and criticism on performance and has found that children who were praised for being smart were more likely to fear being seen as anything else. In contrast, children who were noticed for effort and guided toward improving their efforts developed a passion for growth. But even if we've gotten into perfectionistic parenting habits, **Repairs** can be made. Studies show that parents can reduce their perfectionism in their children by recognizing those perfectionist behaviors and by openly discussing the problems with perfectionist thinking.

That's right—just talking about it can help. Just reflecting on the tendency can begin to shift the pattern. **Reflection** is one of the Five Rs for a reason.

Make sure your child knows that your high hopes for them are separate from your love and support for them. As one of my mentors, the late Suniya Luthar, said, "Our job as parents is to help our children feel unconditionally loved so their self-esteem doesn't rest on the splendor of their accomplishments." If our kids get the impression that our love is wrapped up in their performance, they may strive to keep achieving in hopes of keeping our love—and that's not a growth-oriented motivation.

Make an effort to talk about goals for the long term, using realistic language about the fact that achieving goals takes time, patience, and effort. When you talk about others, make sure you also focus on these values. Also, talk with your child about what they're interested in, what they wish to pursue, and what they hope to achieve. Help them to understand what they can control versus what's outside their control and help them set attainable and realistic goals to work toward.

## Notice When Things Go Right

*When we take time to notice things that go right, it means we're getting a lot of little rewards throughout the day.*

—MARTIN SELIGMAN

Recall five things that have gone right today. Maybe some huge things have gone right, or maybe they've felt pretty basic. Either way, count five things on your fingers. The next time you see your child or partner, ask them what they think is going well. Tell your child or partner something that you notice is going well.

So often we come to parenting books because we're worried something is "wrong," and it might be, but surely some things are also going amazingly well—or at least a little bit well. The science of an "optimistic mindset" has shown that focusing on what goes right reduces stress and increases motivation, as well as overall happiness. As parents, we have daily opportunities to set the tone for how our children are going to see the world within their particular temperaments.

Ask your child or partner, "What do I do that makes you feel good about yourself?"

You can take the conversation further—but you don't have to. Ask your child or partner to tell you what you could do more of. Ask them to tell you what you could do less of. If these little conversations go well, take note. What we focus on expands. By focusing on what goes right, we not only give ourselves little mental rewards throughout the day, but we also set the stage for more positive experiences.

## Give Others Space to Make Mistakes, Too

You can tell your kids you believe mistakes are opportunities for growth until the sun goes down, but if you berate other people for the mistakes they make—to their faces or behind their backs—in front of your children or just when your children are in earshot, all the work that you're doing to teach tolerance of themselves or others goes out the window. This is such a great example of the way parenting makes us better people. It invites us to be mindful of how we treat other humans and whether we want to pass that down.

Instead of saying, "Whoa, that athlete just made a fool of this entire country with that performance," say something like, "Okay, that's a really good example of the fact that people who are amazing at their sport can have tough days sometimes."

## Let Other Adults Do Things Their Own Way

When your partner puts your child to bed and does it a little differently from how you usually do, avoid jumping in to rescue your child—even if you can hear them protesting. Unless there's a real danger, it's more important for your child to see that you trust them to adjust to different caregiving styles, and for your partner to get the message that you appreciate the help, than making your partner feel like you think they're incompetent.

The same goes for the extended family, even though those dynamics are a little different. If you're visiting your crazy aunt, let your kids have their own relationships with her. Obviously, you need to protect your children if your family members are dangerous or violent, and you may need to step in if they have different approaches to hugging-consent, but when it's just about learning to be around different kinds of people, who put different amounts of paprika on the potato salad, ask yourself, *Is it worth it?* Our children are not so fragile. Let them learn through safe experiences that people are different, and some of them are harder to navigate than others.

If someone approaches things differently with your child than you would, see if you can shift into a mode of curiosity: *I wonder why this person is so different from me?* Is there something in their way of showing love and holding boundaries that you can learn from? Maybe not. But allowing yourself to stand by and wonder will shift you out of the control struggle. You can give your child a little nod across the room that says, "Yeah, I know she's different, but I bet you can handle this."

## Take the Fear Out of Failing

The more our kids get to see us making mistakes and learning from them, the more they'll come to understand that life isn't about getting things right the first time. Disappointment is natural, but taking the fear out of failing means remembering that *imperfect people are worthy of love.* Imperfect people are successful. Imperfect people are, well, all of us. Imperfection makes us human. This is why parenting is best not left to robots.

When you see your child struggling because they have a disappointment, try not to falsely take away that feeling. Sometimes there isn't a bright side. Losing can be hard, but it's not the end of the world—and the sooner kids really believe that, the better. If your children are bummed out because they didn't do their best, or they did their best and still didn't win, you can acknowledge "That sucks," or "That's so disappointing." Practice standing in the discomfort of that disappointment for a few moments before you try to lift their spirits.

### Q & A Session

**Question:** I don't know what to do with my five-year-old who suddenly can't stand to lose games. He was okay with it from age two to five, but recently gives up the second he's behind, then immediately starts whining and quits. Help!

**Answer:** Learning to win and lose well doesn't always come naturally. To sidestep the drama, some families call off all competition, and others decide it's easier to just let their kids win. Both options miss opportunities to stay in the game when you're down, to consider someone else's perspective, to manage disappointment, and to persist despite setbacks.

Here are some tips to address competition:

*Model sportsmanship.* Let your child see you that you value sportsmanship, can come back from challenges, use strategic self-talk, and congratulate winners.

*Explain luck vs. skill.* Many games are not based on skill, which can be confusing to young children. Remind them that both winning and losing are temporary, and that certain abilities grow with time and effort. Other games are just based on luck.

*Modify the teams.* Play cooperative-style board games, pair siblings as partners against adults as often as you pair them with an adult.

*Play to win.* Resist the temptation to let your child win to avoid their disappointment. They have to lose in order to become a good loser.

*Play by the rules.* For chance-based games, don't offer second spins or special allowances.

*Set individual goals.* Pick activities in which your child can compete against themselves. For example, time them running a certain distance and then have them do it again to beat their own record. Talk about improvements they have made over time, such as being able to score a goal this season when they didn't last season.

*Praise effort, not outcome.* Help your child turn their losses into motivation to get better. Focus your praise on improvement (including good sportsmanship) and strategies used, not outcomes.

*Teach "bounce back" statements.* Equip them with phrases that show compassion and help them to recover, like "Practice makes progress."

*Encourage empathy.* Talk about being sensitive when things didn't go well for someone else. Remind your child that their win means that someone else lost.

*Acknowledge feelings.* Regardless of how silly it seems to you, let your child know it's normal to have big feelings. Offer compassion, but don't invalidate feelings by trying to offer perspective in the moment.

*Use the word* yet. Stress that with effort and practice, they'll eventually be able to do things they can't "yet."

## REGULATION EXERCISE

### *Making Friends with the Imperfect Present*

Studies show a direct link between mindfulness and self-compassion—a known antidote to perfectionism—so if you've been doing the mindfulness exercises in this book so far, you're likely already beginning to see some growth. If you've been skipping them, well, maybe you're not such a perfectionist after all!

Still, it's never too late to start. As with all aspects of parenting, and growing ourselves into the good humans we want to be in the process, we know that with a little bit of grounding in our own nervous system, we're better prepared to respond to the nervous systems of others. So, let's take this moment and find a posture in which you can feel relaxed and alert.

You can sit on a chair or on the floor. You can lie down or stand up. If you're driving, be sure to keep your eyes open. If any part of your body feels uncomfortable, see if you can shift your position.

Allow yourself to look around where you are, opening awareness to your body and all your senses. Notice the colors in the room, or in the park, or wherever you are. Notice the window and the curtains. Notice the sky and the grass. Consciously notice five things that you're looking at. And then as you look around, take a breath and let yourself just take in the environment.

When you're ready, bring your attention back to yourself. If it's practical, you can close your eyes and relax even more fully. You're safe. Notice if you're straining or holding any part of your body, and just let it go. You're arriving with a sense of dignity and alertness and presence. You're right here. You're certain of it.

Now, you saw where you are, you relaxed into it. And just now you notice the sounds that are around, including what sounds are coming and going. Is it the air conditioner humming? Is there traffic outside?

Are there screaming children? Nothing to do about it. Everybody's safe. Just notice those sounds.

Now, you can notice if there's any sense of smell—maybe some cooking nearby or even thinking the word *smell* might evoke your favorite smell. Or maybe it evokes not your favorite smell. That's okay, too. Just notice your body sensations and areas of ease or tightness, vibrations or stillness. Just notice the feel of this body received with kind attention, no judging, just noticing.

Notice the state of your heart. Is there interest? Is there gratitude? Is there judgment, sadness, excitement, curiosity? Whatever it is, does your heart feel open or closed? No judgment, you're just noticing.

Now, notice your state of mind. What's happening for you? Are you planning what you have to do today? Are you wondering if this exercise is going to get to the point? Are you excited? Are you feeling relaxed? Are you obsessing? Just notice. You are here. You saw, you heard, you smelled, you checked in with your heart and your mind.

Now, feel your body with presence and dignity, and realize that you can notice the play of experiences you have with an open and kind attention. You are fully present.

Open up your eyes if they were closed, breathe in through your nose and out through your mouth, and say to yourself:

*I can tolerate my own flaws and inadequacies.*
*I can tolerate my children's flaws and inadequacies.*
*Our failures, just like our successes, are part of the human experience.*
*When something upsets me, I can keep my emotions in balance.*
*I can tolerate my children's flaws and inadequacies.*
*I can tolerate my own flaws and inadequacies.*

Exhale.

CHAPTER 8

# The Delight Lab

*The Science of Awe and Play*

*When a child walks in the room, your child or anybody
else's child—do your eyes light up? That's what they're looking for.*

—TONI MORRISON

My maternal grandmother collected all things frog—figurines, stuffed animals, necklaces, you name it—because, she said, "Frogs only jump forward."

When my sister and I were growing up, my mother surrounded us with hand-painted folk arts furniture and woven trees of life. An early-elementary schoolteacher, my mom taught me a love of learning. She often worked with kids who were having a tough time, so her patience and humor muscles were champion level. Even though she taught full time, she took every opportunity to make an occasion special. She loved making the breakfast table our happy place. On birthdays, she made me wear a pin that said, "Hug me, it's my birthday!" She used to clap for me so much that when I started preschool she noticed I would look for someone clapping for me after anything I did. She took that cue to back off on her expressions of enthusiasm, but our home remained a delight lab.

As I grew up, no matter what other crazy or challenging stuff I had to deal with in my family or in the outside world, I had that foundation of care to return to. Even now, when it's my kids' first day of school, Grandma sends them a little cellophane bag of Swedish fish to represent the sweetness of a "school of fish." She takes any excuse to make the day a little more delightful.

So often, we look for parenting advice when something feels "wrong," and that's understandable. But let's not forget what experience and hard science has established: in childhood and parenting, delight is right. Children naturally turn to play when they're bored, sad, hurt, happy, and curious—and that's because it's how they learn and how they integrate their experiences.

In the first seven chapters of this book, I've explored the common disconnects we face as parents and caregivers—the hard work of boundary setting, the perfectionism, the sometimes-tricky fits between our children's temperaments and our parenting styles, and the ways our attachment relationships can experience ruptures. Now, I'm going to share with you the fastest, clearest strategy to reconnect and begin to **Repair** when things have gone awry: *shared joy.*

## Plan Delight Time

*You see a child play, and it is so close to seeing an artist paint,*
*for in play a child says things without uttering a word. You can*
*see how he solves his problems. You can also see what's wrong.*
*Young children, especially, have enormous creativity, and*
*whatever's in them rises to the surface in free play.*

—ERIK ERIKSON

What if I told you there's something you can do with just five minutes each day, with each child—even just four times a week—that will bolster your attachment relationship, boost attention span, improve your child's social skills and behavior, and get them to listen more throughout that day? The concept, developed by psychologist Dr. Sheila Eyberg in the 1970s, is pretty simple. For at least five minutes per session, sit down with your child and join them in child-led play of their choosing—anything that doesn't have a right or wrong way to play.

Let your child be in charge. Don't ask questions (harder than it sounds!), and don't give commands. The purpose is to communicate both verbally and nonverbally that you're authentically interested and delighted to be spending time with them. Label the session as "delight time," or any other name you come up with, so that it's delineated from the rest of the day as something special. Roger Harrison, a pediatric psychologist with Nemours Children's Health, in Wilmington, Delaware, just calls it "special time." Other researchers call it "parent-child interaction therapy," but it's still just child-led delight time set aside for stress-free play.

We know that relationships are a key building block of resilience; this delight time has been shown in study after study to strengthen parent-child relationships and heal disruptive behavior tendencies. In the studies, parents are taught to use the acronym PRIDE:

**P**raise—and that's *specific* praise, like "I love the way you pieced those Legos together" or "Thanks for letting me take a turn!"

**R**eflection—which just means reflecting back what our kids say to us. If they say, "I'm reading now," simply reflect that back to them by saying. "You're reading now."

**I**mitation—imitate your child as you engage in this parallel play. If they're stacking blocks, you stack blocks. If they're walking stuffed animals along the windowsill, you walk stuffed animals along the windowsill.

**D**escription—Harrison recommends narrating your child's play like you're a sportscaster. You're not here to coach the game, just to provide the verbal descriptions like, "You're setting up a tea party for your trolls. You're giving the green cup to the green troll." This is a fairly simple way to show your interest in what your child is doing.

**E**nthusiasm—to reinforce appropriate and positive behavior, express your enthusiasm at everything that's going right.

When these studies show the best results, parents are also instructed to avoid leading or intrusive behaviors, like commands, criticism, sarcasm, and any negative physical behaviors.

Harrison also recommends that we make all this easier for ourselves by choosing toys that encourage imagination or creativity, such as blocks, magnetic tiles, trucks, train sets, kitchens and play food, and simple arts and crafts. For delight time, avoid steering your child to toys or activities that have a lot of rules, such as board games, or lend themselves to rough or messy or dangerous play, like pretend sword fighting. You don't want to have to be telling your child to "be careful" all the time. You just want to join them in their world of the imagination and let them show you what's fun for them.

## Try New Imaginative Games

Games you remember enjoying from your own childhood or imaginative activities you and your kids make up today are wonderful. Virtually all imaginative children's play contributes to *regulation*, one of my Five Rs that lead to resilience. Playing together improves your **Relationship** with your child, another one of the Five Rs. And shared joy promotes **Repair**, yet another of the Five Rs. You don't have to play any special science-approved games, but you can. The science of play is rich. You can have fun while building resilience, confidence, and family happiness by borrowing tried-and-true ideas from developmental psychologists and theater educators. Jocelyn Greene, my friend who founded Child's Play NY, suggests these great games.

**What Animal Am I?** This is great for motor skills and self-regulation. Have kids pick their favorite animals and make up poses and movements and ways of breathing like them. Kids can play "What Animal Am I?" with friends, siblings, and parents, or even all by themselves. As you and they make up poses, you can write the name of the animals or creatures down. They can even illustrate their own human-as-animal deck.

**Active Reading.** This helps with developing and reinforcing bravery. Take the exciting moments in your child's favorite storybooks and act them out. Use simple props you already have: a blanket can become the ocean. A chair can be a mountain.

**Body Phone.** This is great for learning how to label emotions to stable them. Use an invisible phone to have kids call into different parts of their brain. Parents can also dial into their kids' feelings and ask to speak with one of their emotions. For example, "Hello? I'm calling to talk to Rosie's angry feeling." Or, "Put Mr. Disappointment-part on the line." You can even dial up physical discomforts like tummy aches or sprains so that kids can use the game to articulate what's going on.

**Silly Chins.** This is awesome for sibling and friend play. Each player draws two eyes on the bottom of their chin—or has their parent do it. Now, have the kids cover their nose and eyes and turn upside down. Take turns interviewing the new creatures. Kids can give their chin face a name, personality, hopes, and dreams.

**Magic Elevator.** This is great for confidence building. Use painters' tape on your floor, or lay down pillows to create a square that you call a "magic elevator." Now, imagine this elevator has doors that close and buttons to choose from. One button might take you to a special forest, another button might take you back in time. Push the buttons and tell the elevator where you want it to go—and imagine that when the doors open, you're there. You can even use soundtracks for your adventure. When you're done exploring one world, you can get back in the elevator and go to a different one. Use settings, characters, and floors that speak to your child's unique interests.

**Magic Restaurant, Magic Stew.** This is great for self-regulation. Each player picks or invents a character and comes to the table to eat with the magic "as if." You can invent a setting, too. Maybe you're all members of an extremely proper royal family having dinner in a castle. Your characters and setting might inspire good habits or funny conversations. Create a magic concoction of invisible ingredients. What would each of your characters add to the stew?

## Look for the "Wow" Moments

Embrace the science of curiosity and awe. In his book *Wonder: Childhood and a Lifelong Love of Science*, Frank Keil notes that pretty much all little kids are interested in science, but by adulthood, most of us have dropped it. Where does our inquisitiveness go? Why do we stop asking why?

Being with children is a beautiful way to start asking ourselves these open-ended questions and to reignite our own curiosity—which is associated with overall well-being. When you follow the path of curiosity, look for the "Wow" moments.

Awe, which can be described as a feeling of reverential respect mixed with fear and wonder—or a sense of everyday magic that makes us feel self-transcendent—has been shown to improve relationships, motivating us toward collaboration and generosity. Humans often find the experience of awe in the natural world, in spiritual engagement, in music, in collective movement, and in unhurried time that allows for the mysterious to unfold before our eyes.

Psychologist Dr. Dacher Keltner, founding director of the Greater Good Science Center, at the University of California at Berkeley, spent years studying the effects of awe and found that, "It makes us humble, sharing and altruistic. It quiets the ego so that you're not thinking about yourself as much." With awe, we're filled with a sense of vastness, which cues our brains to become more expansive, allowing for a cognitive realignment that makes room for whatever new experience we're taking in.

The experience of awe engages a number of internal processes, including shifts in neurophysiology, engagement of the parasympathetic nervous system, a diminished focus on oneself, the release of oxytocin, greater social integration, and an increased sense of meaning—all of which benefit well-being. Awe has even been shown to reduce inflammation.

You can use this science to improve your relationship with your partner by spending time in nature, at a concert, or marveling over your children's awesome growth. Researchers have documented the pattern of facial movements associated with awe, so if you're not sure if you or someone else is experiencing it, look for raised eyebrows, widened eyes, an open and slightly dropped jaw, and vocalizations of "Wow" and "Whoa." Notice how many times you authentically say or witness "Wow" or "Whoa" when you're playing with your kids. That's awe.

Any awesome experience—from wandering among old-growth sequoias to discovering for the first time that water comes out of a faucet—can evoke that sense of mystery and wonder. But you don't have to take your kids to the Grand Canyon or the California redwoods to experience awe. You can simply slow down together to notice the ordinary magic of a caterpillar crossing a path, a long-awaited shooting star cross the night sky, or the sounds that emerge from musical instruments. As kids get older, you can keep that sense of awe and curiosity alive by slowing down to wonder about life's big questions, going to concerts, and taking part in community events that remind you that you're a part of something bigger than yourselves.

## Play "What Makes You Happy?"

The science shows us that what we pay attention to gets re-emphasized in our brains. It's kind to let our kids know when we notice their unhappiness or anxiety, but don't forget to notice and explore the more positive emotions life brings. When you're in the car with your kids or sitting around the kitchen table, you can play a mindfulness game called "What makes you happy?"

Ask the question. When they answer, repeat the question and have them answer with another option. Do this for up to four minutes (keep it shorter for younger kids). Then have them ask you the same. (Warning: eye rolls may start around age ten. Go ahead and make fun of yourself, but keep doing it. At minimum, you'll share a laugh.)

The act of naming multiple things you appreciate forces you to have a present moment of gratitude, even if all you can drum up in that moment is "This coffee makes me happy."

## Q & A Session

**Question:** I feel really guilty about this, but my four-year-old daughter always wants me to play dolls with her, and I just don't like dolls. I was just not that kind of girl and I'm not that kind of mom.

**Answer:** If you are looking for permission, you do not have to pretend you don't have your own preferences. Instead of dwelling on what you don't like to do, you can do two things: (1) find someone other than yourself to play dolls with your daughter (a co-parent, a friend during a playdate, or a babysitter), or (2) find another activity that you *do* enjoy doing with your child (**Relationship**).

If playing with dolls means a lot to your child and can be a way in for connection, try shifting to that perspective and see if you can find some interest in it. But if there are other sources for building connections (which there likely are), ditch the dolls and do something you both like.

## Share the Activities that Give You Joy

So much of parenting is about helping our kids figure out what they're interested in, but it's a gift to share our own happy places with our kids, even if those aren't their happy places—yet. Love an art museum? Bring your kids along and share your delight in your favorite Frida Kahlo pieces. Find peace when you hike? Take your kids on nature adventures whether or not hiking is their idea of a good time—yet.

## Play Pretend: Is Santa Real?

Playing "pretend" is an important part of child development, but many parents worry that cultural make-believe—like Santa Claus, the Easter Bunny, the Tooth Fairy, and others—conflict with reason and may create unnecessary disappointment. Here's what the science tells us.

Magical and rational views of reality coexist throughout development, but until about age eight, children who are given reason to believe in Santa Claus tend to believe. Young children love pretend-play and believe that beautiful sense that all things are possible. After age eight, you may begin to hear some rational inquiry. Kids begin to show a shift in thinking and can correctly judge fantasy versus reality.

When kids want to know if Santa Claus—or dragons or fairies—are real, ask them more questions to see if you can figure out where they're coming from. If your child wants to believe, they may be asking less as a reality check and more because they want you to give them "permission" to keep believing. However, if they're challenging and using scientific inquiry, they may be asking for you to level with them. If your child is disappointed, acknowledge the feeling and help them stay with the magic and the meaning of it by coming up with ways to share traditions and fantasy with younger siblings and family members.

For kids who don't believe, or who don't celebrate, it can be helpful to remind them that every family has different ways of celebrating and believing; and for folks celebrating and believing things that are different, it is kind to respect their beliefs and culture, and not tell them their beliefs and culture are not true. Then you can reassure them that you are available to discuss and wonder so they have a place to process it all without offending others.

### Keep Coming Back to Play

Most of us had kids because we hoped, on some level, that they would make our lives happier and more fun. We imagined the joyful moments. And yet it can be so easy to forget to center the things that make us happy when we're in the middle of the hectic reality of family life, trying to get the food on the table and get each kid to school on time. That's understandable. It's completely forgivable. And it's repairable. Every day brings a new opportunity to find even five minutes for delight time. The *Repair* will begin almost instantaneously.

## REFLECTION EXERCISE

### Engage Your Optimistic Mindset

We know that if we practice speaking a foreign language, or practice playing a new instrument, we'll make progress. The science reminds us that we need to practice the feeling of well-being, too, if we want to make progress toward a more delight-filled life.

Get in a comfortable sitting position or lie down. You're going to scan your body from top to bottom and relax. Begin by allowing your forehead and your eyes to soften. Allow your jaw to soften. Allow your neck and your shoulders to soften. Move down, giving your attention to each part of your body as you allow it to soften—relaxing your arms and your chest and your torso. Soften your belly, your pelvis, your hips. Notice if you're holding anything tightly. Relax that tightness. Allow your thighs and your knees to soften. If you're grasping, let go. Allow your calves and your ankles to soften. Allow your feet and your toes to soften. Envision your whole body to feel at ease.

Allow a half-smile to form on your face. You could have a full smile if you need to, but just notice what happens when you have a half smile. Take a few deep breaths and allow the breath to find a natural rhythm. You don't need to control the breath—just let it happen.

Bring to mind an experience of joy. The image could be a memory of dancing with a loved one, cuddling with your pet, or looking at your child's face. Allow a feeling of contentment and well-being to wash through your body. Don't make anything happen; just relax and enjoy that memory. As you're sitting or lying down and enjoying that memory, notice how it feels in your body. Allow your awareness to rest in that feeling of well-being. Take a breath.

Now, bring to mind some blessing in your life—something or someone that you're grateful for or to—and let that person, or being, or circumstance wash through you and whisper the word or silently say, "Thank you." Take a deep breath and let that feeling of gratitude wash through your body.

Now, bring to mind another blessing or someone in your life whom you're grateful for or to, and again give a silent "Thank you" from your heart, and just feel the feeling in your body.

You can continue to do this a few times, bathing in the relaxed sense of being alive, of feeling the people and animals and other circumstances that give you joy and feel like blessings. Feel the miracle of this radical joy pulse through your body. You are alive. You are capable of this quiet joy. You are present in your body.

Take one last deep breath, open your eyes, and just look around, and notice the first little thing you can delight in.

# PART TWO

# FROM PAGE TO STAGE

*Putting the Science and Your Values
into Everyday Practice*

Now that we've covered the big picture and have considered what developmental psychology tells us about raising good humans, let's look at some ways we can apply this science in our daily lives. While the science applies to children of all ages, including adult children, I will walk you through the years for which I have the most theoretical *and* real-life training: birth to age thirteen. My girls are fourteen and seventeen as this book comes out, so I also don't want to burden them with anything they may currently or imminently be experiencing—not that they're going to be reading Mom's book.

In addition to my training as a developmental psychologist, I've worked with thousands of parents over the years, and I present here the most common questions they have brought to me. This said, each of us has a different bandwidth for listening to parenting advice. Some of us thrive with tons of information, while some of us shut down. I offer you all this in the spirit of serving you, not stressing you out! For instance, if your way of making sure that everyone gets as much sleep as they need is working for your family, I'm not here to ask you to change that. If your limits or lack thereof concerning screen time are not causing you stress, I'm not here to add any stress to the equation. But I know that sometimes we all need support translating the science into action, and so what follows is what many parents have found helpful.

## CHAPTER 9

# Eat, Poop, Love

*Autonomy Without Shame*

*All struggles are essentially power struggles, and most are
no more intellectual than two rams knocking their heads together.*

—OCTAVIA BUTLER

Children thrive when they have room to be individuals.
As kids begin to express their needs to have control over themselves and the world around them, our job as parents is to offer healthy options and then *step back*. While many parents understandably get stuck in fixating on what goes into their children's bodies and what comes out, the important developmental thing that's happening with food and bathroom use actually represents the road to autonomy. That is, as kids develop their independence, they also develop confidence in their ability to take care of themselves. But autonomy isn't *just* about independence. Sensitive caregiving that promotes autonomy helps kids feel comfortable being exactly who they are in their own bodies. From that basic sense of self-determination concerning what goes into their bodies and what comes out, autonomy can bloom in all different directions of their lives.

Professor Stephanie Carlson at the University of Minnesota has extensively studied "autonomy supportive parenting"—the parenting that helps kids solve their own problems, with appropriate guidance. Parents who tend to hover are sometimes called "helicopter parents," while those of us who have a tendency to remove all the obstacles our kids face are sometimes called "snowplow parents." Instead of focusing on criticizing these more extreme styles, let's think about how we can help kids get into the habit of trying challenging things and solving the problems that come up. The science shows that this kind of autonomy support is also a precursor to executive function skills. Autonomy allows kids to develop critical thinking skills, to learn from their own mistakes, to process emotions, and to begin to make decisions independently.

Making things wonderfully cohesive, the five principles of parenting are also the road to autonomy:

**Relationships** that promote autonomy are the opposite of controlling, but they're still firmly connected. Instead of leaning into helicoptering, snowplowing, or resignation, sensitive parenting reminds us that our relationships with our kids are dynamic, and their slow and steady growth into adults who can live without us is the goal.

**Reflection** helps us breathe into that pause between a problem and our response to it so that we can find the middle road between micromanaging our kids' experiences and leaving them to the wolves. Instead of unnecessarily going into fight-or-flight mode, take the moment to reflect on your child's growing abilities and continuing needs for support.

**Regulation** is a key facet of autonomy as children grow from infants who may need constant co-regulation into young adults who can self-regulate *more often than not.*

**Rules** help children feel safe. Structure helps them understand what's acceptable both at home and in the larger world, where they'll have to make daily decisions with more and more independence.

**Repair** is the space in which humans grow and learn, so it's key to autonomy. As kids learn to go to the bathroom by themselves, they're going to have accidents. As they make more of their own food choices, they're going to overdo it on the junk some days.

As parents, we can walk and talk a growth mindset so that they come to see these times of misalignment as necessary steps on the path to greater success.

## The Fundamentals of Being Human

Whenever a parent shows up on my Zoom, or whenever I have a child-rearing doubt of my own, I first check in about two things:

1. Is everybody well nourished?
2. Is everybody getting enough rest?

It might sound basic, but nine times out of ten, human problems can be solved with a handful of nuts, a few bites of broccoli, and a good night's sleep. We are embodied, after all. If our bodies aren't happy, our minds and hearts aren't going to be far behind.

### Start from Your Place of BALANCE

If you notice yourself getting into power struggles with your kids around food and bathroom issues, take the opportunity to get into BALANCE. In fact, as we take all the developmental science that's been presented in Part One of this book, and we look at how we can apply that science to real life in this part, you'll notice I start every chapter that follows with a BALANCE exercise. Seem repetitive? That's the point! It's the repetition of these practices that builds our parenting muscles over time, helping us become more of the parents we want to be more of the time.

**B**reathe: Inhale deeply through your nose. Exhale through your mouth. (No, you still can't skip this step.) Are you noticing that you're getting better at this response? Take the breath.

**A**cknowledge your own baggage: Ask yourself, "What is this moment bringing up for me?" Many of us have a ton of baggage concerning eating, hygiene, and body issues that date back long before we became parents. Then when we did become parents, we had to deal with every aspect of their food and poop. Baggage is natural.

**Let it go:** You can unpack any baggage later, on your own timeline. When you let go of the past and future this moment is bringing up, you can ground ourselves in the present. In this present, your children are becoming more autonomous.

**Assess:** Take stock of this moment. Gauge your own and your child's state of mind. Is your child hungry? Are they asserting their autonomy? Do they have a physical need that needs to be addressed?

**Notice:** Observe what's going on in your own body and what's going on in your child's body. What are these bodies trying to tell you?

**Connect:** Let your child know verbally or with your body that you see them and care about their feelings.

**Engage:** Now that you're in balance, you can decide on your response. What can you do to show your child that their feelings are welcome? Do you need to also share with them that a certain behavior is not welcome? Or is this an opportunity to let them try out their autonomy? How can you shift away from power struggle? What response would inhabit the space between micromanagement and neglect? When you get into the habit of responding from this regulated, balanced place, the clarity will follow.

## Diverse Nutrition Without the Drama

Do any of these voices live in your brain?

*That mother doesn't feed her children enough.*
*That's a lot of carbs.*
*Have some more! But not too much! You don't want to get too big!*

Many of us have so much generational baggage around eating, scarcity, and body image that it's completely understandable that we sometimes bring a lot of extra stress to the table.

In my parent group, Jasmine wants to make sure her kids eat full meals, so she ends up making four different menus at every mealtime and serves them to her kids while they all watch TV from her bed. By the end of the night, she feels frazzled—and she once found her son's half-eaten cheese sandwich under her pillow.

Bridgette, on the other hand, follows the guidelines she got from her pediatrician to a T, and finds herself counting how many bites of cereal each of her three children eats. She feels a lot of frustration when the numbers are off, even though her doctor has never said there's anything to be concerned about when it comes to the growth charts.

For both Jasmine and Bridgette, there's a path back to the middle of the road. But in the absence of a medical situation, we never need to count how many bites of food someone else eats. If you notice yourself paying attention to such minutiae, it's time to give yourself a small intervention.

Here's what to focus on when it comes to feeding your kids: Provide them with nutritious and diverse food options, prioritizing available fruits and vegetables and deprioritizing sugar and processed foods. Establish limits to protect your domestic labor, and don't worry about what other people eat. From a developmental psychology perspective, what matters is that we focus on positive experiences at mealtime. I'm not a nutritionist or a physician, so I won't get into the details about what to eat, but so many of our issues with food and nutrition can be solved with a focus on the experience of eating.

A healthy relationship with food means that we see it as a source of fuel and delight, not as a reward or a punishment, a source of guilt, or even an expression of love. As parents and caregivers, it's our job to provide healthy food options for our kids and to model as healthy a relationship with food as we're able. It's not our job to force kids to eat, to encourage them to override their own feelings of fullness, or to associate whether they're hungry with other issues—like world hunger or whether they're going to get to play later. If you make a special apple strudel for your kids and they don't like it, try to manage your understandably hurt feelings. Just don't force them to eat it.

If food becomes a power struggle, they may feel compelled to push back when they really just need the food. Consider leaving healthy snacks out on the kitchen counter or table. Chances are, the snacks will get eaten. Kids will eat when they're hungry. If they're using food to exert their power, so be it. Acknowledge your feelings, but the best way to get through a power struggle quickly is by *not engaging* in it. When dealing with a picky eater, let them be picky: try to be calm and relaxed when you're offering new foods, offer only one new food choice per meal, and offer new items when you know your child is hungry. In all of this, remember that your job is to set the tone with healthy food options, and then to support your child's growing sense of autonomy as they learn to notice and trust their own internal hunger signals.

If you're having trouble getting your child interested in vegetables, try adding them to foods your child already likes. Put some peas in their mac and cheese, for example, to see if pairing a new food with a familiar food helps.

Many parents in my groups also find themselves needing to take a step back to moderate their own "fear of fat," as Julia Child put it. Don't limit your baby's fat intake, and try not to make a big deal of fat as your child grows. Fats are essential for the healthy development of children's brains and immune systems. Avocado and egg yolks are both great sources of fat. Unless your pediatrician is concerned, full-fat dairy products are fine, too. If you're worried, you can consult a nutritionist, but the vast majority of humans do best when we get to eat any variety of foods of different colors that aren't super processed. Nine times out of ten, any concerns beyond that are our own baggage.

## Body Image Baggage

Willow came to me composed and confident looking, neither fat nor thin, but she had a secret. She'd been on a diet since she was fourteen years old, and she was noticing herself having a hard time watching her eleven-year-old twins, in her words, "get fat."

As with virtually every parenting dilemma, I reminded Willow to take a deep breath and ask herself what was triggering her concerns about her children's bodies. I wondered if she was worried about their health, in which case I would recommend pivoting to focus on nutrition and physical activity. Were her children expressing worries about their own bodies, or was this entirely Willow's stuff?

"Body image" has three components: perception, ideals, and sense of self. *Perception* includes how we see ourselves, whether we see ourselves as others do, and how much we focus on one feature of our appearance as opposed to the whole. *Ideals* refers to our notions of beauty, our ideas around how closely reality should match fantasy, and whether we like the way we look. Our *sense of self* is built on both our perception and ideals, and on what we value about ourselves outside of our physical appearance.

As parents, it starts with us (**Reflection**). Be honest with yourself about how you feel about your own body. Observe without judgment how you move through the world. Are you self-conscious or ashamed? Do you stare at other people's bodies and feel envious, disgusted, or anything that objectifies bodies rather than viewing them as instruments? It's understandable to have negative feelings about our bodies, because we've all been raised in a culture that reinforces perfectionism and judgment. As parents, it's our job to create a sanctuary from that unhealthy world for our kids, not to pile on the negativity.

If you've had struggles concerning body image, start doing the work to make peace with your own experiences, so that you can be present for your child. Try to break the cycle of punishing behavior or negative messages that can follow us into adulthood.

## Food as a Point of Connection and a Path to Autonomy

Instead of worrying about the exact foods your kids are eating, offering your children healthy choices and letting them exercise their growing autonomy is the best way to support their development.

There are so many different and wonderful practices to feed your children, especially when they're very young. Introduce a variety of foods early on. Choose foods of various colors that aren't so processed that they'll never go bad. A moderate approach is to introduce one new food every three days and monitor your baby for signs of allergies from each new food. Some families choose to give babies adult food right away (de-emphasizing purees and being careful of choking.) Even though it may mean introducing many foods at once, this go-with-the-flow technique can make things quite a bit easier. A popular practice called "baby-led weaning" puts the baby in control of what, when, and how much they eat. Babies are encouraged to explore different textures and tastes with very little pressure to actually ingest the food. The term is a little confusing—"weaning" in this case refers to the gradual process of replacing calories from breastmilk and formula with calories from solid food; it doesn't mean that the baby completely weans from breastmilk or formula, which should remain their main source of nutrition in the first year of life.

Your pediatrician may have a more specific view on this, and new research comes out all the time. Most things are pretty flexible, though, so try not to get bogged down in minutiae.

As your baby grows into a toddler, remember to eat with them. So often, when parents call me to discuss their toddlers' eating habits, I find out that nobody is eating with the toddler—they're just watching. The first thing I say is that every time your young child sits down to eat, you eat something, too. Who wants to just sit and eat while someone else stares at them? Mealtimes are a great opportunity for delight time (see page 133). As a bonus, when you eat with your kids, they may want to eat something you're eating that they have historically shown no interest in.

School-age kids need healthy meals and snacks. These kids are growing, mostly slowly and steadily, and usually eat four or five times a day, including snack times. Eating becomes social at school, and family, friends, and the media can influence food choices and eating habits. Don't skip a healthy breakfast—even if it has to be on the go. Virtually any food can constitute a "healthy" breakfast; the lower in sugar and the less processed the better, of course. Provide healthy after-school snacks. And let your children help with meal preparation when you can.

When schedules permit, have regular family mealtimes. Consider designating mealtimes as a device-free time, meaning no phones, tablets, or TV at the table. If you're into a specific diet trend, be really mindful about how you discuss the food you "can and can't have." Family meals aren't about bringing value judgments about food; the more you can talk about other things, the more likely everyone is to form positive associations around this time.

Let kids help prepare the meals. Kids of all ages benefit from getting involved in making their meals. When you can, include preschoolers and older kids in meal planning and preparation. If it's practical, you can try letting each child create the menu once a week and be a part of making it.

Remember that tweens do tend to eat more. Girls typically go through a growth spurt around age twelve and boys around age fourteen. Some kids grow out before they grow up. Some kids grow up before they grow out. Bodies change, and tweens can be incredibly vulnerable. Whether your child feels too gangly or too fat, it's important to take the focus off body image and refocus on the joy of healthy eating.

Tweens also tend to eat a lot of meals out of the house, and being micromanaged doesn't help them feel capable. If you catch yourself fixated on what they ate at the school lunch, absent of a recommendation from your pediatrician, you are likely making food too centered.

## Six Ways to Make Family Meals Easier

Eating together as a family is associated with lower incidences of depression and anxiety, better overall nutrition, better academic performance, and higher self-esteem. Because time spent together improves our Relationships (the first of the Five Rs), it also builds resilience. If the following ideas make your life easier, please incorporate them. (If not, I'm certainly not here to add more work to your week!)

1. **Pick any meal** (it doesn't need to be dinner). Research shows that the benefits of eating together are seen with five meals per week. This could be breakfast during the week, three meals a day on the weekends, or a few special meals spread throughout the week.

2. **Don't get caught up on the location.** Even a shared meal in the car after practice or a snack at the baseball game counts. We have to work with what we've got.

3. **Don't drive yourself crazy about the menu.** Making healthy choices *is* important, but you don't need to make a fancy farm-to-table meal or take individual orders. Keep it simple; keep it something your child is willing to eat (at least one of the offerings), and don't add unnecessary pressure, like cooking new recipes or serving five courses—unless that's totally your thing. Eating together is so much more powerful than the minutiae of what you are eating.

4. **Create new rituals.** For example, tell your highs and lows from the day or play "rose, bud, thorn, and feather" (see page 32), a game about promoting gratitude. Share stories and take turns talking. If things are *really* quiet, try a set of family conversation cards (available online). Asking silly questions can break the tension and get everyone laughing. *The Family Dinner Project* has great conversation starters on their website (like "If you had a superpower, what would it be and how would you use it to help people?" or "If you woke up tomorrow and could do one thing you can't do yet now, what would it be?" or "How do you know you can trust another person?").

5. **Use family meals to share stories about yourself.** Helping your children get to know you through storytelling can be an important way to deepen your *Relationship* as they grow. Share stories from your day, your past, your history, and your culture. Encourage your children to ask you any questions they may have.

6. **Discuss current events.** If your children have *big* ideas about the world, family meals can be a safe place to discuss them. Encourage older children to come to the meal with a topic to discuss and let them practice leading the conversation. Make the dinner—or lunch or breakfast—table a safe space for debate, lively discussion, and an open flow of ideas. Ask questions that get your kids talking, so you can find out more about what they are curious about, where they get their information, and how they process the world around them.

## Q & A Session

**Question:** My son wants to make his own bagels in the toaster oven but I'm afraid he'll burn himself. How do I decide when he's ready?

**Answer:** Autonomy-supportive parenting reminds us to let kids do for themselves what they can already do, and to teach and model things that they can't yet do. So whether it's using a toaster oven now or navigating public transportation later, step back when your kids already have the skills and teach and model the activity when they don't. Show your child how to turn on the oven safely and how to toast that bagel. Next, let them show you how they do it. Offer any safety reminders so they can keep from burning themselves, and then let them toast that bagel alone.

**Question:** My third-grader and fifth-grader aren't helping with cleaning or being cooperative around the house. When I yell at them about it, they might do something grudgingly once, but that's it. I don't have the energy to keep nagging them. I want them to have some sense of autonomy and to make choices for themselves, too, but then how do I get them to do anything? Do I just leave them alone?

**Answer:** You don't need to nag to have clear expectations. These kids are eight and ten years old, and you can plan ahead with them. Sit down with them and say, "We've got a problem. You guys haven't been cool about helping around the house. We need to figure out a solution that works for all of us. But the solution is not to leave your stuff all over. So, let's figure this out together" (***Relationship, Rules***).

## Chores by the Ages

Chores can be a great way for kids to feel they're contributing to the household, but they also train kids for life in the outside world—whether that's offering to do the dishes at a friend's house or building the skills for independent living. Of the chores your child is capable of doing, have them choose one or two that they're going to be in charge of. Kids can have regular chores, or you can make a stack of chore cards that each family draws from each week or a chore wheel.

**Chores for Toddlers:** Most toddlers love helping their parents and caregivers, but they do need supervision and guidance. Some great chores for toddlers include putting their toys away, helping put clothes in the laundry basket, or sweeping a small area with a dustpan.

**Chores for Preschoolers:** Preschoolers can often do the same chores they were doing as toddlers, but they need less supervision. At this age, they may be able to start making their own beds, water the plants and pull weeds, sort the laundry, or dust the furniture.

**Chores for Elementary-Age Kids:** When kids are about school age, they can take on a lot more responsibility, but they also might start whining about those responsibilities. This is just a budding sense of independence, and it's okay to keep your expectations steady through the rebellion. Kids ages six to ten can vacuum, rake the leaves, sweep the floors, clean their rooms, make themselves snacks, and put away groceries.

**Chores for Tweens:** Tweens and middle-schoolers should be able to do any number of things around the house, from laundry and dishes to taking out the garbage or babysitting younger siblings when you're at home.

Kids are often capable of a lot more than parents imagine. When your requests are met with resistance, lean into choice and clear expectations: Do you want to do the dishes or sort the laundry?

### Let Your Child Create a "Freedoms List"

When either of my girls and I find ourselves getting stuck in the tension between their desired freedom and my parental control, I call a moment to regroup. I suggest we problem-solve with a "freedoms list."

For us, this list is one way to talk about desired freedoms, consistent behavior, and their growing autonomy. This isn't an overnight process, but by using the following step-by-step process, you can lead your child through the responsibilities that come with independence.

1. Let your child know you have noticed they have more wants than they are allowed, and suggest a one-on-one sit-down to come up with some solutions.
2. Come up with a list of all their desired freedoms. Young children may need some help with suggestions, but likely the older set have those top of mind. Examples are a later bedtime, attending a certain party or event, traveling alone to school or a friend's house, being able to make their own breakfast, and so on.
3. Arrange the list in the order of what is possible now, followed by what needs to wait until later.
4. Express your excitement for them to have more freedom

and take on more independence. Join them in imagining what fun that independence will be and how it will feel. This establishes you as a collaborator, not a naysayer.

5. Connect the freedoms to readiness. Talk about what skills your child can build upon, the choices they can make that will support their having additional freedoms, and what they would need to do to show you they are ready. Convey optimism for their ability to reach all their desired freedoms, and meet their challenges with confidence and positivity. You are on the same team.

6. Remind yourself: this is not about a power struggle or control. This is about helping them learn the skills needed to take on more and more responsibility.

### Practice Makes Progress

I know it's all easier said than done, but practice does make progress. Only pick consequences you can enforce. Make consequences just and fair. Make a **Repair** (one of the Five Rs) after a clash. Avoid withdrawing or giving the silent treatment. And remember, **Repairs** deepen the **Relationship** you have with your child.

If you've jumped in when your child was in danger, if you've paused to respond with balance and intention, if you've given yourself permission to parent, if you've been clear about your expectations while honoring feelings, if you've made some effort to prevent escalation when possible, if you've made an attempt to understand your child's moral development as likely age appropriate, if you've offered empathy and connection, if you've avoided physical punishments in favor of connected consequences and inductive discipline, then you're on top of this parenting thing! If you've been able to be the parent you want to be *more often than not*, you're a star. This work isn't easy.

## RELATIONSHIP EXERCISE

# Watch the Kite Float Away

Of course, we all have some investment in how our kids eat and how much of our lives we are going to spend literally wiping their butts. We love them and want them to thrive. We love them and don't love the smell of urine on the carpets.

Our concerns are also wired into our DNA, our own histories, and our natural worries about what the people at the next table will think. This mindful exercise is more of a thought experiment that allows us to practice what it would feel like to have no investment at all. It helps us to calm the investment we do have. I learned it from a client who grew up on The Farm, a commune in Summertown, Tennessee, and it originates with author and Farm cofounder Stephen Gaskin.

Start by sitting or lying down someplace where you can be undisturbed and comfortable for however long you've decided you can give to this meditation. Set your timer or mindfulness app for those two or five or twenty minutes. Inhale and exhale. Adjust your posture for comfort and a sense of stability.

Now, picture your child's eating issues or sleeping issues and your own guilt, or other emotions around the issue, as a kite. What color is the kite? What shape is it? As you fully imagine it, breathe in and exhale. Now, picture that kite in the sky. You're holding on to the string. Breathe in and exhale. Visualize yourself cutting the string. Breathe in and exhale. Watch the kite as it floats away.

CHAPTER 10

# The Science of Sleep

## *Getting Enough of the Best Medicine*

*Sleep that soothes away all our worries. Sleep that puts each day
to rest. Sleep that relieves the weary laborer and heals hurt minds.*

—WILLIAM SHAKESPEARE, *MACBETH*

Kids spend up to half their early years asleep. So much developmental magic happens when we're asleep! With more public policy attention on early childhood education these days, researchers are scrutinizing this developmental need. Should kids spend more time learning in the classroom—or more time sleeping? The answer may often be sleeping, as researchers are finding that naps mean better memory-network development and more efficient memory storage (but those benefits are observed only after kids have gotten sufficient overnight sleep!)

The healthy sleep habits our kids learn before they're eighteen can serve them well for the rest of their lives. And if they have gotten into any unhealthy patterns, it's never too late to do the work to correct them so that everyone can get the rest they need.

The most important thing I can tell you about sleep is that it matters *that* kids get consolidated sleep, but it doesn't really matter *where* they get that consolidated sleep. While there are some slightly increased dangers associated with bed-sharing, there is truly no difference between co-sleeping, sleeping in one's own in a room, or having a bed in the corner of the living room, so long as the lights can be dimmed and kids can have the quiet they need to fall asleep.

There's a lot of controversy about how we get our littlest ones to sleep through the night—to sleep train or not to sleep train?—so let's clear away that noise, too: in terms of developmental psychology, it doesn't matter. You need to do what works for your unique family. Lots of my clients let their older babies "cry it out" for a few nights, and that's how those children transition to sleeping through the night most nights. This is admittedly stressful to both parent and infant, but it is a temporary stress in the context of a warm, loving, and otherwise responsive household.

This approach is sometimes mistakenly compared to other experiences, when infants are neglected in more chronic and harmful situations. Those are simply not appropriate comparisons, and just amount to more unnecessary burdens placed on parents, predominately mothers, who will likely be more present, more attuned, and more functioning when their baby is sleeping through the night.

If that situation still feels uncomfortable, you can avoid it all together and still help your baby learn to sleep. To be clear, we are not talking about hours of crying for multiple nights; if the crying is lasting for that long, it is a cue that your baby is not ready for this or is not necessarily up for this kind of learning to sleep. But a well-rested parent is worth prioritizing. You need to do what works best for your family and not let any outside feedback push you toward anything else.

## Sleep by the Ages

We know that getting enough sleep is key to brain development, mental and physical health, memory, mood, and behavior—but how much sleep is enough?

The National Sleep Foundation offers these guidelines for the total number of hours humans should typically sleep in each twenty-four-hour period. Notice these are ranges, and nothing more exact:

Newborn (zero to three months old): fourteen to seventeen hours

Infant (four to eleven months old): twelve to fifteen hours

Toddler (one to two years old): eleven to fourteen hours

Preschooler (three to five years old): ten to thirteen hours

School age (six to thirteen years old): nine to eleven hours

Teen (fourteen to seventeen years old): eight to ten hours

Adult (eighteen years and up): seven to nine hours

### Newborns Do Sleep a Lot

Newborns' brains are growing so fast it's literally exhausting—more than a million new neural connections per second! It can feel like cosmic jetlag for the caregiver, so be gentle with yourself. Most babies need to sleep every couple of hours in their first few months, and it's easy to confuse their sleep cues for hunger or boredom. If your baby seems to be disengaging, having a far-off stare, pulling on their ears, rubbing their eyes, or suddenly crying out, they're tired. It's time to slow things down and start the sleep routine—no matter how recently they woke up.

Once your baby falls asleep, it's normal for them to be able to sleep through pretty loud noises, like vacuum cleaning and even sirens, and it's normal for them to twitch and smile while they're dreaming of whatever newborns dream about.

During these early months, babies sleep around the clock, for minutes or hours, with their sleep-wake cycles interacting with their need to be fed, changed, and nurtured—and not interacting at all with whether it's day or night in the town the stork dropped them off in, and whether you're at your wit's end. Human circadian rhythms, or the sleep-wake cycle, are regulated by light and dark, and they do take time to develop, so your baby's irregular sleep schedules are normal and will pass. By six weeks, babies should begin to distinguish between day and night.

You can begin to help your newborn distinguish day from night by allowing them to sleep in a room with the curtains open and with typical daytime sounds, and then making sure the environment at night is quieter and darker, with less activity. You can also make nighttime interaction during feeding and diaper changes pretty limited and uninteresting, so your baby starts getting the cue that you're not going to be throwing a Lizzo dance party *every* night.

In these first few months, offer your baby any soothing they need to get to sleep. Babies this age cannot be "spoiled," and they're too young for sleep training. Crankiness and out-of-synch sleeping tend to peak around the six-week mark, and it's especially important during this time to be gentle with yourself as a parent so you can be gentle with your baby. By roughly ten to twelve weeks of age, circadian rhythms begin to develop, and many parents can see a glimmer of light at the end of the sleep-deprivation tunnel.

### Babies Four to Six Months Old Still Sleep a Lot

Babies this age will continue to get sleepy after being awake for what may seem like a relatively short period of time. They'll take about three naps a day. It's completely normal for babies this age to wake during the night—whether it's related to nighttime feedings, separation anxiety that typically starts around age six months, or developmental milestones like rolling over.

When your baby starts rolling over onto their stomach around age four or five months, you should still place them on their back before bed, but you don't need to keep flipping them over throughout the night. At this point, you can begin "sleep training" if you want or need your baby to start sleeping through the night without you.

A typical schedule for infants four to six months old may look something like the following (but if it doesn't look like this, don't panic; babies have a huge range):

| 7 a.m. | wake up |
|--------|---------|
| 9 a.m. | nap |
| 12 p.m. | nap |
| 4 p.m. | nap |
| 6–8 p.m. | bedtime |

If you have only one baby and you're flexible, the schedule can be flexible, too, shifting with your baby's sleep cues; but if you've got twins or need to run a more time-conscious ship, it's fine to clock naptimes starting at this point.

### Sleeping Through the Night at Seven Months

Between seven months and one year, most babies can start sleeping through the night without a nighttime feeding—even breastfed babies. A typical schedule for babies ages seven to twelve months may look something like this:

| 7 a.m. | wake up |
| --- | --- |
| 10 a.m. | nap |
| 2 p.m. | nap |
| 6–8 p.m. | bedtime |

At this age, daytime naps can be as short as forty-five minutes, but if you don't have to wake your baby, it's fine to let them sleep for as long as three hours at a stretch during the day. Neuroscience tells us that sleep during naps is a critical part of brain development, and many studies have shown that infants' daytime naps are beneficial in language learning and memory.

Avoid keeping your baby up in hopes that they'll sleep through the night. When babies aren't given opportunities to sleep during the day, they get overtired, sometimes expressing it in a kind of hyper or manic "I am *not tired*!" vibe and actually making it more difficult for them to fall asleep at bedtime and to sleep through the night. As Dr. Marc Weissbluth says, sleep begets sleep.

### Nap Transitions for Toddlers

Sometime between fifteen and eighteen months, most toddlers drop from two naps a day to one. Toddlers should continue to have at least one nap per day until age three, and some will continue to nap until around age five.

Take your cues from your child about when it's time to shift from two naps to one. Some kids stop falling asleep easily for that morning nap, and we find ourselves pushing it later and later, until there really isn't time for an afternoon nap at all. Some kids doze off easily in the mornings but are less tired in the afternoons. Others continue to get tired and nap twice a day, but then don't seem tired at night, resulting in a bedtime that's later than 8 p.m. All these are signs that it's time to shift to a one-nap schedule—usually around midday for an hour and a half to three hours.

While many children ages three to five may still be napping successfully, issues with a delayed bedtime—later than 8 p.m.—may mean it's time to eliminate the daytime nap altogether, allowing for more consolidated sleep at night. That said, research shows that toddlers generally drop their naps when their brain's hippocampus is more developed, and this happens for different kids at different ages. If it works for your family to let your child lead their own naptime schedules, that works for me.

### Age Three for the Move to a "Big Kid" Bed

Switching from a crib to a "big kid" bed—or whatever you like to call it in your family—is best around age three. The reason for this is that kids under three years don't typically have enough impulse control to follow the rules of staying in their own bed, and they don't necessarily possess the language skills to understand the directions of staying in your bed until a grown-up comes to get you (instead of walking into the grown-up's room at any point).

Transitioning too early can result in a host of bedtime issues and safety concerns. So, keep those toddlers in the crib, if possible. For most solutions and strategies for sleep, you can lean on strategies responding to behavior at night and connection during the day.

### *Grade-Schoolers Thrive with Routine*

As kids get older, keep leaning into a bedtime routine, even if that routine changes. Maybe you'll transition from reading to your child to both of you reading your own books side by side. Maybe after a bath, you'll spend some special time with your child before turning the lights off, sticking to low-stakes topics that won't upset or excite. Maybe you'll listen to music.

It's okay to use a night-light, but make sure lights are dim at night and the bedrooms aren't too hot or too cold. Set an alarm clock for morning wake-up time.

### *Tweens Do Sleep More*

As kids reach puberty, sleep patterns may change. When children go through a new developmental stage of cognitive maturation, they may even sleep more than they did during their grade-school years.

Your tween may also want to sleep longer in the mornings and stay awake later at night, even though the time they need to wake up for school hasn't changed. It's helpful to set clear limits, like what time devices and lights must be turned in and turned off.

Keep your child active during the day, but avoid strenuous exercise before bedtime. Try not to schedule too many activities, especially at night. Make sure your child avoids drinks with caffeine, like sodas, energy drinks, coffee, and tea—especially in the afternoon and evenings. Avoid a big meal before bedtime. Your tween shouldn't go to bed hungry, but a light snack is a better idea at the end of the day.

Make sure to remove screens from the bedroom. We know that the light from screens between 11 p.m. and 4 a.m. lowers dopamine, messes with focus, and generally disrupts our capacity to get a good night's sleep. Ideally, everyone in the house should ditch the phones and screens at night in the service of better sleep. We know it calls us; why not remove the obvious culprit?

Set an alarm clock for morning wake-up time. If your kids like to sleep later on days they don't have school or other morning activities, don't worry about it. But if you notice that they struggle to readjust to waking up for school during the week, you can limit sleeping in to an additional two hours. If kids need to get up at 6:30 a.m. for school on weekdays, for example, have them get up by 8:30 a.m. on the weekends. On the other hand, if they seem to be thriving and are well rested, it's fine to leave them alone to sleep in as late as they want. The more structured solutions are for the kids who are not getting proper sleep—you know who they are.

## Q & A Session

**Question:** My baby falls asleep fast when I have my white-noise machine on. Will this damage his hearing or cause other problems over the long term?

**Answer:** Your baby is in the majority on this one. In a randomized trial, 80 percent of babies exposed to white noise fell asleep within five minutes, while only 25 percent fell asleep that fast without the white noise. In a different trial, white noise significantly outperformed swinging as a way to soothe babies with colic. That said, whether you use a white-noise app or a machine, it's best to keep the levels in the seventy to seventy-five decibel range. To achieve this, you may want to keep your white-noise machine across the room instead of directly next to the crib. You can also download a sound-level monitor app from the CDC to measure decibel levels. It's kind of fun!

### Kids Need Predictability, But Not Rigidity

Sofia wanted her kids to be flexible, so she let them stay up when the family had company—but not when they didn't. This worked with her oldest child, but her second child couldn't quite process that the **Rules** changed on a night-by-night basis. He got fussy when he stayed up past his regular bedtime, and then didn't understand why he couldn't stay up a little later when he felt like it. It comes back to the solid science behind authoritative parenting. Permissive parenting—what might feel like forced flexibility—doesn't tend to work that well. Rigidity, on the other hand, is associated with authoritarian parenting. We're looking for that Goldilocks sweet spot in between. When in doubt, stick to a consistent bedtime. Even if things can't be consistent, let them be predictable. Let your kids learn to trust your steadiness. For those more biologically sensitive kids, help them thrive by leaning in.

### Too Much Accommodation Only Increases Anxiety

Abby came to me because her seven-year-old daughter was having a hard time falling asleep if Abby fell asleep first. The daughter had created a lot of different barriers to falling asleep—for example, she needed certain doors open, then she insisted she needed Abby in the room with her, and now she needed Abby to be in the room with her eyes open. Abby wanted to help, so she worked hard to make sure her eyes stayed open, but her daughter would start sobbing if Abby accidentally fell asleep first.

While Abby's goal in going along with her daughter's requests came from a place of love, allowing the process to get in the way of her own need for sleep had turned the bedtime process into what psychologists call "accommodation," and accommodation can actually increase anxiety. The SPACE (Supportive Parenting for Anxious Childhood Emotions) program at the Yale Child Study Center emphasizes that parents can respond more supportively to their children with fewer accommodations. The other extreme would be dismissiveness, which also increases anxiety, so as usual what we're looking for is the space between those two extremes.

I asked Abby what happens to her when her daughter gets sad, and she said "I feel scared that she's having such intense emotions." I challenged her to think about whether it might be helpful to her daughter to find out that her mom is not afraid of her sadness because she knows that a sad feeling is temporary and manageable. After some *Reflection*, Abby shared that she herself was afraid of pretty much all intense feelings—that she would do almost anything to make sure they went away—but she agreed to stop making the accommodations that weren't working—that were in fact just leading to need for further accommodations.

Instead, she would help her daughter with a comfort box that has pictures that made her smile, a journal, and a soft shirt that belonged to Abby. She agreed that she could talk to her daughter about the fact that it's okay if she needs to cry a little to get those sad feelings out but that everyone needed more sleep.

## Sleep Tips: Troubleshooting

Use these sleep tips if they make your life easier. If what you're already doing works for you, keep doing it and skip this part.

### When in Doubt, Shift Bedtime Earlier

Many babies and toddlers get super fussy, frustrated, and even inconsolable toward the end of the day—the dreaded "witching hour." When a baby is overtired, their body, like ours, produces a variety of hormones to stay awake. Once a baby has these elevated levels, they're more difficult to soothe to sleep and more likely to have episodes of intense crying. By the time this happens, we've missed the sleep window and that accumulated sleep debt can have an impact on schedules and behavior. If this is happening in your family, shift to an earlier bedtime, consistent with the onset of that "witching hour."

### Look for Early Sleep Cues

Putting a child to sleep later at night won't make them sleep later in the morning. It's worth repeating: when babies are overtired, their bodies, like ours, produce a variety of hormones to stay awake. This natural response makes it more difficult for an infant to fall asleep.

Avoid trying to overtire your baby in hopes of improving their sleep duration or quality. This runs contrary to many parents' instinct that children should be "tired out" or made to go to sleep later, in an attempt to sleep later in the morning. Instead, look for early sleep cues and avoid intentionally exhausting your baby.

### Keep Evenings Calm and Quiet

Whenever possible, keep the room where babies and children sleep dark, calm, and quiet throughout the night. This can help avoid overstimulation or children becoming too alert when feeding or changing diapers during the night. The benefits of everyone having a dark and quiet sleep space—adults and older siblings included—are real. Our sleep is deeper and more consolidated.

Consider rethinking TV use overnight, or bright nightlights, distracting noises, or devices. You can even experiment with using a free white-noise app on your phone, although ideally you can get a white-noise machine so you avoid having a phone in the room, even when you control it.

### Have a Bedtime Routine

Kids love routines, even if they might seem boring to adults. Research has shown that having a consistent bedtime routine is related to better sleep and better behavior. Develop a routine that includes three or four calming steps, like giving a bath, putting on PJs, feeding, and reading a book—and do these steps in the same order every night.

The content of the routine isn't important, but the consistency helps kids learn how to predict what will happen next. This sends a cue to children's brains that it's time for sleep and helps them feel secure and in control of their world. And this is true not just for younger babies and younger children but also for your older kids. Finding a soothing bedtime routine works wonders for everyone. This routine can evolve with age and for tweens may include some hygiene rituals and other habits that they associate with night, even if you are not involved.

### Have Kids Go to Bed Drowsy but Awake

When we put babies and young children down to sleep drowsy but awake, we give them a chance to learn to self-soothe and fall asleep independently. If they don't depend on us to fall asleep, they'll be less likely to need help in the middle of the night, when they inevitably wake up.

This tip is meant to be helpful, but if you prefer rocking your baby to sleep and cuddling and falling asleep with your child, there's absolutely nothing wrong with that, either. It will be harder to get them to fall asleep on their own, though, should you eventually tire of that process; just be prepared to deal with the challenge when they are a bit older and everyone feels more comfortable.

### Avoid Motion Dependence

On-the-go, "motion" sleeping, like in a stroller or a car, can make a child dependent on that motion for sleep. Of course, life happens, and the occasional on-the-go nap isn't going to be a big deal at all, but if the majority of a baby's naps happen while in motion, it may hinder their ability to learn how to self-soothe on their own later.

## A Note About Co-Sleeping and Room Sharing

We know that consolidated sleep is important for children of all ages. After infancy, it doesn't really matter where that sleep happens, but sharing a bed with your infant can be slightly more dangerous than letting them sleep in their own crib or bassinet. The American Academy of Pediatrics recommends sharing a room, but not a bed for the first year; but they acknowledge that different cultures and parental preferences might mean you share a bed. Under certain circumstances, bed sharing is more dangerous, such as if anyone in the bed has used drugs or alcohol.

Wherever your baby sleeps, place them on their back and make sure their sleep area is clear of blankets, stuffed animals, pillows, and inebriated people.

Whether your child sleeps in a co-sleeper next to the bed or in another room in a crib, whether they share a room with a sibling or not, consolidated sleep is far more important than where your child sleeps and—barring safety issues—anyone who tells you that where your child sleeps is going to impact their development or attachment relationship is not giving you a scientific opinion. I keep repeating this because there is so much misinformation out there, and I want it to be clear: procedural choices are not associated with your attachment relationship.

## Waking Through the Night Is Normal

It's common for people of all ages to wake several times in a night. Most adults have just learned to put themselves back to sleep. For infants, the problem isn't that they wake up, which is natural and expected, but rather their inability to go back to sleep without assistance. In the middle of the night, they'll look for the same environment they initially fell asleep in at the beginning of the night. If they were rocked, they'll want to be rocked again. If they were fed, they'll want to feed again. If they went for a long drive, they'll want to get back in the car.

If they were able to fall asleep without assistance, they'll be able to do it again in the middle of the night—and that's what we're looking for. Maybe more for your sanity than anything else?

### Q & A Session

**Question:** My second-grader has been having nightmares, so I want to start sleeping in his room with him again. Will this help or just cause regression?

**Answer:** That you want to comfort your child is natural, and letting him know that you care about his feelings is a wonderful place to start, but you don't need to change where you sleep (**Relationship, Rules**).

All kids have dreams, and sometimes they have scary ones. Nightmares in particular tend to peak in the preschool years, when fear of the dark becomes common, but they can reappear throughout childhood during periods of change, when a child is processing a trauma such as a natural disaster, after taking in a scary movie or book, or sometimes for seemingly for no reason at all. When nightmares occur, it's a good time to hold onto predictable routines and rituals, and not try to change things up (**Rules**).

These frightening dreams, like most dreams, happen during the REM stage of sleep, when the mind is very active. Instead of returning to co-sleeping with your child, unless you just really want to go back to that longer term, you can go to them when awakened and reassure your child that you're there (**Relationship**). You can place your hand on their back and help with your co-regulated calm. (**Regulation**).

Label what has happened; you can remind your child that the scary thing that happened in the dream didn't happen in real life. You can also remind your child that everyone dreams and it's natural to feel upset when the dreams are scary. You can keep some "monster spray" by the bed for anyone young enough to believe in the tooth fairy, and show your child how to use it to keep the scary dreams away.

Finally, you can try using a night-light to change the mood and help your child transition back to sleep, so that you can go back to sleep in your own room, too. You can also make a "brave box," which is a box that during the day the parent and child can fill with things that the child finds comforting—maybe that picture of the pet dog, cute animals, mom's shirt, some special worry dolls, a note with a mantra like "I'm safe at home. My dreams are stories in my head. Mom is home, my sibling is home, grandma is home [or whoever is home—fill in the blank]." Talk to your doctor if nightmares seem to be stopping your child from getting enough sleep, but rest assured that for most kids, nightmares only happen now and again.

## Three Tips to Encourage Sweet Dreams

1. **Stick to those routines.** I know I keep saying it, but repetition is the point! Have a regular bedtime and stick with it whenever possible. Have regular sleep routines, too, so that kids can slow down and feel calm before they drift off. These bedtimes routines might include a bath, a snuggle, calming reading, or quiet talk about the pleasant events of the day.

2. **Avoid scary movies, TV shows, and books right before bedtime.** Some kids—especially the ones with wonderfully vivid imaginations—are more susceptible to scary media than others.

3. **Make sure your child's bed is peaceful and cozy.** A favorite stuffed animal, a night-light, or a dream catcher can help.

## REGULATION EXERCISE

*Progressive Muscle Relaxation*

To get a body primed for sleep, it helps to increase the parasympathetic nervous system activity—that's the part of the nervous system in charge of digestion and resting. To do this consciously, use a progressive muscle relaxation exercise.

Lie down in bed, or someplace else where you can fall asleep. Focusing on one part of the body at a time—in any order that feels intuitive to you, say, starting with your toes and moving up through your legs and torso, then through your shoulders and down your arms to your fists—clench and release each of the muscles in the part of the body you're focused on. You can do this for yourself or with your kids, moving through the body with this squeeze and release.

In addition to helping you relax in the moment, studies show that this kind of body scan meditation done every day for as little as a few weeks improves sleep quality and decreases irritability.

## CHAPTER 11

# A Disciplined Approach to Discipline

*All Feelings Are Welcome, All Behaviors Are Not*

> *If there is anything that we wish to change in the child,*
> *we should first examine it and see whether it is not*
> *something that could better be changed in ourselves.*
>
> —CARL JUNG

The meaning of the word *discipline* is "to teach," but the feeling of the word is "to punish." Science tells us that punishment doesn't ultimately yield compliance, but *teaching* will get you into a relationship with your child that can help them learn how to move through the world with more ease, more thoughtfulness, and a better capacity to regulate themselves, so that they can stop doing the things that drive you crazy and stop doing the things that might get them kicked out of school.

When we have no consequences, we feel like we're being permissive, allowing our children to "walk all over us" or "get away with things." But when we overcorrect and have consequences that are harsh or unreasonable, we risk damaging our relationship with our child. It comes back to the consistent science regarding permissive, authoritarian, and— Goldilocks here—the winning *authoritative* parenting, the latter being that which has been shown in study after study to be most effective.

Approaching discipline with the intention to teach will set a more effective tone than approaching it with the feeling of imposing punishment. Leading with punishment sometimes makes us feel temporarily in charge, but it doesn't actually serve us or our children. Luckily for all of us, there's a large space between indulgence and punishment, and that space includes understanding, curiosity, guardrails, room for self-compassion, and **Repair**. This chapter is about how you create that space.

## Pause to Respond with BALANCE

You're with your child at a neighborhood joint, meeting up with a friend or two, with their children in tow. You've been looking forward to coffee and a conversation about the latest book club reading or whether skinny jeans are ever going to go out of fashion for good. You figure the kids will entertain each other. You've picked a spot with a little play area in the back, complete with a wooden train set and a few headless Barbies. You order your cappuccino and pastry, find a table, and make room for the others.

That's when it happens: your kid decides to throw himself on the dirty floor and have a meltdown. There was no warning; but either way, you feel partly embarrassed and partly annoyed. And in the moment, you have no idea what to do.

Whether your child is two and a half and having a temper tantrum in public or a disengaged tween checked out on their phone during family dinner, the consistent feature here is more than just kids behaving "badly"; it's the relentless challenge parents face, trying to answer the question: What's my job here?

In any moment when you feel your nervous system kicking in, pushing you into a fight-or-flight or a freeze response, take a breath. When there *is* immediate danger, like running into the street, not only is raising your voice forgivable but it's also probably necessary. But if there's no bloodshed or immediate danger, you can take yourself through the seven steps: BALANCE.

**B**reathe: Remember, there's rich neuroscience behind the power of the breath, and no, you can't skip this step. Take a breath. Teaching your child to behave from a place of calm also means modeling this quick method for getting there yourself.

**A**cknowledge your own baggage: Ask yourself, "What is this moment about for me?" For example, is your guilt, anger, frustration, or shame the filter through which you're seeing your child's behavior? Can you separate your feelings about the child's behavior from your feelings about how that behavior reflects on you? Maybe you're experiencing a flood of memories from how you were responded to as a child, and the instinct is to overcompensate for that. No judgment here. You can just reflect—and let it go for now.

**Let it go:** Leave the big-picture lessons for later. Neither you nor your child is going to be responding to big picture lessons right now.

**Assess the present moment:** Gauge your child's state of mind—calm, curious, frantic, distraught?

**Notice:** Observe what's going on with your child's body. Ask yourself what your child is trying to tell you—behavior is data.

**Connect:** Let your child know you see them and want to have a connected moment. If they want nothing to do with you, you can connect with them via your breath and the way your compassionate, curious nervous system permeates the space.

**Engage:** Now that you're in balance, you can decide which response you want to throw your weight behind. Do you want to pick your toddler up and calm them? Good. Now you can co-regulate with them from your regulated state. Do you want to distract them? Also fine. You know how they respond best in those moments. Do you want to remind them that the dinner table is a phone-free zone and that the consequence might be that they lose access to their phone for at least that meal? Good. Do you want to give up and worry about this whole parenting thing tomorrow? Also fine.

When you get into the habit of responding from this regulated, balanced place, the clarity will follow. Whatever you decide to do—

The 5 Principles of Parenting

whether or not it ends up "working"—you'll do from a place of intention, and that will bolster your relationship with your child. We know these seven science-backed steps work on mechanisms in the brain-body so we can better manage tense scenarios.

## Give Yourself Permission to Parent

Lin came to me, resigned to the chaos in her household. She'd given her fourth- and fifth-graders phones, and really had no idea who they were talking to at this point. The kids' teachers had started assigning homework the previous year, but the family hadn't established a time or a place for schoolwork. Lin wanted to talk about some boundaries for the future, but when I asked her about what already wasn't working, she shrugged, "I'm afraid that ship has sailed."

I gently reminded her that she's allowed to change her mind, turn that ship around, and establish new expectations. Sometimes we think everybody's ready for something new, and it turns out they're not; the kids weren't ready to manage their phone and homework time, and Lin wasn't ready to monitor it. It's okay to regroup and reevaluate.

Lin sighed. "I'm not sure if my kids will let me."

I actually hear that line all too often, and it's a line I hope parents can stop repeating. If you find yourself saying that your child won't *let you* parent them, ask yourself what you mean by that. Do you mean physically? Your children are pinning you down? Do you mean your child won't approach you with a smile on their face? What do you mean?

It's never too late to implement **Rules**—that is, boundaries and appropriate limits—but it also might be time to get comfortable being the bad guy. As long as your children are living with you or spending significant time with you, that ship has most certainly not sailed. It may even be a time to ask yourself if saying that the ship has sailed really means "I'm not comfortable dealing with the extreme reactions and feelings that will come from my kids, so in order to keep myself comfortable, I'm going to just accept defeat."

Practice saying no in the mirror. How does that no feel on the body for you? Practice standing your ground—it will get easier!

## Be Clear About Expectations

Setting appropriate limits means making clear your expectations of your child's behavior. An example of an expectation is a parent telling their child to keep their hands to themselves, not to text at the dinner table, or that there are five more minutes until bedtime. This gives children a sense of safety and predictability, and with practice and reinforcement, children can learn to meet the expectations set for them. Guiding children about the *Rules* of society—both in the household and in the larger context—helps them understand what is expected of them.

When you need your child to do what you say, the instructions need to be clear. Get close to your child, make eye contact, and in a loving or neutral voice, tell them—don't ask them—what to do, one step at a time. You can say "please" because saying "please" is just a nice habit to model.

For discipline strategies to be most effective, there has to be a foundational relationship in which children feel loved and secure. Discipline that focuses on teaching rather than on punishing can strengthen a parent-child relationship and build the necessary skills children need to function effectively within their family, at school, and within their other relationships.

Here are two questions to ask yourself when you respond to your kids:

1. Did I honor my child's feelings?
2. Did I make my expectations clear?

When you're wondering if you've given the right response to your child's behavior, just ask yourself, "Did I honor their feelings?" "Was I clear about the behavior that I expect?" Think back to the last conflict you had with your kid, and think about how you might answer those questions. Asking these questions won't mean you get to live in a world of no fights and no challenging feelings; it's just a way to know how you can check yourself and examine the way you play your part.

How your unique child responds isn't your job. It may become your *problem*, but it isn't your job. The more you allow those questions to guide your parenting behaviors, the more easily you will be able to put your hand on your heart and remind yourself: *parenting is a long game.*

## Come up with House Rules

My own house **Rules** are pretty basic:

+ No physical harm to humans or animals; no breaking bones, no breaking skin
+ No disrespecting property
+ No dehumanizing language
+ Each person is entitled to personal things they don't share, which go into a private drawer or private bucket, depending on the age of the child
+ Electronics are turned in at agreed-upon hours and not used during mealtime

You can have a family meeting at which you go over your house **Rules**, and you can decide together what consequences feel appropriate.

## Q & A Session

**Question:** At home, I'm getting good at breathing into a place of balance before I respond to my kid's behavior, but yesterday when we were out in public and my daughter pushed another child, I snapped at her and marched her off the playground. I feel like I forget everything I've been practicing when I'm on the spot in public!

**Answer:** We can all get so mortified when things don't go well in front of other people, and then we can lose our parenting center. When your child is acting out in public, you might have the inclination to go into shame and panic. Instead, take the moment to reflect; remind yourself that you're reacting based on what the other adults around you might think and your worry that they might be judging you. Remind yourself that you're raising this kid, you're not raising those people; you probably won't even see them again.

Or, if they are people who are in your life and in your child's life and they're invested in your child's growth and development and in you as a person, they will understand that you're centering your child and what your child needs, in that moment and in the long term. It can be helpful to remind yourself that part of why others judge your parenting is that if you are making different choices than they are making or once made (think about your in-laws), they have to either judge your parenting or question the choices they once felt were right.

Apart from special occasions with Grandma, or someone for whom you feel you need to make an exception, try to let go of the sense that you need the approval of anyone else, at the expense of being true to yourself and your children.

Lead with compassion, and assume others do, too; and if they don't, it's not really your business. What people think of you is their problem. You might even keep this phrase in your back pocket for quick access: "I'm raising my child; I'm not raising the folks around me. What matters most to me?"

## Embrace Connected Consequences

We can't protect our children from the consequences of their actions and expect them to learn. *Connected consequences* make things right. A punishment shuts your child's system down, meaning there is no learning opportunity. A consequence, on the other hand, may not be something your child is thrilled about, but it creates a cause-and-effect feedback loop in which they can learn through experience. When the consequences fit the behavior, there's no shame.

Connected consequences can be divided into *natural* consequences and *logical* consequences, if it's helpful to think about them that way. They're both connected to the child's behavior, and they're both effective. Natural consequences are ones that you have very little to do with as a parent. If your child was banging a toy against the wall and it broke, now they no longer have a toy. If your child decided not to study for a test, and then failed it, natural consequences allow them to feel the responsibility of making a wrong choice; it's not about punishment from you. All that's required from you as the parent is that you refrain from going into "fix it" mode. Don't replace the toy. Don't call the teacher and threaten to sue them. Let your child live with the results of their decisions.

Logical consequences, in contrast, take a little more proactive response from us. We can set a consequence that's directly related to the action. Maybe your toddler used their toy wand to hit their younger sibling, and you take the wand away for a few days until they are ready to learn to use it properly. Maybe your child sneaks their phone or iPad into their room for extra use at night, and loses phone privileges until you feel you can trust them again. That is, logical consequences reinforce what you're teaching your child about what you expect from them in a given situation, and they allow the child to understand the connection between their own decision-making and the loss of a privilege.

When your child breaks a rule or exceeds a limit, you tie a logical consequence to that misbehavior. For example, if your child runs away when walking down the street, you might say, "If you want to continue to walk, you need to hold my hand to keep your body safe. Running away is dangerous. Or we can use the stroller."

As kids get older, it can be helpful to start mapping out "collaborative consequences" in advance. For example, you can collaborate on the expectations and consequences at a family meeting or just in a conversation by asking, "What do you think the consequences should be if you don't follow this plan?" This way, kids start to feel like they have some control over their experience. In another example, if you're establishing expectations for online behavior, you can say, "If you bully someone online, what do you think the consequences should be?" And they might say, "You should take away my social media and my phone for three weeks." Then, if they make the choice to bully someone online, they know what's coming.

## Set the Stage for Success

### Catch Your Child Being Good

Many of us ignore good behavior and focus on the negative, so the majority of feedback our kids get from us are things like "Don't do that," or

"Put that down." Positive reinforcement, on the other hand, shifts the focus to what we *do* want to see.

For example, when your child shares a toy with his sister or spends some time playing quietly with his own books, you can notice and comment, "That was so nice of you to take a turn with your sister." Or, "I see you're looking at your books while you wait until it's time to go to school." This kind of specific and positive praise makes children more likely to repeat the positive behavior in the future, and helps kids understand what is expected of them as they navigate sharing the world with other people.

General praise like "Great job" doesn't seem to have much impact, though. Studies show that praise is most effective when it's specific and comes immediately after the behavior.

### Introduce Interoception

We all know about the five senses—sight, hearing, smell, touch, and taste—but a lesser-known sense to be aware of is *interoception*, a sense that helps us understand and feel what's going on inside our bodies. Kids who struggle with their interoceptive sense might have a hard time knowing when they feel full, cold, hot, hungry, or thirsty. Having trouble with this sense can make self-regulation extra challenging.

You can help your kids begin to develop their understanding of their body-mind connections by labeling them in yourself, such as by saying things like, "I feel so nervous; it's like I have butterflies fluttering around in my tummy." You can also try reflecting back your observations about your child's body-mind connections by saying things like, "Oh, you were so stressed out about that test that you got a headache." Or, "Your stomach growled because you're hungry."

Just a note: for a lot of kids, the space between hunger and anger or other emotional responses can be pretty small, so it's helpful to teach kids to have a snack on hand and to recognize a mood shift as possible hunger.

## Meet Big Feelings with Calm Connection

Big feelings have the capacity to shut down rational thinking, no matter how old you are. Calmly connecting with your child helps their brain move from a reactive and emotion-driven "survival brain" to a more receptive "sage brain." When parents are attuned to their child's emotional state–making them feel seen, safe, and supported–they are better able to diffuse those big feelings.

*Connecting* doesn't mean we condone our child's decision to eat their bubble-gum Chapstick; it just means that we understand they are a good human and that they were curious, but we can still give them a calm hand as they learn to shift from survival mode to developing-sage mode. No one can learn, problem-solve, or take accountability when emotions are running high without their sage partner.

Emotions are a wonderful data source. When we get in balance and feel calmer, we can interpret that wonderful data and determine the next best steps. So, save teaching for later and calmly connect in the moment.

### Follow Predictable Routines

When children know what to expect, they are less worried, feel more secure, and are more likely to behave pro-socially. When parents plan and execute consistent routines—such as at bedtime—they build executive function skills by giving children opportunities to predict what comes next, so that they can plan and act appropriately. For families where caregivers work multiple jobs, this may be difficult, but focus on whatever is predictable.

### Prepare for Transitions

Being aware of what is coming next, especially if it's not typical, decreases the intensity of emotions that escalate when children feel surprised by a change. Offering children frequent reminders and having a schedule can help kids handle transitions more flexibly. For example, a five-minute warning if it is almost time to leave the house, such as "Remember, we have to leave to go to dinner in five minutes," can help to avoid some of the tension that transitions often bring. Even if your younger ones can't quite grasp what five minutes actually feels like, they'll learn to understand what to expect.

### Anticipate and Prevent When Possible

While even the calmest, most authoritative parent can't prevent every tantrum, we can learn to anticipate what sets off our unique children, and then set up the environment and schedule accordingly. For example, if tantrums frequently occur in the late afternoon, avoid overstimulating activities at that time of day. If seeing cookies ignites too much temptation, keep the package in the closed cabinet.

Validating a child's feeling early in the reaction can often prevent escalation. You can say something like, "I know you really love cookies and we're about to go to pick up cookies for Aunt Molly, but we won't be getting cookies for ourselves. Do you think you can pick out your favorite cookie and we can take a picture so we remember to get it next time we go to the bakery and are buying ourselves a treat?"

### Plan Ahead with Big Reactors

If your child is a "big reactor" and your attempts at connection are met with ever more intense tantrums, violence, or spitting, then connection may not be their thing. Spend some time with your big reactor when they're *not* upset, and discuss what would help them self-soothe when they're having those big reactions. You might consider setting up a safe space for them with comfort items that can help them regulate when your presence escalates the situation or when you have two other kids to attend to and may need to physically protect their bodies.

## *Offer Choices*

Giving kids choices (when choices are a reasonable option) allows them to exert some control over the world around them and encourages co-operation while decreasing power struggles. For example, offering a child the choice to get into the stroller themselves or for a parent to put them in the stroller may help to avoid the tantrum when a parent chooses for them. You might say something like, "Do you want the blue cup or the red cup?" for a younger child, or "Do you want to take your screen time before dinner or after dinner as your break?" for an older child.

## *Introduce Contracts*

Older elementary-school kids and tweens can begin to understand specific expectations, obligations, and previously agreed-upon consequences. By formalizing these into a written contract, you make the expectations that much clearer, and you help kids start practicing what it's like in the larger society to make commitments that may even be legally binding.

You are ultimately the parent, but this has to be done collaboratively to a certain extent, and it feels good for kids to be able to ask for what they feel is reasonable. When invited to collaborate, they will also be more likely to feel respected and respect the plan.

## Understand Their Moral Development

When our kids act out, it can be helpful to understand where they're coming from developmentally. After all, kids don't know the social contracts when they get here. They rely on us to guide them as they learn how to act appropriately in various contexts.

American psychologist Dr. Lawrence Kohlberg has a theory of moral development that gives us insight into the decision-making process when humans are presented with moral choices. This can help us manage our expectations by considering not *our* moral understanding (e.g., only a selfish brat would steal that toy from his sister) but, rather, the understanding of a particular child's developmental phase, cognitively and ethically.

Kohlberg interviewed people of various ages and analyzed how they justified their behavior when faced with moral decisions, and he came up with six stages humans typically go through as we mature. He called the first two stages *preconventional* morality, the next two stages *conventional* morality, and the last two stages *postconventional* morality. Before our kids become teens, they grow through the first four stages. As adults, they may mature into postconventional morality.

### Preconventional Morality

Preconventional morals are typical in childhood through about age nine, and among adolescents and adults when under pressure. The preconventional stages are as follows:

**Stage 1: Obedience and Punishment.** In this orientation, humans figure that if they get punished for something, it must be bad and if they get rewarded, it must be good. An example of leaning into preconventional morality is when a kindergarten teacher tells students that they are not allowed to leave the classroom during class time or they will have their name put on the board. Because the rule has an associated punishment, most kids will obey it without thinking about the whys and the nuances of the rule.

**Stage 2: Self-interest, Individualism, and Exchange.** At this second level, humans are driven by fear, reward, and self-interest. Think about it for yourself: *What would make you override the fear of punishment when you were making a decision that might get you in trouble?* Your answer might be on the high road because you're much further along in your development, but sometimes the answer is going to be more basic: there's something in it for me. As for children, it's completely normal and appropriate for them to weigh fear of punishment with self-interest.

### Conventional Morality

Humans tend to develop into the conventional level of morality at around age nine and stay here at least through adolescence.

**Stage 3: Interpersonal Accord and Conformity.** At this stage, it's developmentally appropriate for kids to start caring what other people think. They also internalize the moral standards of their adult role models. Often that's you, but if tweens seem unexpectedly conventional, approval seeking, or suddenly embarrassed about the things that make your family unique, know that they're just doing their developmental work as they learn more sophisticated ways of navigating social norms.

**Stage 4: Maintaining Social Order.** This is a super-interesting stage when children really come into their understanding of the wider rules of society. Their judgments take into account concerns for obeying the *Rules* in order to uphold law and order, and avoiding guilt. Authority is internalized and not questioned, unless that questioning is really a part of their culture or subculture.

### *Postconventional Morality*

Postconventional morality is rare among adolescents and slightly less rare among adults. Kohlberg established that only 10 to 15 percent of humans ever get to stages 5 or 6—but it may be something to strive for. Postconventional morality means we understand universal, abstract ethical principles based on personal, nuanced values like the preservation of life or the importance of human dignity. A person with postconventional morality is someone who doesn't need a parent, a police officer, or even a law to tell them how to behave.

**Stage 5: Social Contract and Individual Rights.** Here, we understand that a rule or law may exist for the good of the greatest number of people, but there are times when it makes ethical sense to break it. For example: Would you steal to save a life?

**Stage 6: Universal Principles.** At this stage, humans literally don't need laws because their own ethical compass and moral guidelines are consistently on point. Weighing issues of human rights, justice, and equity, a person at this stage is prepared to act to defend these universal principles, even if it means going against the rest of society and having to pay the consequences. For example: Would you refuse to serve in a war you thought was unethical, even if it meant imprisonment?

---

What's salient for parents is to remember that the preconventional level our kids are in lasts until they're about nine, and that's normal. The conventional level our kids move into as adolescents is also normal, and a perfectly acceptable place to stay. Having adult children who can engage in postconventional morality might be one of your goals or hopes, but it's not likely something you'll see in them until adulthood.

One way to help get them to the next level is to make it a practice of noticing together how your stomachs feel when an ethical conundrum comes up, when anyone causes minor harm, or when they lie to cover up breaking a rule. Rather than telling a child how they should act, you can help them pay attention to what their body tells them when their inside values don't match their outside behavior.

## Effective Discipline Helps Shape the Growing Brain

As a parent, you've set the stage for success, you've made your expectations clear, you understand childhood moral development, but your child is still acting a fool. It's time to step into your authority and practice some *intentional discipline.*

Studies in neuroplasticity—the brain's ability to adapt—have shown that repeated experiences *change* the physical structure of the brain. With effective discipline, the parent's goal is to strengthen the connections between the back and front parts of the brain—for both the children and caregivers—so that everyone's responses can be less reactive and more thoughtful.

### Think About Your Discipline Goals

As parents, we all have to find healthy patterns for responding to our kids when they don't meet our expectations. Of course, we're not going to respond perfectly all the time, but we're looking for *more often than not,* and that's something that, with thought and practice, most parents find manageable. If you have a spouse, partner, or co-parent, talk to them about your values and how you will address unacceptable behaviors, as well as what your goals are in disciplining your child. This requires coming to terms with your own childhood and how you feel about it, then creating a vision and plan for your own parenting moving forward.

The most common follow-up response I get when I talk to parents about boundaries is this: "But I don't want to shame my child." That's a great place to start, because we know that children don't learn well when they're shamed. Shaming calls into question someone's worth as a person; it implies that the mistake is who they are, as opposed to something they did. But there's nothing shaming or shameful about setting a boundary or a limit around a behavior—and staying focused on why that behavior is unacceptable.

Having conversations with your kids early on—whether it's about family values or simply discussing different scenarios where you have expectations—is an incredibly useful way to set a limit or define a boundary *before* it gets tested. If your children disappoint you or they do something dangerous, you can remind them of those previously established limits and implement consequences, but your responses needn't be fear based. You don't have to come at them with a shaming attitude, because that can leave them feeling like there's something wrong with who they are. Instead, you can say, "I have expectations about behavior that you are not meeting right now. We're going to tighten the walls a bit."

I know it can be frustrating when kids aren't compliant, and we want a quick fix to get them to behave, but raising a child who will eventually be able to hold up their end of life's social contracts is a long process. Here are a few examples of how you might respond in an authoritative way when you need your child to change their behavior:

**If there's imminent physical danger.** That's exactly when you're supposed to sound the alarm. If your child is running with scissors, you can say, "No!" You can grab your child to stop them from getting injured or from injuring someone else. You don't have to have a peaceful, measured response. When there's real danger, we do want everyone's adrenaline to respond.

**If there's no imminent physical danger.** If your child is pushing through the limits in a way that creates something other than a crisis situation, like ripping the head off their sibling's beloved stuffed animal, you have time to go through the BALANCE steps (see pages 8–9):

*Breathe.*

*Acknowledge your own baggage.* Maybe the stuffed animal cost a lot of money or was a gift from your mother. Maybe you never got stuffed animals when you were a kid. Maybe you are aware that this was their siblings' only way of falling asleep without you. Maybe you're making up a future and deciding that this behavior will lead to your child becoming a serial killer.

*Let it go.*

*Assess the current situation.* Your child is cutting off a stuffed animal's head and that's a behavior you don't want to tolerate. (Maybe "no destroying property" is even on your house rules list.) Notice what's going on in your child's body. Are they upset? Are they calm?

*Connect.* You can reach out to your child physically or say something like, "It looks like you're upset."

*Engage from that point of balance.* No one is in imminent danger—I mean, except maybe Pooh Bear—so there's no need to increase the adrenaline in this moment; but you can still say, "We don't destroy toys in this house. Let's figure out what's going on here."

## Q & A Session

**Question:** My seventeen-month-old constantly puts things in the toilet even though I've told her a million times not to. I know she's just doing it to irritate me. She gives me the most gleeful little look when she does it! What can I do to show her who's boss?

**Answer:** Children are scientists. Your child is likely fascinated by the whole concept of the toilet—in something goes, flush, and watch it disappear! It's pretty normal and expected for toilets to become one of a toddler's favorite toys. Because it does get your attention, they've also learned that for some reason, when they go near the toilet, it's a guarantee you'll follow and engage. At this age, it is a lot to expect not to party with a fun toilet toy when there's so much fun and attention involved.

When we view toddler behavior as manipulative or defiant, it's understandable that our automatic reaction is to come down harder and harsher. But trying to punish away challenging behavior misses opportunities to strengthen the very skills toddlers lack, like self-regulation and frustration tolerance. Besides, punishing in these kinds of situations is unlikely to be effective (**Relationship**, **Regulation**, **Rules**, **Repair**).

When we take into account how kids' temperaments can make parenting more challenging, it becomes a little easier to stop taking their behaviors so personally and start noticing whether our "asks" might be too big for them to carry out (**Reflection**).

It may be, in this case, considering her age and her interest in doing something too destructive to keep allowing, it's time to set her up for success by keeping the bathroom door closed and off limits to her until a grown-up can be with her. When you're in the bathroom together, you can practice showing her what *can* go in the toilet and how it is important to only put a little bit of what can go in (e.g., toilet paper), because you also don't want to waste water. Then you show her something she can put objects into (e.g., the trash can) and you can thank her for keeping to that plan (**Rules**).

**Question:** My thirteen-year-old just walked in the house smelling like a chimney! My father died of lung cancer, and I'm freaking out. Please help.

**Answer:** If you discover your teen is doing something that *is* physically dangerous, like smoking, but not immediately so (like getting ready to jump off a diving board into an empty pool), you have time to get into balance and avoid flipping out. Remember, too, that it's okay to be BAD: Breathe, Assess, Deal (see page 10). But since this matter is bringing up other issues for you about your own father, you'll want to go through all seven steps of BALANCE:

> **B**reathe. Breathe in through your nose and out through your mouth to give yourself that moment to reset your nervous system. You know that all feelings are welcome, but all behaviors are not. This is

bringing up your grief and other feelings about your father's smoking, and that's natural.

*A*cknowledge that baggage.

*L*et it go for now (**Reflect, Regulate**).

*A*ssess the current situation. Your child has obviously been smoking and you're clear that's something you cannot allow (**Rules**). That's all that's going on in this moment.

*N*otice what's going on. Check your child's body. Do they seem stressed out? Are they strutting like they've just figured out how to be cool?

*C*onnect with your child. You can reach out and touch their shoulder. You can say. "I love you and I need to tell you that you smell like you've been smoking" (**Relationship**).

*E*ngage. Finally, from your balanced, intentional place that sets aside your deeper associations with smoking, you can deal. You can say some version of, "This behavior tells me that you're really pushing limits, or you're really stressed out, or you're feeling peer pressure, or you're feeling curious. How can I help you satisfy those needs emotionally, which are very valid, without doing this thing that is so harmful I cannot allow it anymore?" (**Relationship, Regulation, Repair, Rules**).

Because you've taken the time to get in BALANCE, you can lay out the logical consequences—or you can tell your child that you need some more time to consider the logical consequences because you recognize that this particular infraction is also quite scary and painful for you, and you want to make sure you are thinking clearly. You might say, "I'm going to go through your room and all your private spaces to make sure that you don't have anything dangerous, and I'm going to walk you home after school until we figure out a new plan." Or you could say,

"I'm going monitor you a little bit more until we figure out what's happening. I get that you are going to make mistakes. I just want to make sure that I'm here to keep those mistakes from getting too far" (**Relationship**, **Rules**, **Repair**).

## Present a United Front with Parenting Partners

When it comes to discipline, most parents aren't on the exact same page with their partner, but presenting a united front means having the same basic parenting goals. Unless your partner is placing your child in imminent physical danger, avoid undermining their authority in front of your child—that diminishes your own authority and sends the message that the adults don't really know what they're doing, and that consequences are always up for debate.

Even if you're part of an in-agreement parenting partnership, chances are at some point you still won't be thrilled with a punishment your partner blurts out in anger, or a limit they set—or one they ignore. They probably feel the same way about you sometimes. We're all only human, after all, and we have our own histories, temperaments, and triggers.

The problem isn't conflicting opinions but, rather, how you handle them in front of your child. When something starts with your child but spirals into an argument between you and your partner, that lack of unity can be confusing, even anxiety-provoking, for your child. Lack of a unified front can also present an opportunity for your child to get off the hook by playing one of you against the other, distracting the focus from the fact that they called the nice neighbor lady an old hag to her face. So, even if you disagree with your partner's parenting in the moment, try to save your thoughts for later, when you're out of earshot of your child and you've both calmed down.

Also, it's not bad for kids to know you sometimes don't see eye-to-eye with your partner. But it's harmful for them to see you continuously handle your disagreements poorly, especially right in front of them. If you do end up undermining one parent or regretting that an argument ensued, take the opportunity to **Repair** and show your child how you resolve conflicts respectfully. We are only human, after all, and luckily you will have plenty of opportunities every day to show *Repair* in action.

## Discipline Practices that Don't Work

*If we can share our story with someone who responds*
*with empathy and understanding, shame can't survive.*

—BRENÉ BROWN, PhD

As you continue to think about the ways you want to use discipline in your family, it's helpful to look at the science and understand that many traditional discipline practices have been debunked as ineffectual—and sometimes downright harmful. In fact, understanding why some common discipline strategies are *ineffective* can help you troubleshoot effectively when you find yourself in a pattern that isn't working.

### *Physical and Emotional Punishments*

Basically, discipline strategies like physical and emotional punishments, threats, yelling, shame, or illogical consequences may make parents feel more in control in the moment, but decades of research have shown that the undesirable behaviors usually reappear once these punishments are withdrawn and then the severity of punishments has to increase over time in order for parents to maintain control.

Importantly, the science doesn't support physical punishment of any kind, including spanking or hitting. Spanking still happens in some 35 percent of households across the country, but it isn't effective—and any kind of physical punishment can be potentially damaging. Even when done with the best of intentions, it's scary, ineffective, promotes more aggressive behavior, and is associated with poorer cognitive, social, and emotional outcomes.

Here's why. A brain that thinks it's under attack can't learn. If you raise your hand to a child because it feels like that's the only way they're going to learn how important it is that they change their behavior, their brains go into a primitive "survival brain" mode, where it shuts down all learning and just tells them to get to safety.

Think of spanking as saying to your children, "Hitting isn't acceptable for you, but it's okay when I want to do it. It's my solution when I'm frustrated with someone's behavior." That's how spanking teaches children to become more aggressive. Instead of modeling a calm, sensitive, and thoughtful approach, spanking models the use of corporal punishment as the most effective tool in managing behavior.

Studies do show that in families where spanking is part of the discipline practice, parental support can mitigate the negative impacts of physical punishments. This may be helpful to know if you have a co-parent who insists on using physical punishment, or if you have used physical punishment in the past. As with everything else in parenting, the meaning of a particular practice depends on the broader context of the parent-child relationship.

Threats, yelling, and criticism also don't work. These are generally reactive responses parents blurt out in the heat of the moment, rather than their coming from a place of intention and balance that serves their relationship with the child.

### Unconnected Consequences

If the consequences you come up with aren't clearly connected to your child's actions, take that as a red flag: maybe you're just reacting from your own discomfort with the situation. For example, if your toddler doesn't listen well at bedtime and therefore loses out on going to the birthday party they were supposed to go to the next day, well, there's no connection between those two things, so there's not going to be any lesson learned. In contrast, with connected, logical consequences, the line between the action and the result is quite clear:

*You made a mess and now you have to clean it up.*

*You stole your friend's toy, so you need to give it back.*

*You texted something cruel on a group chat while you still have training wheels, so you need to check with your parent before you send something out to a group.*

*You took the car and stayed out past curfew, and now you have to surrender the keys.*

### Ineffectual Time-Outs and Negotiations

Sometimes when we're trying to move away from the yelling and physical punishments that may have been wired into us as children, we instead turn to punishments that seem quieter and less violent, like time-outs, logic, and negotiation. These strategies may all have their place, but they're overrated.

*Time-outs* are a popular discipline technique used by parents, and often recommended by pediatricians, to prescribe a nonviolent and minor punishment in instances where parents and children would otherwise escalate to something damaging. To be clear, time-outs are not associated with long-term negative outcomes, and the science has found no significant difference for children whose parents reported using time-out versus those who did not.

They may be a good option if you, as the parent, need a moment to calm down so as not to react with violence, but the one-minute-per-year of the child's age that used to be recommended has not been shown to be effective, and if the time-outs aren't helping you as a parent, or if you don't feel you are at risk for further escalation of your own self-regulation, you can go ahead and let go of them.

Another ineffective response when a child is angry or in a reactive state is to appeal to their *logic*. By definition, a child's ability to think rationally when in "survival brain" state is limited. Later, when your child has calmed down enough that their brain is back in a receptive "sage brain" state, using logic to explain your reasoning is important in helping them understand your intention and in their making better decisions in the future. For example, you can say, "When you ran away earlier, it was very scary, and I yelled because I thought you could get hurt. When we're on the street, we need to hold hands to be safe."

## Shift into Connection and Empathy

*The number one thing you can do in the moment if your child is falling apart is connection and empathy.*

—TINA PAYNE BRYSON, PhD

The most effective discipline strategy comes from connection and positive reinforcement, with clear structure and expectations that build a solid foundation for emotional and behavioral growth. These strategies may also serve to prevent some—although, let's face it, not all—outbursts and tantrums. Clearly defined and consistently enforced limits allow kids daily opportunities to practice managing their emotions and their bodies when they don't get what they want, or when they have to deal with change or challenges.

At any age, parents can handle these behavior challenges by having empathy for a child's experience, acknowledging and validating their feelings, setting fair and just consequences, and most important, tolerating their disappointment. Moments of **Repair** deepen the parent-child relationship and provide learning that can be applied to other circumstances.

If your children have multiple caregivers, it may be helpful to share the clearly defined limits and consequences with all the adults involved. This way, discipline strategies can be consistent and effective. That said, we can't control how other people respond to our children, and the science is clear: Even one caregiver—that can be you—who uses effective discipline strategies will benefit a child's developmental outcomes.

## REFLECTION EXERCISE

*Act from Intention*

Remember that pause between stimulus and response we talked about in Chapter 1? In that pause, we get to choose the response we're going to throw our weight behind. So, that moment—those brief seconds between your child's action and your response—is the space where you'll find a new opportunity every day to pause and reflect.

Breathe in through your nose and out through your mouth. Simply recognizing that space can give you the pause you need to BALANCE and respond to your child in a thoughtful way, instead of an impulsive one. In noticing the moment, you're also co-regulating with your dysregulated child and modeling the mature self-regulation you're hoping they'll eventually internalize. Most of the parents I work with have a predictable next question: "Okay, but then what?" Now that you've given yourself that moment to reflect, now that you've gotten yourself into BALANCE, what should you do? Essentially, anything you want. If you've calmed yourself down—even with just a moment's breath and assessment of the situation—you can act from intention, and that's everything. The following tips make most parents' lives easier.

### Say It to Slay It

Daniel J. Siegel and Tina Payne Bryson coined the phrase "Name it to tame it." In the same vein, as I mentioned earlier in the chapter, I like to say, "Say it to slay it." Just like it's helpful for us as adults to pause and remind ourselves that our feelings have names—*I'm angry* or *I'm sad*—helping kids label their emotions is the first step in helping them slay "it" as they start to understand those feelings and accept that they're normal and manageable. Eventually, emotional fluency will allow our kids to consciously choose their responses to their triggers, but just like linguistic fluency, emotional fluency begins with a few key vocabulary words.

Often kids aren't even aware of what emotion they're feeling during an outburst, so it can feel comforting to have parents validate them directly. For example, "You're angry because I said you can't have the ice cream right now." Or, "I wonder if you're sad because you didn't get invited to a party. That makes sense. It's hard to feel like your friends are doing something fun and did not think to include you." Giving kids a chance to label their feelings and share with you what they're upset about creates space for everyone to respond thoughtfully, rather than react mindlessly. As younger children need more direct labels, older kids need guidance to find their own labels. That's when naming becomes a matter of wondering and guiding.

Another aspect of emotional fluency is being able to connect how we are feeling with where in our bodies we feel it. You can model this by noticing and saying where you feel things in your body, and by encouraging your child to notice their own feelings-body connection. If you're already clear in your language concerning feelings, take a break from that for a while and practice asking your child where in their body they might be feeling a feeling. What part of their body are they feeling in the moment? Do they feel nervous in their tummy? Do they feel unfairness in their throat?

This strategy isn't usually effective in the heat of the moment, but once everyone is regulated, it's an interesting way to teach children to pay attention to their bodies when their bodies send them signals. You can start with something simple, just by pointing out obvious feelings connected to our bodies such as hunger and building from there.

### Opposites—Tell Your Child What You'd Prefer

Every negative behavior that you want to get rid of has what psychologists refer to as a positive opposite. Instead of yelling, "Don't jump on the couch," try, "Please jump on the floor." Instead of saying, "Don't throw your food on the floor," try, "Please keep your food on the table or in your mouth."

### Label and Stabilize Your Own Moods, Too

Just like we teach our kids to "Say it to slay it" when it comes to their emotions, you can also start talking to your kids about your own affective state—or your mood. You might say, "I feel stressed out because we've got company coming, so if you've noticed I've been short with you, know that it has nothing to do with you! I'm actually going to go for a walk so I can feel a little bit more at ease."

Explaining your affective state takes the guesswork out of it for your kids and helps them feel more aware of saying what they're feeling. It normalizes finding healthy ways to address and slay these emotions. It also makes it clear that they are not responsible for your mood, which is a gift that cannot be overstated.

When you underscore that you have strategies for taking care of your own feelings, acknowledging what is going on can make more sense than pretending you are fine and then lashing out. Keep in mind that for younger kids you would probably want to use fewer words while you can get more sophisticated with older kids.

### Practice Inductive Discipline

In contrast to shame, a little bit of constructive and appropriate *guilt* can actually help encourage empathy. When you ask your children to reflect on how their *intentional* behavior may have caused harm to another person, you're not shaming them for who they are but, rather, invoking an adaptive feeling that will encourage your child's sense of remorse. That will in turn help them develop their moral and ethical standards. Empathy-based guilt—when we've intentionally done something that ended up causing harm—can help us learn how to **Repair** our **Relationships**.

Psychologist and professor Dr. Martin Hoffman defined three common approaches to discipline in parenting: There's power assertion, when a parent uses physical punishments, privilege deprivation, or threats. There's love withdrawal, when a parent gives their child the cold shoulder or the silent treatment. And then there's what Hoffman called "inductive discipline," associated with the best outcomes, including empathy building.

Here's how to use inductive discipline:

1. Step back and ask yourself: What am I trying to achieve? What values am I trying to instill in my kid? If you've already got your family values written up, you've got the answer at your fingertips.

2. Take a moment to model empathy yourself. You can say something like, "I can see why you wanted to hit your

brother because he seems to be getting all the attention right now."

3. Call out why your child's behavior was unacceptable to you. You can say simply, "I love you, but that [name specific behavior] was unkind." And then explain why.

4. Specify the behavior as the source of your disappointment— *not* your child. You can say something like, "The behavior was unkind because you did not consider your friend's feelings. I know you are a kind person and I expect you to think about how another person might feel. Let's think of how we can do it another way." Rather than making a child feel shame for who they are, this approach sets boundaries within which kids can feel safe to be themselves as they grow into more caring and self-disciplined young people.

### Let Your Expectations Grow with Your Children

There is no one-size-fits-all approach, but the optimal discipline strategy stems from a parenting style that balances love and connection with clear, consistent, age-appropriate expectations. This approach to discipline helps children feel a sense of connection and consistency, is kind and firm, and teaches valuable life lessons and social skills that children need to control their own behavior.

Often, our misconceptions about what our children can "control" leads to our increased frustration and possible punishment. We assume that our young children "know better" than to make a mess with their food or bite their friend, but we forget that they are only beginning to learn how to control their bodies. Even if they know something is wrong, they may lack the ability to stop themselves each time. Their brains are only beginning to make the connections between what they know and what they do. If you can connect with your child and redirect their behavior, it may not mean they will be able to stop themselves from doing the same thing the very next time, but through repetition they will eventually learn.

In this vein, consider how to handle this situation in the following age groups.

**Infants and young toddlers:** Under age two, they lack a lot of the skills required to be able to control their behavior and manage their emotions. When infants are upset, they can usually be easily distracted. You can often just replace the thing that's upsetting them, or the thing you've taken away from them, with something else. "I know you like to play with that, but it isn't safe. You can have this instead." When this isn't possible, acknowledge their feelings before quickly moving their attention to something else.

**Preschoolers:** Kids can't hear you when they're screaming or crying, and they first need physical soothing and space to calm down. Offer them an initial empathic response. You can discuss the details and possible consequences to behavior later—after they are regulated. State your intention: "I'm here to help it go better next time." Instead of leaning into time-outs, think about a "time-in" connection to give the child and parent an opportunity to settle down. They should not be used as a punishment but, rather, as a strategy to help you and your child learn how to self-regulate through the pause.

Develop a comfy corner to help your child calm their body with your support. Have them pick out soft furniture like a beanbag chair, some books or stuffed animals, maybe even some music. Let them build it! Having a safe place to go to when they feel out of control can help your child practice the skill of self-regulation. This should be the opposite of feeling like they have been sent away; it should be a place that gives them a sense of ease so they can decide to invite you to join if it is helpful, or if they want to be left with their lovey and glitter jar. That's okay, too. For the kids who actually feel more dysregulated when you try to join them, respect their need for space and don't get hung up forcing a connection. In that case, you are respecting their boundaries of a desire to have some distance.

Later, when you and your child are calm, have a conversation. Use your voice to convey, "I will help you with this even if I may be upset about what happened." Invite your child to state what happened, and to shed light on their reasoning. You can also reflect on what you observed. You might say, "I know you knew that that could break, but it was so tempting and so hard not to touch." Talk about what can be done differently next time and come up with new solutions together.

No matter what approaches you take to help guide your toddler's behavior, remember that they won't work the first time. Discipline requires consistency, repetition, and patience. Remember also that your child isn't trying to be difficult; it's that they are new here and in the process of learning.

**Elementary-age children:** Though there are many different types of challenges, one common one is a child's wanting something so badly that desire overrides what they know about "right" and "wrong." They may know they're not supposed to steal a friend's chocolate granola bar, but they really *want* it! Kids this age may tell a lie, cheat in a game, or take something they really want. Understand where your child is developmentally. Say something like, "I can see how much you wanted that and how hard it was to let it go." Give or allow a natural consequence directly connected to the behavior you don't want to see. Have your child return anything they may have stolen and apologize. Talk about the way being stolen from makes people feel. It's okay to connect the challenging behavior with the future by saying something like, "When you swipe someone's toy and don't return it, it makes it hard for them to feel comfortable playing with you when you are ready to play."

**Tweens:** While it may have worked to just tell them what to do when they were younger, now it's more effective to engage them in a conversation about why their behavior is not acceptable and what they think you can do about it as a family. With so much going on—intense self-consciousness, awareness of self, body development, outside expectations, and age-appropriate sexual drive—it's important to have compassion for the tween in your life.

That said, as kids enter adolescence (emerging adolescence begins around age ten), they're much more capable of engaging in cooperative problem solving. This is also a time when behavior contracts become especially appropriate and effective. If you lose your cool as the parent, it's okay to apologize. Try something like, "I thought about what happened and what I said or did and I feel bad about it. I think that I could have done it differently, and that's what I'm going to try to do from now on." Focus on modeling the importance of humility and self-reflection, and rest assured that this will not undermine your authority. Show you care by paying attention to your child's moods and behaviors, and get to know their friends' parents.

## Q & A Session

**Question:** I don't want to embarrass my kid by reprimanding her in public, but I don't want to change established rules just because other people are around. Any suggestions?

**Answer:** You can set up a signal when you're establishing and talking about the **Rules**—something as simple as pulling on your ear to remind your child of the limit or the rule. Importantly, don't talk about a gesture that will come across as a threat but, rather, as a point of connection and a secret sign that says, "Hey, we don't have to get into it verbally right now, and I know you really want to stay on this playdate, but remember that we said it was going to be hard to leave when it came time but we have to get home in time for dinner" (**Relationship**, **Rules**).

## REPAIR EXERCISE

### Picture a Blue Light of Compassion Amid the Conflict

Sit down or lie down someplace where you can get comfortable. Notice where your body is in contact with the floor, the bed, or the chair. Take an intentional breath, and exhale. Take a few moments just to focus on the flow of your breath.

Now, bring to mind a situation in which you didn't handle a conflict in a way you feel super-proud about. It can be something fairly small. Allow the conflict to play back in your mind's eye like a movie. Recall how you felt in your body. Now, imagine compassion as a blue-tinted light, and imagine that light surrounding yourself in the conflict. Keep breathing. Now, focus on the other person or people involved in the conflict. As you play back the conflict, notice what was going on in the other person or people's bodies. Expand that blue light of compassion to include them.

Breathe in and breathe out. Now, if you can, try to shift into the other person or people's perspective, seeing the conflict from their point of view.

Breathe in and breathe out. What would it be like to be in your child's or your partner's body and state of mind? If the people involved in the conflict were sad, angry, or afraid, just notice that. Picture your blue light of compassion encompassing the whole interaction. Send a silent message of acceptance toward all the people involved. See yourself apologizing, if that's appropriate. Place your hand on your heart and say, "I send compassion to myself."

Now, if it's appropriate, you may want to reengage with your children or partner.

## CHAPTER 12

# Common Points of Conflict

## *Apply What You've Learned to Tricky Situations*

*Man must evolve for all human conflict a method
which rejects revenge, aggression, and retaliation.
The foundation of such a method is love.*

—MARTIN LUTHER KING JR., NOBEL PEACE PRIZE ACCEPTANCE SPEECH

Humans, like strong trees, can sway without snapping. And that's what we rely on as human parents. Psychologist Edward Tronick, who was mentioned in Chapter 5, has extensively researched why some children become sad, withdrawn, insecure, or angry, while others become happy, curious, affectionate, and self-confident. He learned that the kids who tend to grow up happy and curious aren't the ones who've never experienced negative interactions with their parents; rather, they are the ones who've learned to trust that their parents are well-meaning humans who are willing to make things right when they go temporarily wrong. It's not the conflict or the ruptures that hurt us—it's the lack of *Repair*.

So, what does *Repair* look like in everyday life? It might be a simple verbal or a nonverbal apology. We *Repair* our relationships by being warm, calm, gentle, respectful, connected, empathic, loving, accepting, curious, and playful. We know when *Repair* has happened; sometimes it's just a shared laugh or a knowing glance, while other times it is an explicit conversation.

When you set a limit, you can absolutely expect pushback, but as the parent you can still make your expectations clear. Conflict comes with the territory, but just as all couples argue (and successful couples *Repair*), all parents and kids have points of conflict where the bond can feel ruptured. What builds relationships isn't that there's never rupture; it's when the rupture is followed by **Repair**. Children actually learn to feel more secure when they learn that good things can follow bad things, when they experience being forgiven, when they see that humans make mistakes or have conflicts and that it isn't the end of the world—it's not even the end of the relationship. When emotions run hot, we have an opportunity as parents to practice our own emotional intelligence. When facing conflicts of any kind, I find it helpful to know what we can expect from our kids developmentally, and over the years I've learned a few helpful hacks I share with you.

## When Approaching a Conflict, First Get in BALANCE

I know I sound like a broken record with all this talk of BALANCE, but consistency and repetition are what child-rearing is all about. As we keep practicing **Reflection**, **Regulation**, and reason, we get better at it. We keep modeling pause and intention, and eventually we—along with our kids—become the best-regulated version of ourselves.

**B**reathe: By now you know that regulation begins with the breath. Inhale with intention and exhale. That's how we reset our nervous system.

**A**cknowledge your own baggage: When kids lie, cheat, refuse to do their homework, and talk back to us, it's easy to get our feelings hurt and think we've lost control of this whole parenting thing, and the kids are obviously going to grow up to be criminals. This is just baggage. Give it a little nod.

**L**et it go: You can unpack your fears of criminality some other time.

**A**ssess the present situation: What is really going on in the here and now? You might not like what's going on, but it also might be developmentally appropriate. Most likely, it's something we can work with.

**N**otice what's going on: Check in on your child's body and your own body. Is your child under pressure and acting from a place of fear? Do they just seem to be testing the boundaries in a spirit of curiosity? Bodies give us information.

**C**onnect: Show your child with your body and with your words that you see them and you care about their feelings.

**E**ngage: From this balanced place, you can make an intentional decision about how you're going to respond.

## The Healing Power of Distraction

Conventional wisdom encourages venting and catharsis when we're angry, but studies suggest that distracting ourselves when we're super angry may be more helpful. When conflict makes you feel angry or resentful, try doing something else before returning to your interaction with your child so that you can shift from that spirit of rupture into a mood that has room for making *Repairs*. In one study, researchers pissed off college students and then had them hit a punching bag. One group was told to ruminate on their anger and take it all out on that punching bag. The other group was also told to hit the punching bag, but they were told this was a different activity and now they were in getting into shape. Perhaps surprisingly, it was the participants who were beating the punching bag while *not* ruminating on what they were angry about who diffused their rage. So, consider getting your anger out by running around the block, telling yourself it's to get in shape, or by gardening, listening to a podcast, or otherwise distracting yourself into a calm mood from which you can cuddle and *Repair*.

## Apply What You've Learned

Every family has its own recurring points of conflict, but let's apply the principles of parenting that pertain to some common sore spots my clients bring to me every day: interrupting, whining, lying, cheating, and not doing chores. With some imagination, you can use these scenarios to imagine how you would implement the same principles in other situations.

If it helps, here's an acronym: CUDDLE can heal the conflict:

**C**onnect.

**U**nderstand the developmental moment.

**D**iscourage unwanted behavior without fixating on it.

**D**istract yourself or your children.

**L**et go of the shame.

**E**ngage with your child without yelling or shame (clarify expectations, expect pushback, hold your ground, and move on).

### Whining, Lying, and Cheating

These are hardly *all* the points of conflict you're likely to encounter as a parent, but they're common examples and ones for which the lens of developmental psychology can help.

#### *Whining*

Kids whine for all sorts of reasons, though usually it's because they're upset about something, or because in the past whining has helped them get something they wanted. Children are also more likely to whine if they're coming down with an illness or are overtired. It's one of those things that isn't harmful, but it *is* annoying. So annoying, in fact, that it's easy to let it push us over the edge into anger. Instead, try taking a breath, getting down to eye level with your child, and saying something like, "I really want to understand what you're trying to say, but it's hard for me to understand when you're whining. Can you try that again in your real voice?"

Whining makes most of us a little nuts. To make sure you can keep it together when you hear the whining (remembering that our children co-regulate with us, so if we are bubbling over with irritation we will likely water the whining plant), try taking a breath before you respond. Just one breath (or a nice four-count breath) can help you respond with intention, not out of annoyance. When you take a breath, remind yourself, "This is annoying but not harmful."

## Q & A Session

**Question:** What do I do after I've acknowledged them, prompted them for that "real" voice, and they just keep whining?

**Answer:** You can do everything I or any other parenting coach out there suggests, and it doesn't mean the behavior will stop. Especially not the first time. Most parenting moments aren't one and done. After you've been sensitive, handled it with that breath, and said it once, it is perfectly okay to move on. You don't have to ignore your child, but you can ignore the request. For example, once you have said that there is no ice cream for breakfast, and asked your child to tell you what they would like in their "real" voice, you can move on with the meal and avoid any more engagement around their whining.

### Lying

*A lie would have no sense unless the truth were felt dangerous.*

—ALFRED ADLER, MD

It can be alarming that first time your child lies to you. You might feel betrayed, angry, or concerned about their budding sense of morality. On the other hand, it might be funny because they are so easily caught. "Did you eat that cookie?"

"No," they'll say, smiling, with crumbs on their cheeks and a chocolate chip in their teeth. But for what it's worth, this early lying signals a positive milestone in child brain development. They are beginning to understand that you can't always see them, that each individual person has their own beliefs, and that we can form beliefs based on what we're told. Before around age four, kids don't generally have the cognitive function required to understand deception, so when those executive function skills and theory of mind do come together, expect kids to experiment with fibbing. It doesn't mean they're going to become pathological liars!

You can discourage lying without making a big deal out of it. As kids get older, you can make a point of setting them up to tell the truth. You know those moments when you find yourself asking your child a question that you already know the answer to? And then you feel like they're lying to you, and you're offended and you have to punish them? Here's the solution: *Don't ask kids a question you already know the answer to.* Instead of catching your kids in a lie, set them up to tell the truth by stating what you know, what you've observed, and go forward with a solution from there.

For example, instead of saying, "Did you brush your teeth?" when you know they didn't brush their teeth, you just say, "I noticed you haven't brushed your teeth—what's your plan?" If they ate a cookie, instead of saying, "Did you eat that cookie?" try "I noticed that you ate the cookie that we had said you were going to have after lunch." That way you don't have to add your frustration with their lying to the fact that they didn't brush their teeth or wait to eat the cookie.

If you find that your child's lying is pushing you into anger or even rage, this can be a good time to engage the power of distraction. Lying is usually not an emergency situation, so go hit that punching bag, telling yourself you're doing it to get in shape. Or go listen to your favorite album from long before you had kids.

### Cheating

Just like lying, cheating is a normal stage of development. Around age six—and it'll be different for different kids—humans typically start experimenting with cheating. This is part of their development of theory of mind, which was discussed in Chapter 1. It basically means they've realized that no one can tell what they're thinking, and they can give themselves an edge in competition by getting sneaky. Peer pressure usually takes care of the issue as kids start scolding each other for being cheaters, but you can discourage it at home, too. Are the games you're playing within your child's skill set? Do you model honesty even if you can get a free cupcake for pretending it's your birthday? Aim to provide contexts in which your child can win and succeed without cheating. If they get caught cheating at school, you can remind them that you know they're honest and that there can be serious consequences for cheating in a school setting. Avoid harsh punishments for first infractions, though. This is all part of typical development.

## Allow for Do-Overs

You're trying to get out the door for a perfectly planned, fantastic day of fun for all. You've been waiting to show your family what an awesome rock-star parent you are, but nobody's listening. Now you're officially late for this outing, so you keep reminding your kids about what you'll miss the later you are. Time is ticking, everyone is ignoring you and fighting with each other, and now you've gone into the fight-or-flight stress response and you yell something you immediately regret. You haven't even arrived, and this perfect day is already a mess.

In that moment, you may wish you could just hit the Reset button and start over. Well, the good news is that you *can* hit that button. It's a moment to call for a do-over to diffuse the conflict and shift directly into **Repair**. You might say something like, "Yikes! This doesn't feel like the Sunday fun day we've all been so excited about, does it? Let's call in a do-over! What do you think? Let's try this again: Who's excited for today? I am!" Do a little dance. "I can't wait to put my toes in the sand. What are you guys excited about?" We know that **Repair** is facilitated by play, so you can absolutely make it more playful, adding a funny "rewind the tape" sound to lighten the tone and take the opportunity for a little silliness.

Everyone makes mistakes, and what better place than home to practice the idea that we're all human and we can bounce back from cruddy moments. Do-overs give us the chance to learn from those moments, and do better the next time. This is a concrete strategy to turn things around and start again. We call do-overs when we're hopeful for a fresh start, and aware that we all say and do things in the heat of the moment that we regret. It doesn't excuse previous behavior; it simply offers a chance to take accountability and to practice a better way forward.

Here's how to call a do-over:

1. **Breathe.** Get back in the moment. You're getting the pattern, right? Everything starts with breath.
2. **Name it.** "This seems like it needs a do-over! Let's try this again."
3. **Connect.** Try to see things from your child's perspective and let them know you get it. Apologize if you overreacted or did something you regret. If it was your child who said something you can see they regret, give them a chance to let it go without a lecture. Make sure your kids and family are onboard. Be careful not to come off as dismissive; this is more about being on the same team.

## Let Go of Shame

If you accidentally say something that's shaming to your child in an overall loving household, and you just had a moment, this is not going to scar your kid for life. Just say you're sorry. A true "sorry" engages **Repair**. In the long game, your self-loathing is going to be the bigger issue to heal from. Put your hand on your heart and say, "*More often than not*, I'm the parent I want to be." Self-empathy is the antidote to shame. Empathy and self-empathy are the keys to turning conflicts into **Repairs**.

## RULES EXERCISE

### Self-Forgiveness

It's common to feel uncomfortable making **Rules** and enforcing consequences. It's also super common to feel like you've pushed too far and respond with self-loathing. Ideally, we all learn from our mistakes, but it's important to normalize self-forgiveness. Find a comfortable place to sit. Take a few moments to relax and connect with your intention—to open your heart.

Bring to mind some aspect of yourself that has felt unforgivable. Maybe it's that you yelled at your child or you feel like you hurt someone. You might even feel disgusted by your own behavior. Ask yourself what feels so wrong or so bad about what you did or thought or felt. Allow yourself to feel that aversion. Don't fight it. Just allow yourself to feel it.

Gently ask yourself what's driving this part of yourself that feels unacceptable. What need are you trying to satisfy? If, for example, you yelled at your child, ask yourself: What fear am I trying to soothe?

Often when we're criticizing or judging ourselves or our child, it's because we're feeling fearful. See if you can identify that underlying fear. If you feel like you've wounded your child, did you act out of hurt and insecurity? Did you act out of a need to feel powerful or safe?

As you ask yourself these questions, you're opening yourself up to the vulnerability of this moment, so bring to mind your most loving, wise, and understanding friend or relative or ancestor or imaginary being and intentionally see yourself through their eyes—with all their compassion. Visualize their face deeply understanding the way you feel you've made a mistake. Even though you dislike your behavior, hold the compassion of this wise loving friend or being.

Put your hand on your heart and whisper something compassionate to yourself. You can say something like, "I see how I've caused myself suffering and I forgive myself." Or you can just say, "Forgiven." Remind yourself: It is my intention to forgive myself when I'm able to.

## CHAPTER 13

# Your Child in the Outside World

### School and Beyond: Staying Grounded as Children Become More Autonomous

*There are only two lasting bequests we can hope to give our children. One of these is roots, the other, wings.*

—JOHANN WOLFGANG VON GOETHE

At the end of the imperfect day, we're not trying to raise kids who'll never need therapy—c'mon, is that even interesting? We're just trying to raise humans who aren't going to lose their cool at the barista because they ran out of half-and-half. One way we can help our kids grow into adults who aren't going to lose their cool is to let them practice autonomy.

It's incredibly challenging as a parent not to get in there and try to fix things—whether your child's pal didn't share a toy during the playdate or their algebra teacher is giving them a B when they're *so close* to an A— but the best choice is often to do nothing, and simply support our kids as they learn to navigate people and consequences in the larger world.

We know that in old-growth forests, trees that are sheltered by their mother trees tend to grow stronger and more resilient. But there's a difference between sheltering and overprotecting. The University of British Columbia ecologist Suzanne Simard has observed that mother trees in the natural world reduce their own root competition to give their little ones extra space to grow their roots deep and strong. How cool is that? Similarly, as our human kids grow, it's important for us to scoot over a little bit so our saplings have room to stretch and grow.

## Breathe into a Place of BALANCE

When our kids go off to daycare, then to school, then to playdates with other families, or to sleepaway camp, and perhaps eventually to college or their own apartment—or to become the captain of a ship we ourselves don't know how to sail—it's more than natural to go into panic mode every time the phone rings. So, let's keep practicing getting to a place of balance. It's from this place of BALANCE that we can best see and act in the space between neglecting them, which makes kids feel unsupported, and micromanaging them, which makes them feel like we don't think they can handle things.

**Breathe:** You know you can't skip this step! Inhale deeply through your nose, and exhale. Good job resetting your nervous system.

**Account for your own baggage:** Take a moment to reflect on when you can remember feeling this way before. *Is there a chance you're overreacting based on past experiences?*

**Let it go:** Catastrophizing is totally understandable, but go ahead and let it go.

**Assess the present moment:** What is truly going on here and now? Is it a grade that maybe doesn't matter in the scheme of things? Is it a person we wish our child didn't have to engage with? Is it not the end of the world? Even if the moment is terrible and impactful, it's key to come to it from your most regulated place.

**Notice:** What's going on in your body? What seems to be going on in your child's body? Focusing on bodies helps us stay in the present. Our future selves don't yet have bodily sensations. Our memories don't have bodies, either. Notice the embodied now.

**C**onnect: Connect with your child, letting them know that you care about who they are and what they're going through. It's okay to remind them, too, who you are and what you're going through—and model being able to handle that.

**E**ngage: From this balanced place, see if you can put your finger on the space between neglect and hovering. I promise, it will continue to get easier.

## Don't Hover at School

The science is clear that parental involvement in children's lives and education improves success, regardless of our income levels or family backgrounds. What doesn't help, however, is hovering, constantly correcting, or contacting teachers about every little thing. These actions generally make children feel like we don't think they can handle their own experiences. We don't want to abandon our kids as they make their way through the world, but we hurt them if we micromanage. There's a space between the extremes.

When and if you can, volunteer in your child's classroom, attend parents' nights and open houses, or chaperone field trips. Show an interest in what your kids are learning at school. Instead of just asking "How was your day?" try digging deeper and asking, "What was the coolest thing you learned today?" Or, "What subjects are you finding challenging?" Reinforce a positive attitude toward school and education, and avoid projecting negative beliefs about class time, recess, and individual teachers.

When you want to instill confidence in your children, remember that it's not just about the specific life skills they're learning—like tying their shoes or reading; that it's a general belief in their own ability to be gentle with themselves and trust themselves as they grow into ever more mature people who can handle themselves when you're not around. If you have advice or observations, try beginning your shares with "I wonder . . ." For example, "I wonder if you're feeling a little uneasy about how your friend group is shaking out?" instead of projecting what you think you know.

## Focus on Inner Efficacy over Self-Esteem

We all want our kids to feel good about themselves, but conventional wisdom doesn't always point us in the right direction when it comes to figuring out how to achieve that. Dr. Michele Borba, an educational psychologist and author of *Thrivers: The Surprising Reasons Why Some Kids Struggle and Others Shine*, says there's actually very little evidence that boosting kids' self-esteem increases academic success—or even their long-term happiness. Several extensive reviews of school-based programs have concluded that trying to raise self-esteem "had no discernible effect on students' grades or achievement."

Studies do show, however, that kids who can make the connection between their grades and their own efforts are more successful than kids who think academic outcomes are based on intrinsic abilities. In one study, psychologist Dr. Carol Dweck and her colleagues taught students that by pushing themselves out of their comfort zones to learn something new and challenging, they were activating neurons in their brain to form new, stronger connections, so that over time they would get smarter. Students who were not taught this growth mindset showed declining grades when faced with new challenges, while those who were taught this lesson showed a sharp rebound in their grades.

*Self-esteem* refers to a basic self-love regardless of accomplishments. Confidence is more closely related to competence and the belief that we can do things. But what I call "inner efficacy" is more focused—and it's what we want to aim for if we intend to help our kids succeed. Inner efficacy is an individual's belief in their own capacity to do what it takes to meet their goals. Self-esteem might say, "I'm amazing!" but inner efficacy says, "I have the capacity to figure this out and achieve what I set out to."

Kids with a strong sense of inner efficacy are more likely to challenge themselves and put in the effort to meet goals and complete tasks. Rather than blaming external circumstances or some immutable lack of talent for their failures, kids with inner efficacy tend to focus on factors that *are* under their control. With this sense of empowerment, our children can acknowledge mistakes and make course corrections. Students with inner efficacy recover from setbacks pretty quickly and are likely to achieve their personal goals. Students with low levels of inner efficacy, on the other hand, assume they can't be successful—and that becomes a self-fulfilling cycle because they have no real motivation to put in the effort.

Research shows that students gain efficacy from four sources: the experience of getting things right, watching others get things right, verbal reminders that they have a history and ability to get things right, and a sense of calm confidence in their bodies.

> **Experience:** For our kids to have the experience of getting things right, they have to be challenged at the right level. Pushing kids into educational experiences they're not ready for can be counterproductive.

> **Watching:** Our kids need to be given a chance to do well. Watching peers modeling a task can also have a strong influence on developing inner efficacy. It's important that kids see others they consider similar to themselves in at least some specifics, like age, race or ethnicity, gender identity, ability, interests, clothing, social circles, and achievement levels. The peer modeling doesn't have to come from people exactly like our unique child, but watching a much older child of a different race and gender do something might not have the same effect.

> **Reminders:** The stories we tell ourselves about the past create our sense of competence about the future. Studies show that people who believe in themselves, leaning into optimism and growth mindsets, often don't have such different past experiences than their pessimistic peers; they just remember successes more vividly than they remember failures. Reminding our kids of past successes can help them get into the habit of focusing on their efficacies.

> **Calm:** If children feel overstressed or anxious in their bodies when faced with challenges, it can be difficult to perform without first taking care of that physiological response. Teaching

our kids self-soothing practices like mindful breathing will go a long way to help them become competent at whatever they focus that mindfulness on.

### Eight Ways to Help Kids Build Inner Efficacy

Here are some helpful ways you can build your child's inner efficacy.

1. **Encourage kids to try.** Remind your child that success is within reach when they make an effort, persist, and lean on strategies they've already learned. Instead of saying "Practice makes perfect," because we know that's not always true—and we're not actually looking for perfection—remind your child that "Effort makes evolution." Whenever kids worry about not being able to do something, you can promote a growth mindset by adding the word *yet*.

2. **Remind them of recent successes.** When kids can see that their new task or goal resembles a past task or goal they were able to improve or succeed at, the assignment can feel less overwhelming. To bolster confidence, ask your child how they can apply previously learned strategies.

3. **Clarify to correct.** Instead of just marking mistakes with a red pen or saying "Wrong again, pal!" try restating, rephrasing, changing the question, clarifying directions, and going over previously learned skills. Even with young children who point to a red apple and say "blue," you can say, "Oh, yes, blueberries are blue and this is a red apple" instead of just correcting them or saying, "That's not blue, silly."

4. **Praise with specificity when it's earned.** Specific, authentic, earned praise is the ticket. When we say "Good job!" it's got be sincere, and it's got to be specific. Tell kids when you recognize their real effort, persistence, creativ-

ity, independence, and competence. You don't have to completely erase the phrase "good job" if it feels too ingrained. Just add something specific and you are good to go. Try something more like "Good job applying that chess opening you just learned."

5. **Point out strategy.** Help kids draw the line between the action and the achievement. If your child does a good job writing an essay they've outlined, for example, you can say, "I noticed you made an outline. I bet that's one reason you did so well." Or, alternatively, you might need to say, "I noticed you didn't do an outline. It can be really tough to write an essay when you don't have an outline. Let's try writing one together." When kids understand that their failures aren't due to permanent limitations, there's an opening for future achievement.

6. **Encourage your child to find their own advice.** Any time your child has a dilemma, try asking them what advice a friend who cares about them would give. What might a crappy friend say? Help them to develop the ability to distinguish among all these voices in their head, so that they can find their own guiding light.

7. **Teach micro-mindfulness.** Just like we can't parent from a place of balance when we're feeling overly anxious or distressed, our kids don't learn well when their bodies are sending them into a flight-or-flight or freeze response. Teach your kids a memorable breathing exercise like "Smell the flower, blow out the candle" (see page 48) as a calming strategy when they're feeling achievement panic.

8. **Be trees together.** Practice a quick visualization together in which your child imagines themselft a growing tree, their roots firmly in the ground. Picture being a mother tree nearby. You can say, "I'm sending you my confidence

that you can succeed through my roots in the ground, but you're growing your own roots, too. You can do this."

## A Sense of Mattering Matters

Another core component of self-concept that's often overlooked in favor of self-esteem is a sense of mattering to other people. The science of mattering has shown us that it's a unique and vital psychological construct that protects against depression and strengthens our **Relationship** and **Repair** muscles. Researcher Gordon L. Flett describes mattering as "the personal sense of feeling significant and valued by other people," and he's found that "the person who both feels and knows that she or he matters is likely someone who is happier, healthier, and more interconnected with other people" (**Relationship**). Researchers even found that a sense of mattering was a key resource and a predictor of resilience during the COVID-19 pandemic. During the public health crisis, mattering helped protect against feelings of loneliness and safeguarded mental health.

You can bolster children's sense of mattering by listening and by making a point of showing them they're cherished simply because of who they are, and not just because of what they do. Tweens' and young adults' feelings of mattering can also be improved by doing things for others, like volunteer work or mentoring.

Jennifer Breheny Wallace, the author of *Never Enough: When Achievement Culture Becomes Toxic—And What We Can Do About It*, shared with me a fun and tactile way to remind children that they matter. When a child comes home from school feeling disappointed that they haven't done well on a test or didn't get the part in the school play—basically feeling deflated or even invisible—show them a twenty-dollar bill and ask them what it's worth. They'll probably say it's worth twenty dollars. Now crumple it up and flatten it out and ask them what it's worth. They'll probably say it's still worth twenty dollars. And here's where you can remind them that even if they feel crumpled up by their experience, nothing can change their worth.

## Stretch Your Own Capacity for Discomfort

*If you can't stand to see your child unhappy,*
*you're in the wrong profession.*

—MADELINE LEVINE, PhD

Charlotte's five-year-old doesn't want to swim and cries every time her mom takes her near a pool. It gets to be so exhausting that Charlotte finally gives up and says, "You never have to swim, and we'll never go near the pool—or the beach or the lake or the river or even a very big puddle ever again." Charlotte—as the mother—feels like she's being cruel by making her child suffer through swim lessons that she so obviously hates. Charlotte's co-parent, who is also very uncomfortable with their child's crying, says, "It's not scary—I'm throwing you in the water and you'll thank me one day." And in she goes.

If we know our child has a history of reacting well to smaller but similar rip-off-the-Band-Aid tactics, this might be the sensitive thing to do. On the other hand, is this going to help a fearful child feel comfortable? Probably not. Just like we don't learn when we're shielded from experience, humans don't learn when we're terrified.

There's a space between the two extremes. Charlotte's instinct to keep her daughter away from pools all together is completely understandable, but it isn't going to make her child feel more independent. Instead, it says, "Yes, fear should rule your life." Her partner's instinct to just power through and remove their child's agency in the matter may appear to "work" in some ways, but it doesn't help this child begin to learn what well-adjusted adults tend to do when possible: push into their fears and inexperience in a slow and sustainable way, increasing their capacity to endure discomfort until it's not quite so uncomfortable.

The way through the swimming debate that I recommend is to take things slowly. In our example, together as a family they worked out a schedule that would eventually lead to getting into the water, but at a timetable that was predictable, previously agreed upon, and consistently messaged. They decided that they would just spend their pool time sitting by it on the first day, regardless of whether everyone was happy. The next day they would sit a little closer. On the third day, Charlotte got into the pool and her daughter agreed to dip her toe in. Notice that this isn't just about stretching their fearful child's capacity for discomfort, but also that of stretching her parents' *capacity for discomfort*.

This is "Goldilocks parenting" in practice. The next time you experience someone else's discomfort—whether it's your child or an adult—practice making it through the experience without trying to fix it. From your place of balance, you can come up with the moderate approach that allows everyone to feel like their boundaries are being expanded in ways that are safe and predictable.

## Five Ways to Say "That Stinks"

Supporting kids without shifting into "fixing" mode can feel challenging, but practice makes progress. If your child says that a friend made them feel sad, instead of reacting to the friend or trying to fix your child's problem, you can say, "I'm so sorry. That must have been so hard." Or you can say, "Yes, I can see you're feeling very sad." Or you can say, "That sounds hard. I think it would make me sad if that happened, too." You can ask your child to expand on what stinks, saying, "How are you feeling about that?"

Try simply mirroring back what your child is telling you. If words don't make sense in the context of what your child is sharing, you can just hold their hand and give it a little squeeze. You don't have to repeat the same script all the time if it makes you feel like a zombie robot, but it's fine to repeat the same sentiment: I see you, I care about what you're experiencing, what happened does stink, and I'm here for you.

## Talk About Racism

*We don't need perfect antiracist parents; we need parents willing to practice antiracism with curiosity and commitment.*

—BRITT HAWTHORNE

Sadly, being in the larger world means facing the cultural biases that persist. Conversations about racism will look different for every family, but the research tells us that the earlier parents start conversations about discrimination and injustice, the better. If possible, let your child experience the diversity in your community. Buy inclusive toys and books, so kids can see positive depictions of humans of all races and ethnicities.

Even babies as young as six months notice differences, including skin color. And that makes sense. Our differences make us each magical and amazingly good humans. The trouble comes when children start to learn bias from the larger culture, and maybe they don't have the understanding or moral development to recognize it and push back against it. Research tells us that by age five, children can begin to show signs of racial bias.

It's never too late to start talking to kids about equity and social justice and sharing your antibias values, but it's never too early, either. With children of all ages, and with ourselves as ever-evolving adults, we can use the Five *Rs* of parenting to shift into and stay committed to antiracism:

**Relationship** in an antiracist context means that we make an effort to connect with people who aren't like us. Bias, by definition, exists in relationships, so antibias must also be relationship based. Shift away from shame and toward curiosity and empathy. Global-majority children experience systemic racism, but they also routinely experience interpersonal racism from their white peers.

**Reflection** means acknowledging that, if we've grown up in this society, our worldview is very likely tinged with at least some racist ideas, regardless of our own racial identity. By reflecting on our own baggage, we can start to think critically about the harm we might be causing by centering our own comfort. What are your own early memories of noticing people with a different skin color than your own? Did you have any adults in your life who helped you think about racial differences? What messages did you get from your family members and the outside world about diversity? What did you learn about talking about differences? How do you feel talking about differences and race now?

**Regulation** comes into play when we commit to breaking old patterns because it allows us to behave not from reactive bias, internalized racism, fragility, or guilt but, rather, to pause, breathe, and act intentionally.

**Rules** can become an important part of our commitment to raising children who can become global citizens. Studies show that in school, rules are enforced differently according to race. For example, black students are still three times more likely than their white peers to be suspended or expelled. Instead of thoughtlessly perpetuating this kind of bias, take time in all your communities to identify what all the individuals in the group need to feel safe and supported, and establish ground rules that honor those diverse needs.

**Repair** means asking for a do-over when we make mistakes, and making amends when we cause harm.

### *Talking About Racism with Toddlers and Preschoolers*

Children typically begin to notice and point out differences in the people they see around them. If your child asks about someone else's skin color, you can use it as an opportunity to acknowledge that people do look different even though we have a lot in common. You can say, "We're all human and we all look different. Isn't that wonderful?" There's no need to shush kids into feeling like noticing differences is taboo. Often, white parents will try to avoid these conversations whereas global-majority parents understand they're inevitable. It's okay not to get things exactly right in approaching these sometimes-tough topics; just stay committed and curious—and keep the conversations going.

### *Talking About Racism with Elementary-Age Kids*

By about age five, children typically understand the concept of fairness, and that's a context in which to talk about racism: It's unfair, it's unacceptable, and humans need to work together to create a more fair and equitable world. As kids continue through the elementary-school years, they typically get better at talking about their feelings, and they're also likely to have exposure to racism in action. Ask kids what they're learning at school or via media. Discuss stereotypes and racial bias. Talk openly. It's okay not to have all the answers, but encourage your kids to come to you with any questions, and prioritize discussion.

### *Talking About Racism with Tweens*

Tweens can understand complex and abstract concepts and express their views. Use news stories or experiences to start conversations about racism. Ask your children what they think and introduce them to different perspectives. Encourage action as kids find ways to comfort or defend others who are being bullied, participate in activism, or otherwise engage with racial issues. Focus on areas where you can be proactive: shopping in stores that are owned by people of different races and ethnicities, and buying dolls that represent the global majority. Kids can feel overwhelmed if they feel like they have to take on the world, but even small choices can emphasize an antiracist approach.

## Extracurricular Activities: More Isn't Always Better

When it comes to extracurricular activities, seek a balance. Like all of us, when kids have too much on their plates, it can become too challenging to manage time and prioritize where to put their energy. Sure, we want our kids to engage in opportunities for fun and learning, but it's also totally okay to allow your children to experience boredom sometimes. A person who can stand being bored is a person I want to know—and yes, that's also a person less likely to lose it while they're waiting in line. On the other hand, we don't need our kids to be so bored that they get into trouble! As always, look for the space between and remember: temperament matters.

**Question:** My daughter wants to quit soccer, but she's really good at it! Should I let her give it all up?

**Answer:** When your child wants to quit an activity, try not to jump to conclusions, but ask them open-ended questions like "What's up?" and validate the feelings by saying something like, "That sounds hard and frustrating" (**Relationship**, **Reflection**). Hold off on making a hasty decision. Maybe they can try it a few more times. As psychologist Angela Duckworth reminds us in her bestselling book *Grit*, "Don't quit on a bad day." See if you can figure out their motives for wanting to quit by talking to their coach or observing the class. When you've got a better understanding of what's going on, you may be in a better position to brainstorm with your child about ways to stick with the activity until the end of the season or when reaching another natural stopping point.

Ultimately, when it comes to whether we should let our children quit something, the decision depends on them—taking into account their age, temperament, and interests; their reasons for wanting out; their goals for participating in the first place; and the "fit" of the class itself. If you spent money on something they agreed to do and you told them they could do, it makes total sense to explain at the start that it's a semester-long commitment (or whatever it is). Then you can say, "We are still going to keep going until *X* date," and maybe if they don't want to join in they can just watch. Likewise, if their teammates are counting on them you can say, "You've got to show up for *X* number of games."

As parents, we can give ourselves a pass if we have one thing we just feel invested in that our kids learn—maybe you always wished you knew how to play tennis or always felt a little bad that your parents let you quit piano. It's okay to push your kids to continue that one thing. You can say, "Look I'm pulling rank as a parent and making you do this because I just have a feeling you will be the better for it. I totally recognize that I'm imposing my own childhood wishes on you in this moment." But choose wisely, because if you do that with tennis *and* piano *and* karate, now it's going to start looking like you're living vicariously through your child and not allowing them to focus on their own interests (**Reflection**).

Of course, waning enthusiasm in anything is to be expected and often, after doing some detective work, you'll uncover easy ways to tweak the experience so your child feels more comfortable, in control, confident, and so on, in at least sticking with things until the natural end.

---

## Normalize Moving On

Decisions about whether to let young children quit things aren't as weighty as they often feel. Toddlers, preschoolers, and even school-age children don't have a real sense yet of what they're interested in, so it's natural that they might be super excited to try something out, only to find that it's just "not their thing." We don't want specialists; we want kids to try stuff out and then move on if it doesn't suit them. That's different from quitting every time something is a little uncomfortable.

If your child wants out of an activity–and after some investigation and weighing the pros and cons, you decide to let them quit–it doesn't mean they'll probably drop out of college, too, or that you're raising a "quitter." As kids get older, you can make advance plans when they decide to sign up for something for how long to commit to it and what the plan is for deciding if it's time to let go.

---

## Humans Thrive with Choice

When parents support their children's autonomy, it bolsters executive function. Specifically, University of Minnesota researcher Stephanie Carlson found that parents who give their kids choices tap into an especially relevant aspect of autonomy support. In her study, Carlson created live mazes in her lab and invited toddlers to choose among mazes of varying complexity. All the mazes led to the same prize—a goldfish cracker—but more often than not, the kids chose the more difficult maze to get to the goldfish because it had more choices.

Choice, it turns out, is inherently rewarding. Choice motivates. Choice makes kids feel autonomous.

Mauricio Delgado, who runs the Delgado Lab for Social and Affective Neuroscience, at Rutgers University, has done adult research and found that even when it's just "perceived control," when adults *feel* they have a choice of any kind, they thrive. I think we can all relate to that. It's really hard to feel you have no control in this world.

Do you want to keep reading this chapter or skip to the next one? It's up to you!

Ultimately, we want our kids to live as independently from us as they can, within their abilities. More than having a particular skill set, that means raising children who are comfortable with their own autonomy, who can face their experiences with curiosity and confidence, and who can ask for help when they need it. Choice supports that growing sense of autonomy and confidence as kids learn to push themselves out of their comfort zone in healthy ways.

Choice isn't about letting your home become a free-for-all; you're not going to give a choice of whether or not you go to bed, for instance. But you might give your child a choice about whether to brush their teeth or take a bath first. Seems small, but choice makes a big difference.

It's the same thing with mealtime. It's not that you're not going to sit down at the meal, but does your child want to sit in this chair or that chair? Does your child want water or milk? Choice gives agency wherein a child can **Reflect** on their options before responding. These small moments serve to build confidence—a foundation of autonomy.

## When Big, Scary Things Happen

When hearing devastating news feels like the norm, it might seem disingenuous to keep telling our children they're safe. And yet we must. We don't talk about plane crashes every time we're headed to the airport—at least we shouldn't—and we don't need to express our panic every time we drop our kids off at school.

It's understandable to want to completely shield our kids from the realities of our world. And yet we can't. By the time kids are in grade school, they're going to start hearing about current events. My teenagers both knew about the latest school shooting before I picked them up from school. What struck me was that my children were completely fluent in how to talk about school shootings *because it has happened so much*. In fact, it was too easy to talk about. It should not be that easy. In addition to recent surges in anxiety and depression, a majority of teens now say they worry about school shootings. Young people are on high alert, the nearly constant media coverage of the events amplifies fears, and the stress is reaching toxic levels. It's understandable that kids' mental health is on the decline, so when there's anything we can do as adults to alleviate that stress, it's our job to do it.

It's up to us to be a place where our kids can process what is going on around them. We can support them and make sure that if the information they are going to encounter isn't accurate, they know we are a trusted resource. The science tells us that children can handle almost anything (though there is much we would not wish for them to have to handle) if they know they have the presence and support of their adult caregivers. For example, studies show that maternal warmth buffers the toxic stress of growing up in poverty.

Adjusting for our kids' temperament, age, and exposure, we can balance the truth of what's happened with the fact that they're safe. We can assure them that the adults in their life are on the job protecting them, and that they're allowed to just be kids. Even our young children easily sense when something's going on around them or when things aren't right with us. Without an adult to explain in age-appropriate language what they're sensing, children's imaginations often create scenarios that are even worse than the realities. Validating that something is going on also helps kids learn to trust their gut.

For older children, giving them avenues to take action can help. Service is the antidote to hopelessness, and getting informed is the antidote to apathy. One way to start is to get involved with a youth service or activism organization. Tweens can volunteer with parents or community organizations. This is why it's more complicated, but equally important, to decide on what, when, and how to respond to your school-aged children who are too old to shield from the news, but too young to process the scope of it all.

## *Tips for Conversations About Scary Things*

If you have preschoolers, you don't need to share bad news that doesn't impact them directly—unless you have reason to assume they'll have exposure from another source. In that case, you can lightly modify the language to be age appropriate. They are young enough to protect from such difficult to process events, and it's hoped that you can do that.

With elementary-aged kids, you can begin by saying, "Something really sad happened today," and then give them just the broad strokes of the event. By starting the conversation in this open-ended way, you can find out how much they already know and encourage questions. If you have tweens, you can directly ask what they think before you share your own reactions. Our tweens are learning to understand the world for themselves and may very well have a lot to teach us. We can support them in thinking more deeply by asking thought-provoking questions. We also have to get comfortable acknowledging for our teens that we just don't understand why certain things happen, but we can share with them what change we would like to see and what actions we're taking to create that change.

With humans of all ages, you can use this nine-step process to face the news from a place of regulation:

1. **Take a deep breath, so you're calm and regulated.** It can help to physically put your hand on your heart to soothe your nervous system. This is the first step before any difficult conversation.

2. **Acknowledge your own emotions.** If you're thinking about these events, reading about them, and regularly watching the news, keep in mind that it's okay to have strong feelings and for your children to see your emotions, but they need to know that you can take care of yourself. Try saying something like, "I bet you noticed that I'm sad, and that makes sense. I know how to take care of myself when I'm sad, and I also know how to take care of you. We are safe."

3. **See what they know.** "You may have heard about what happened in _____. I'm curious what you know and I'm here to answer questions." When they do have questions, be honest and clear in your responses.

4. **Take a moment to pause.** Let the information about what has happened land. Avoid oversharing or adding unnecessary details. Resist the urge to talk through uncomfortable silence and see what your child has to say.

5. **Listen and make room for any response.** Your child does not need to be interested, have a strong reaction, or even express sadness. You're also having this conversation in anticipation that they'll hear from other sources, and you want them to know that when possible, you're always doing your best to share things with them first.

6. **Describe the age-appropriate facts.** If your child has questions, provide simple answers, or look up answers together on child-friendly news sources, like Newsela. If your child is repeating misinformation they've heard, help them to think through more reliable sources. Answer only the questions they've asked and resist going into longer explanations.

7. **When you can't answer a question, admit it.** These are complicated issues that present an opportunity for critical thinking and investigation. They also require all of us to accept a reality where we don't always have answers. We don't want violence and disasters to feel normal to our children, or like something we have to accept, but we also need to admit to them that we can't always understand the thoughts and actions of others.

8. **Stick to routines.** Whenever things in the world feel uncertain, it's important to lean on routines to keep things

as stable as possible for your child. This is also helpful for *you* to manage your own emotions and be present for your family.

9. **Strategize together.** If you notice your child is having anxiety around this discussion, this tragedy, or other current events, let them know that you're here to support them. Strategize ways for them to remain informed *and* take care of their own emotions. Reassure them that their anxiety makes sense given the circumstances, and that we all feel similarly.

---

### Ask About Guns

One concrete way we can assure our children that the adults around them are thinking about their safety is to normalize asking about guns. The questions can be awkward, but experts agree that we've got to ask. There are thousands of accidental gun deaths and injuries among children every year. In fact, gun-related injuries have become the number one cause of death among children in the United States. Safe firearm storage is proven to reduce youth suicide and unintentional shootings.

We have to get more conscious about keeping guns from children, and we've got to be honest with other parents. While the number of households with guns is declining, there are still an estimated 300 million guns in the United States. Normalize asking about guns and gun safety when you set up a playdate with another parent. Be open yourself, so others don't have to ask. You can say, "For peace of mind, I wanted to let you know that we don't have any guns in the house and we're very safety-conscious," or, "We do have several guns in the house, and they are stored in such-and-such a way, and I wanted to make sure that you're comfortable with that and let you know that we are very safety-conscious."

## Become a Sanctuary Parent

When our kids come to us with big news, they're offering us an opportunity to support them and show them we know how to walk our talk when it comes to inclusion, diversity, and unconditional love. If your children are dealing with life changes still stigmatized in the larger culture, you can make sure your home is a safe haven. As our kids enter the middle school and high school years, they may even start to bring friends over who need a safe space to be themselves. Within the boundaries of safety and the law, you can be there for the young people in your community. Psychologist Susan Silk and mediator Barry Goldman developed a concept they call "ring theory," in which they see a support system as a series of concentric circles surrounding the vulnerable center.

Draw a small circle in the middle of a page. The individual going through the life change or crisis—in this case, your child or their friend—is seen at the center. Draw a circle around that circle. The individual's immediate family and intimate partners are in that ring closest to them, so this circle would include you and your child's other parent, as well as your child's closest companions. Draw a third circle around these two circles. That's where your own trusted friends are. Draw a fourth circle. Therapists and other support people might be in this fourth circle. And so on.

In ring theory, Silk and Goldman advise that comfort should be aimed inward, while dumping, stressing, criticism, worrying, and venting can be aimed outward. If you think your child's life change may just be a "phase," for example, you can tell that to your own friends in confidence, aiming your doubt outward. If you find a resource you think your child will find comforting, you can aim that inward, at the center. If your child loves your carrot cake muffins, you can make a batch. If you're angry, hurt, experiencing a grief response, terrified for your children's long-term health and safety, or just plain needing to vent, you can take all of that to anyone further out from the center than yourself—a counselor, say, or a nonjudgmental friend or spiritual advisor. This allows you to get the support and comfort you need without adding stress to your child's experience or harming your relationship with them.

## REGULATION EXERCISE

# "I Cannot Control the Outside World; I Can Control My Response to It"

Sit down someplace where you can get comfortable and set your timer for as long as you can give to this meditation—three minutes or ten minutes or twenty minutes will all suffice.

Stretch your neck a little bit by rolling your head in each direction. Notice anywhere else in your body where you might be holding anxiety. As you breathe, send flutters of calm to those tight parts of your body. You are a mammal, and it's absolutely natural to feel anxiety about your child in the outside world. As you breathe, imagine yourself connected to every human mother and mammal mother in history, exhale with them as you whisper, "I cannot control the outside world." Breathe in again, and exhale: "I can control my response to it."

Continue to breathe in the strength of the whole mammalian history of worried parents who nevertheless made it through, and breathe out: "I cannot control the outside world." Breathe in the strength, and breathe out: "I can control my response to it."

If you notice any specific anxieties bubble up in your mind, quietly acknowledge them with a little nod: "Hello, anxiety." And then, like the anxiety is just a billboard on the highway, drive on by. Continue breathing.

## CHAPTER 14

# Friends and Siblings

*Learning to Be Flexible with Other Kids*

*Teddy said it was a hat, so I put it on. Now Dad is saying,*
*"Where the heck's the toilet plunger gone?"*

—SHEL SILVERSTEIN, *WHERE THE SIDEWALK ENDS*

You thought having one child on the playground was fun, so you've decided to invite another.

Why not? The more the merrier. Right?

Well, yes. Often. But as we grow our friend circles and our families, interpersonal dynamics get more complicated. We often talk about raising kids as individuals, but we aren't just raising individuals, we're raising children in the context of a family committed to caring for one another. We are also raising individuals in the context of the larger world of peers and community. One child is one thing, but siblings and playmates introduce new opportunities to navigate boundaries, deal with comparisons, and exercise empathy.

As with everything in parenting, I like to start by getting to a place of BALANCE.

## Start from BALANCE

**B**reathe: Breathe in through your nose. Bring the calm of all the trees in this world into your own body. Breathe out through your mouth. *Good job resetting that nervous system.*

**A**cknowledge your own baggage: If you identify as a younger child, you may notice that you have more empathy for your baby. If you were bullied by a classmate, you may have a lot of anxiety about your child's interacting with other kids at school. You may even notice yourself overreacting to squabbles and roughhousing. All your responses are understandable. Give them a silent nod.

**Let it go:** You're the parent now, and your kids are their own people, not the ones from your family of origin or your own hometown. You can let go of your baggage for now.

**Assess the present moment:** What fresh drama have the children cooked up for you today? Do you even need to get involved?

**Notice:** What's going on in your body? Are you unnecessarily going into fight-or-flight mode when there's no imminent bloodshed? What's going on in your children's bodies? Are they overexcited?

**Connect:** Using your body or your words, show the children you're dealing with that you see them and care about their feelings.

**Engage:** If one child does seem to be treated unfairly, address their hurt first. Either way, with BALANCE, you'll be able to engage intentionally from your regulated place that exudes calm.

## Sibling Relationships

We know that all positive relationships build resilience, so both sibling relationships and friendship relationships contribute to that underlying ability to bounce back from hard experiences. Positive sibling relationships thus build resilience. As our kids grow into adulthood, their warm relationships—those that are high on affection and low on conflict—tend to become a source of both practical and emotional support, and they can protect against depression and loneliness.

More than 80 percent of kids live with at least one sibling, and the science tells us that these horizontal connections can improve confidence, emotional regulation, and communication skills—and decrease stress. Sibling relationships are potentially some of the longest relationships our kids will have in their lives. These bonds provide lifelong avenues for mutual support. While sibling relationships tend to be both more intimate and more charged than friendships, the research shows the most positive outcomes when siblings can also be friends.

### Sibling Relationships Can Be Complicated

Studies show that even through their conflicts, siblings can develop skills in perspective taking, emotional understanding, negotiation, persuasion, and problem solving. These competencies carry over beyond the sibling relationship and are linked to later social competence in their friendships and other peer relationships. As our kids grow into adolescence, siblings keep contributing to positive developmental outcomes, including prosocial behavior and better academic engagement.

On the less positive side, research also shows that coercive interaction styles between siblings can and do extend to aggression with peers, so if things seem to be getting *way* off balance for a prolonged period, or if kids seem to spend more time reinforcing antisocial behaviors or colluding to undermine your parental authority than they do inspiring each other to improve their communication skills, well—it's worth addressing. One way to do this is to call a family meeting to calmly discuss the behaviors that will no longer be allowed and why. Validate that it's totally normal to fight and to disagree and argue in any relationship, but that families are on the same team, which means not saying things to tear each other down or intentionally hurt, no matter how angry.

Preventing sibling bullying from causing harm in your own home needs to begin with you. Here's how to initiate a family meeting:

1. State the problem without placing blame.
2. List as many solutions as everyone can come up with.

3. Evaluate how and if the solution will work for all parties involved.
4. Try the solution, acknowledging that it is a process and won't necessarily work right away.
5. Start over if the first solution does not work.

In order to make your home feel safe for everyone, and to also ensure lots of chances to learn and practice constructive ways of handling negative feelings and conflict-resolution skills, sometimes it's necessary to begin with some concrete **Rules** about how family members treat one another.

## Reduce Sibling Conflict and Increase Sibling Closeness

To avoid going completely bonkers and generally feeling like a failure, you should note that research suggests siblings experience some form of conflict up to six times per hour. No parent could possibly have the bandwidth to intervene every time—and it's not necessary. You can pick your battles. The research shows that when parents intervened during the most intense fights between siblings—those fights where children were in physical or emotional danger and where their coping strategies were inaccessible—siblings learned more sophisticated negotiation strategies.

In addition, some studies have shown that family cohesion and equal treatment of siblings is linked with fewer hostile conflicts between siblings. Keep in mind that equal treatment isn't about making sure every child's cookie is exactly the same size, it's about making sure that each child receives the same sensitivity of care—and when there is differential treatment, it's named and contextualized so it doesn't breed resentment.

## Support Your Children as They Form Friendships

As an adult, I think of a friend as someone who will tell you when you've got broccoli in your teeth—and say it in a caring way rather than a mocking way. More broadly, friendship is an association between people that includes care, respect, admiration, and concern. A friend is a person who, *more often than not*, you can trust to have your back.

Friendships can benefit children by creating a sense of belonging and security—a support system that can in turn reduce stress. Child psychologists have found that early childhood friendships contribute to a child's quality of life, as well as their resilience and flexibility. Children often start meeting other children right away in life, and by around age three, they may start being able to name their friends. By age four, kids usually start having friends at preschool or daycare, if they attend.

Remembering that children watch us, we must be conscious about modeling good behaviors in our own friendships so our kids can see what it's all about. As kids are learning not to mistreat their friends, show by example that you have care, respect, admiration, and concern for your friends. Support your kids in keeping up their connections with friends who have become important to them—even if those friends end up at different schools. And remember that all humans are unique; try not to compare children's friendship skills, development, or unique personalities.

## Avoid Comparisons, Labeling, and Playing into Good Kid/Bad Kid Dynamics

Each of our children and each of their friends is a unique individual. They may grow up to be super close, or they may grow up to forget each other's birthdays—there's not a ton we can do about that. But we *can* do our best not to complicate their relationships with unnecessary competition and resentment. When we come from a place of fear and scarcity, we often feel like there isn't enough love to go around, and it's so important that children understand that a parent's love is not something that is felt in comparison. Different kids, even if they're the same age, are going to have different skills and interests. When we start labeling and—consciously or unconsciously—pitting siblings and playmates against each other, we perpetuate the scary idea that there might not be enough love to go around.

## Avoid Comparisons

It's easy to get in the habit of saying things like, "Annie's so good at eating, I wonder if you could do that, too." It might even get the results you're looking for in the short term, but the science tells us that comparing and competing can decay relationships over time. Instead of saying, "Well, I see *one* of you put your dishes in the sink," say, "I see you put your dishes in the sink. Thank you. I really appreciate that."

Even when the comparisons feel small or positive, saying things like "This doesn't come as easily to your friend Abe—he doesn't have the attention skills you do," might impart some self-confidence for your child or some pity for Abe, but it doesn't feed the relationship. Instead, try to keep things separate. You can say, "I noticed that you're really focused, and it's wonderful to see how much you can accomplish when you stick with something." You don't have to bring Abe into it at all. Instead of saying something like, "Your three-year-old sister knows how to tie her shoes. You're six, and it's time for you to tie your own shoes," keep it separate by saying, "It looks like you're having trouble tying your shoes. Let's take a little time to practice."

Similarly, instead of saying, "It's a wonder that your cousin manages to get his homework done before dinner and you haven't even started yours," try saying, "Let's figure out how we can set up a schedule for you so that you can get your work done in time for all of us to have dinner together. Would it help if we sat together while you do your homework and I answer my emails?"

The same goes with compliments. I might say to my child, "You have such beautiful posture; your sister looks like a hunchback," when I could just leave it at the posture compliment and not make my kids feel like there's a posture competition.

## Avoid Labeling

Jesse has one child who's been focused on art her whole life, and when his other child started doing it, she was doing it kind of secretly—she didn't want to step on her younger sister's toes as "the artist." The other child had become really good at gymnastics—so much so that "the artist" didn't want to sign up for a tumbling class. It's natural for parents and kids to label themselves and then not want to go near the other sibling's "thing," but childhood—all of life if we're lucky, but especially childhood—is a time of exploration and infinite possibilities. Our kids don't need to specialize, and they certainly don't need to own particular activities.

### Avoid Playing into Good Kid/Bad Kid Dynamics

It's common for friends and siblings to get physical, and it's natural to place blame on the bigger one, saying things like, "You know your friend can't handle that," or "Why are you hurting her?" But it's important to avoid labeling one child as "bad" or "the bully."

Conflict doesn't typically happen because one of the kids is a bad person; it's because they need to work on their self-regulation and new ways of expressing their anger and frustrations. If one child does have more self-regulation issues, it's easy to count on the more capable child to do better, but you don't want to play to the weakness of the other child any more than you want to label one the "bad seed." When you're in the moment, you can say things like, "I'm not letting you hurt your brother. Let's figure out how you can show these feelings some other way." Or you can say, "I'm going separate your bodies to keep you both safe." Once tempers have settled down, you can say, "Let's try that again. What were you trying to tell your brother?"

## Allow for Boundaries

Relationship is the first of the Five Rs of parenting, and all good relationships allow for boundaries. Often, older siblings are taught to share everything with their baby brothers and sisters, so it's important to remember that it's all right not to share everything. Allow all siblings and friends not to give everything over. Will baby sister be sad if she can't play with her brother's truck when she wants to? Probably. But it's okay to say, "Your baby sister is sad. We can help her with her feelings without letting her play with the truck you don't want her to play with." This is just another expression of the truth that all feelings are welcome, but all behaviors are not.

## Validate All the Feelings

Simply validating feelings can go a long way to boost relationships. If your nine-month-old takes a toy from your preschooler, you might be inclined to say, "They're just a baby; they don't know what they're doing." Instead, you can validate your preschooler's upset by saying something like, "It really feels like they took that toy to irritate you." You don't have to fix the issue, but by acknowledging and affirming the feelings, you normalize the full range of human emotions.

Often, an older sibling will adore a new baby—for a little while. When the initial cuteness gets boring, they might want to send the baby back. Instead of saying, "You don't mean that. You love this baby," you can validate their frustration by saying, "Yeah, you wish sometimes you had a break from her and that she would just go away. That makes sense." Then you can move along without making a big deal out of it.

When kids start spending time with friends, the same types of push and pull will come up. It's not your job as the parent to fix everything between kids. Feeling left out is common. Instead of trying to convince your kids that it's not a big deal or saying, "Those kids do martial arts together, so they don't want to spend time with you because you're more into bowling," say "It's hard to feel left out." Because it is. When kids are old enough to write, you can even give them a blank journal in which they can express all their feelings about friends and siblings that would be hurtful to express openly. In short, validate the feelings, redirect the harmful behaviors, and give kids new ways to express themselves—and the permission to express themselves in non-harmful ways.

## Allow for Roughhousing

*Half the time when brothers wrestle,*
*it's just an excuse to hug each other.*

—JAMES PATTERSON

Roughhousing and play fighting are very different from real violence. The science shows that roughhousing is good for kids, helping them learn to get physiologically amped up and to settle down in a regulated way.

## Give Kids a Safe Word

As caregivers, we often want to stop the madness because it feels aggressive, but in this context it's perfectly contained and safe. Give kids a safe word they can use when they're not having fun anymore. "Banana!" can mean that everyone has to wind down and stop the play fight.

Bickering and play fighting are part of how kids navigate communication and relationships. You don't need to do anything. It's when it becomes dangerous or threatening that it's a problem—and you may have to intervene. If there's a physical or verbal power play, where one person is clearly taking advantage of another, it's time to intervene, acknowledge the distress and the anger, and again help the kids settle down to a place where they're going to be able to problem-solve without any injuries. To stop impending bloodshed, you can get in there and say, "I'm going to separate your bodies and help you settle down to a place where you can problem-solve." If words won't be heard, just say it in your head while making sure everyone is physically safe.

## When to Act as Mediator

It's typical for friends and siblings to fight, but that doesn't mean there's nothing you can do about it. Handle conflicts by being the mediator, not the judge. When you act as an impartial mediator, everyone can feel heard and can learn to listen to different perspectives. You can also teach important conflict-resolution skills for the future.

You can support all the kids in your care by coaching them through the process of having a disagreement without taking sides, so you're just stating observations. You're a witness, not a judge, and you can name what you see from each child's experience, or you can ask them to explain. It's also often helpful to ask them to tell you what's happened from the other child's perspective. This helps them understand the experience of "other," even if they don't agree with it. This can even be playful if kids are up for role playing, almost a Trojan horse for indirectly getting into perspective taking.

Finally, you can come together when everybody's calm and make a plan for moving forward from the situation. The other option, if no one's getting hurt, is to think to yourself, *I don't have it in me right now; I'm going to let them sort this out. I know they can do it.* Both options are fine. It just depends on where you, the adult, are at in the moment. Some days you don't have time to be an emotional coach, and that's okay.

## Q & A Session

**Question:** My nine-year-old and seven-year-old fight and tattle all the time. I don't want them not to tell me when they've got a real problem, but I'm sick of hearing about their bickering.

**Answer:** Tattling is designed to get another kid in trouble. "Telling" is about protecting oneself or someone else who's being harmed. Teach your kids the difference. This way, when they come to you with a tattle you can say, "I know you'll be able to work that out," and when they come to you with a tell, you can intervene appropriately to protect bodies (***Relationship***, ***Rules***).

For instance, you can ask, "Is this something you want to share because you want me to help by listening or intervening?" (***Relationship***). Then you can be open with them when they need to tell you something, so they always know to come to a grown-up when it's for help; but you can resist responding to the tattling so they stop the habit of tattling on each other, which can be exhausting and unproductive (***Rules***).

## Encourage Perspective-Taking

When kids have a minor blow-out—meaning that no one's in tears, but one or both of them is eager to tell their side of the story, ask them to tell the story from the perspective of the other person. They may resist at first, but it is an incredibly powerful tool to help them build perspective. In the first scenario, they might tell you they were innocently singing a favorite song when their sibling pushed them out of the room and slammed the door. Speaking as the other person, they might shed a little different light on it, saying, "I was talking on my phone and this bozo came in and started singing at the top of her lungs just to interrupt me." With the new perspective, they may be able to start working the problem out together.

## Sometimes You Bite Your Tongue

When kids go to school, they don't just study; they also start socializing with kids you don't know. When your child or tween inevitably comes to you with a friendship problem, it can be hard not to give them *all* your thoughts. I mean, any kid who does our kid wrong has got to be a fool and a bully, right? Well, maybe and maybe not.

The problem is that childhood and adolescent relationships change daily. When you hear a story that makes you mad, and you share your outrage with your kid, and then hold it against the friend who, for some reason now is back on your kid's friend list, they might stop sharing with you. It's not healthy for you or your child to remember every bump and divot on the long road of friendships your child is traveling. Kids are figuring out how to connect with each other, finding each other's boundaries, and are going to get things wrong sometimes.

Your kids need you to be a steady, consistent supporter and advice-giver *when they ask*. Getting involved every time you hear something you don't like teaches your child that they can't navigate their world. Of course, if they need real help, and the friend is truly a bully or a danger, step in with a plan that your child knows about. Absent that, it serves the longer-term relationship to let them go through their experience, be there to support them, and keep your commentary to yourself.

Child psychologist Dr. Michael Thompson has said, "Don't interview for pain," which is a good reminder about our tendency to keep conflicts alive long after our child has moved on. Here's a familiar example: Your sixth-grader was reeling from a conflict with their bestie last night. When they got home this afternoon—without even noticing their mood or leaving space for them to either talk or get some quiet— you jump in with "How did things go with Maya today?" Instead, consider reading the room and just saying hello. If she wants to bring up the wound, you're there; but if she wants to move on because she and Maya worked it out, no need to dwell on it.

## Q & A Session

**Question:** Do you have any suggestions on how to help little ones cope with feeling left out? This is all new territory for our six-year-old daughter. We are doing our best with listening and sympathizing, but I want to make sure we are saying the best things to help her along as well. It's so hard to watch her little face when she feels disappointed!

**Answer:** Being left out is a painful reality. Adults often assume that any child who leaves their child out of a game, or rejects them on the playground, is being mean, but often children aren't applying adult notions about friendship to their playing. Rather than simply giving a solution to your child such as "Play with someone else" or "Yell back at that mean kid on the playground," learning how to manage the day-to-day drama of early friendships is much more complicated (*Relationship*).

It's worth teaching kids that not everyone is going to be their friend, and that they're not required to be everyone's friend, either. They're expected to treat people thoughtfully, but part of that includes being able to turn down an offer to play and gracefully accept it when someone else doesn't want to play with them. This lesson can take a lifetime to learn, but it's a bit easier when we can normalize the reality. You can't fix it so that the playground is all joy and no drama, but you can help prepare your kids to navigate social situations, and you can prepare yourself to lean in with empathy. If your child is seeking advice more than empathy, you can help them role-play different ways to approach and make friends, how to read social cues, and when to bow out gracefully.

## Seven Ways to Navigate Tricky Friendship Drama

This is a good time to go through the seven steps to get into BALANCE, or to take the shortcut and be BAD: Breathe, Assess, Deal (see page 10). This way, you give yourself a moment to set aside your own baggage and deal with the very specific situation at hand.

1. **Check in with your own feelings.** Take a breath, hand on heart, and regulate yourself before responding. This will stop you from overreacting, bagging on the other child, or imposing your own feelings of rejection on your child's experience.

2. **Validate your child's feelings.** Make space to hold their hurt while being a safe place for them to express themselves. This may look like "Ugh, it sounds like you felt hurt when you were left out. You thought Stephanie was your friend, and when she didn't invite you, it makes sense that your feelings were hurt." Then pause so your child can let it land. Avoid telling them what they *should* be feeling. It may make us feel better to say, "Well, Stephanie is a loser anyway and you are so much cooler." *Bite your tongue.*

3. **Ask permission to participate.** Try saying, "Do you want a suggestion or do you want to just vent?" before you leap in with a recommendation. My daughter and her friends taught me "rant or advice."

4. **Tread lightly.** Avoid getting too involved. Before you offer a suggestion, ask them if they have any ideas about how they want to handle this. Once they are open to your suggestions, offer a suggestion that empowers them, like a strategy for telling someone that their feelings have been hurt; a mantra to help them remember that it was only one bad day; or a plan for something else they can do at recess.

5. **Don't make this about the other child.** Calling another child "mean" or "bad" won't help your child build empathy, and that ignores the fact that your child may still want to spend time with them. It also doesn't consider other perspectives and the reality that we can like someone *and* not be able to include them. So many interpretations get rejected when we go right to assuming the other child is mean. Instead, help your child be curious about what is going on with that child and why they would be acting this way. Help your child to understand that this type of behavior is more about the other child than about them.

6. **Talk about how friendships feel.** Telling your child that friendships should feel good is an important way to help them set expectations around their relationships. You can also help kids understand that friendships don't all feel the same. Some friends are fun to play with on the playground, but not the friends you share your feelings with. Some friends are good at making you laugh, some are good for long talks, some are good for shared interests. Not all those things lend themselves to being included and may be context dependent. And if your child is being treated in an unkind way, ask them to pay attention to how they feel when someone treats them that way compared to how they feel when someone who is a good friend treats them. Give them permission to notice that some people do not make them feel the way they want to feel, and that they do not need to be friends with people who constantly hurt their feelings.

7. **Gain street cred.** Notice and check in for some of the positive qualities of a friend whom your child is in conflict with.

## Bullying Defined

There are lots of reasons that children may start to act aggressively toward others. Sometimes they're looking for attention or trying to indicate that they're struggling. Other times, a child may be having trouble with self-regulation and controlling their behavior. Still other times, children see themselves as a victim and their actions are a result of a heightened stress response. Some children lack perspective-taking skills (understanding the thoughts and feelings of others) or are being bullied or feel powerless in other settings (like home or school). Notice that "because they are bad" is not on the list. Understanding that a bully may be hurting themselves is a key to gaining understanding and help for their behavior.

The term "bully" is often misused in the course of normal child development. Often, what we really mean is that a child is being a jerk. Let's look at what makes bullying different from the normal ups and downs in an otherwise healthy friendship or acquaintance.

1.  **Power.** Bullies are seen to be in a more powerful position than their victims. A power difference between two parties can stem from differences in age, size, strength, popularity, or other status.
2.  **Repetition.** Bullying is targeted behavior, with ongoing mistreatment that is consistently directed at one victim.
3.  **Harm.** Bullying is an intentional act that has a direct and negative impact on another person or child.

### If You Believe Your Child Is Being a Bully

If you suspect your child is bullying others, here are seven strategies for dealing with the problem:

1.  **Talk openly and honestly about what you know** (incidents at school, reports from teachers or other parents, or what you witnessed). Ask your child what they think may explain why they are engaging in this behavior, where they

feel it comes from, and make space for them to express themself as much as they can. If you have trouble uncovering this information from your child, you may need the support of a mental-health professional with experience working with children concerning these behaviors. Ask your school or healthcare provider for help finding someone with a specialty in this field. Understanding if there are any underlying issues can help both you and your child move toward healing (**Relationship**, **Reflection**).

2. **Engage strategies to handle situations differently.** If you've gotten to the root of your child's bullying (for example, wanting to feel powerful because they otherwise feel unnoticed, or they have an impulse-control problem in heated moments), work together to find alternate behaviors. Find ways they can feel seen and heard, noticed or powerful *without* hurting others and engaging in bullying (**Relationship**, **Reflection**, **Rules**).

3. **Reflect at home.** As parents, we may need to take a bird's-eye view of the conditions in our home (**Reflection**). Are we watching violent content or shows? Are we watching comedies that contain behaviors requiring sophisticated humor to understand? Do we tease each other? What kind of boundaries do we have for fighting or name calling? Often unknowingly, we can find some of these patterns in our homes and we can work to replace them with positive messages. This is not an indictment of home; it is just helpful to notice if what may seem harmless is getting misinterpreted by developing humans.

4. **Monitor the situation closely.** Once you know about bullying, it *is* your responsibility to monitor chats, online behavior, and other actions, and to communicate with teachers and school administrators regularly. Bullying does not often disappear overnight, and it will take time

and attention to help your child to create new patterns of behavior. Your child needs appropriate consequences for bullying behaviors. This may mean a loss of privileges and additional supervision while you are ensuring that the behavior improves. It may also mean mandatory participation in counseling or therapy to help to address your child's underlying challenges (*Rules*).

5.  **Make amends.** It's important to also talk to your child about those they have hurt and to take steps to make it right. Focus on empathy. Involve your child in what those amends can be, from writing letters of apology to taking steps to *Repair* the *Relationships*. Talk about the experience the victimized child has had and help your child to understand what the bullied child has gone through and suffered. This is not meant to build shame, but instead to help your child develop empathy and perspective taking. It is not bad if your child feels guilty; guilt is there to help people develop a moral compass (*Repair*).

6.  **Spend more time together as a family.** Children who are closely connected with the adults in their family, who spend time together regularly, and openly discuss thoughts, feelings and events, are less likely to engage in bullying behavior. Try to stay connected to your children's inner and outer lives—their friends, their moods, and their needs (*Relationship*).

7.  **Bring in reinforcements.** I know that the first step is often the hardest, but once you know that your child is in need of help, don't hesitate to get it. Ignoring it, fighting about it, or waiting for them to outgrow it won't help. It may turn out that it was just what they needed to thrive.

### *If Your Child Is Being Bullied*

Knowing your child is being bullied is painful. It is excruciating to see your child suffering, to feel helpless to make it better, to worry about their well-being and safety. It can also bring up painful memories from our own social experiences, our own hurts, and our own vulnerabilities. As a reminder, our children will be teased, they will be left out, they will get their feelings hurt. That isn't necessarily a sign of bullying. Bullying is meant to *hurt*, it is *intentional*, it is *directed* at a particular target, and it involves a *power* imbalance. We have to remind ourselves that this isn't about us, our experiences, or our anger. Jumping into high gear and tackling this problem from your end won't help. This is a journey you have to make *with* your child, not *for* them.

Here's where to start:

1.  **Believe your child.** Practice being a listener who wants to understand, not the type of listener who wants to respond. The easier you make it for your child to talk to you, the more they will share and the easier it will be for you to stay connected.

2.  **Ask questions.** Ask your child to tell you the complete story before you rush to intervene or make a judgment. Empower your child to share their story, and their description of the experience. Ask them how they responded, what worked and what didn't. When you have the facts, you can help assess whether it sounds like bullying is happening. If it is, name it.

3.  **Stay neutral.** If you become distressed, it will likely increase your child's distress. So as hard as it is, take a breath to signal to them that you can handle hearing this. Then you can assure them that you will help, and that together this situation can improve. If you have a big reaction, it will make it harder for your child to share with

you in the future. Focus on building their confidence in your ability to help them when they find themselves in harm's way.

4. **Avoid retaliation.** This is not the time to talk about revenge, but instead to focus on problem solving.

5. **Talk to teachers, parents, and administrators.** Make sure to have all the facts about what is happening, how often, and who is involved. Help your child to share their experiences, and work to support them in finding their voice to speak out about what is occurring. Make sure your concerns are heard, and that you have the attention and support that you need from school. If you don't, reach out to other parents in the school, or parent organizations to help with advocating for action.

6. **Make a plan.** Work with your child to plan for alternate ways to handle situations at school, lunch, or recess. Role-play what your child can do in response to, or to avoid, bullying behavior. Talk about safe people and places or discuss having a buddy system. Think about the ways they can reach you, or another trusted adult they can go to, if they need to.

7. **Express confidence in your child's ability to problem-solve and try new strategies.** A child who is being bullied can feel hopeless. Talk about all the skills they do have, the power they do have, the change they can make. Regaining their voice and confidence is an important step in helping them to work through the bullying behavior.

8. **Work together to find allies in the community.** Finding places for your child to feel passionate and capable is an important counterbalance to the powerlessness that bullying can create. Help kids to try new things and "find

their thing" as a way to support them. Observe their skill sets and expose them to activities where they can shine, even if they show a little reluctance at first to try something new.

9. **Monitor and communicate.** Bullying isn't solved overnight, so constant communication with your child, teachers, other adults, and friends will help you keep tabs on how things are progressing. Don't ignore or sweep issues under the rug when they persist. Stay vigilant and continue to communicate with your child in a way that feels open and without pressure.

10. **Create a safe space.** Make sure your child knows that being bullied is not their fault and that you are there to support them. Spend time together when you don't talk about it. Do fun things together that your child enjoys and share quality time. Work to support and build your relationship in a way that lets them know that you are their partner in making the situation better.

### The Role of the Bystander

In most bullying situations, in addition to the bully and the person being bullied, there are bystanders. But common advice like "Stand up to the bully!" tends to be unhelpful at best and dangerous at worst. The research shows the opposite reaction might be more effective: when bystanders walk away unimpressed—maybe with a shrug or an eye roll—they deprive the bully of the audience and attention they may be looking for. Bystanders can instead focus their attention on the *target* of the bully, even after the fact, and show compassion.

## Give Kids Humanizing Language

Just like when we talk to our kids about behaviors we don't like—focusing on the fact that we're disappointed in their behavior, rather than who they are as people—we want friends and siblings to treat each other with a basic sense of humanity.

If one kid knocks over another kid's blocks, you can give them language to say something like, "Those are mine; you can't touch them," which is different from hitting them, or locking them in a closet, or calling them a garbage pail. It's always okay to say that someone's behavior was not acceptable, but it's not okay to say that they *themselves* are not acceptable. Intervene to remind kids to use humanizing language. If they say, "I'm going to kill you," you can say, "Wow, you're pretty furious. You're not just mad. Instead of threatening your friend, tell her that you're furious."

## Do I Love My Thumb More than My Index Finger?

"Which one of us do you love more?" It's an awkward question, especially when you do feel more drawn to one kid than another on a particular day. You want to say, "I love you the same," but of course that's not quite true. I like to think of it in terms of *equity* rather than equality. As my grandmother used to say, holding up her hand, "I have five fingers. Do I love my thumb more than my index finger? My love for my pinkie doesn't diminish my love for my ring finger."

What's important is that each sibling experiences love—unmeasured. Each of your children will have uniquely different needs and uniquely different qualities you'll delight in as a parent; you're going to love them each for their uniqueness. But not everything is going to be exactly equal. If you had four kids and you gave them each a cupcake made in a factory that also processes peanuts, and one of these kids is allergic to peanuts, well, you've given them equality but you haven't given them equity, because the child with the peanut allergy would not be able to safely eat their share.

We have to stop trying to pretend that everything will be equal and the same. If you're giving each child a pile of crayons for an art project and one inevitably whines, "He got more than me!" instead of counting out the crayons to prove the distribution is pretty close, you can remove the tension by saying, "Do you need more crayons?"

If it's one child's birthday and you're worried the other child is going to get jealous because they aren't getting any presents, you can validate their feelings by saying, "Today might be hard because we're excited to celebrate your sister's birthday," and you can include them in all the preparations. You don't have to make sure to get presents for everyone in order to protect everyone from the hard feelings. Support without fixing.

### *The Glass Child: When One Friend or Sibling Has Special Needs*

As adults, spending time with disabled and differently abled kids does remind us to appreciate abilities we may take for granted, but young kids don't usually think that way—and it isn't helpful to expect them to. As difficult as it is, it's important not to minimize the experience of one child because you think they have it easier.

Acknowledge your typically developing child's wants and needs as developmentally appropriate for them. When one child in the house has higher needs, it can accidentally render a sibling what has been called a "glass child." Sometimes, when we're so focused on the higher needs of the one, we can see right through the needs of the glass child and forget to take care of their needs as well. While it can be exhausting, cultivating a relationship with your children who don't seem to need you as much, and making sure that their role is not to disappear and be easy, will render them more compassionate and more able to empathize with and care for their differently abled or disabled sibling.

Common challenges include holding a distorted view of the typical behavior of less high-needs children. Of course, they still have tantrums, outbursts, struggles, and challenges. Of course, they aren't "good at that yet"; they may only be a toddler. What often happens to parents who are so focused on the needs of one particular child is the "adultification" of the sibling. We may assume, as compared to their sibling, that they are more capable or more independent than their age and developmental stage suggest, and therefore we place unrealistic expectations on their behavior and emotional wellness.

Another issue here is that we may inadvertently ignore the toll a family crisis is taking on the siblings. Even in the closest parent-child relationships, it's easy for children to fear adding burdens to their already taxed parents. For instance, in the service of protecting you and your feelings, your children may hesitate to tell you about their own struggles. That's why the role of our extended networks and community is so critical. If you have family friends who are dealing with crises or ongoing high-needs situations, offer support. Prioritize "normal life" experiences like holiday dinners, outings, and family traditions. Consciously create safe spaces for the glass children to "not be okay"— and instead to be seen. These are all-important contributions that friends, extended family, and other community members can make.

Hearing about the feelings of your glass child—or even considering that you're too taxed to parent them in the way you would choose—can be devastating. I don't want to add to your stress by elaborating on the issue, and I want you to remember to be gentle and forgiving with yourself.

---

### The Strengths of "Glass" Children

A beam of light. Studies show that glass children have tremendous strengths, including being more empathetic, having more understanding, and being more resilient because of their unique sibling experience. Alicia Maples gave a TED Talk on her own experience as a glass child and said, "We are some of the strongest children there are. We have to be in order to survive the things that we survive."

---

## RELATIONSHIP EXERCISE

### Loving Kindness

When our own **Relationships**, or our children's **Relationships**, with friends and siblings are strained, it can be easy to stumble into a place of resentment. I find that a loving kindness meditation specifically focused on the self, the "other" in the **Relationship**, and the **Relationship** itself, can calm us.

Sit someplace comfortable and close your eyes if that feels safe and natural. Keeping your eyes open is okay, too. Breathe in through your nose and out through your mouth three times. Say to yourself or out loud: "May I be filled with loving kindness. May I be well. May I be safe. May I be loved. May I live with ease."

Breathe in through your nose and out though your mouth three more times. Picture the "other" in the **Relationship**. Bring their name to mind. Then say to yourself or out loud: "May _____ be filled with loving kindness. May _____ be well. May _____ be safe. May _____ be loved. May _____ live with ease."

Breathe in through your nose and out though your mouth three more times. Now picture the two people in the **Relationship**—whether yourself and someone else, your two children, or your child and their friend. Keep breathing as you picture a glowing thread that each person is holding on one end. Keep breathing in through your mouth and out through your nose as you say to yourself or out loud: "May this connection be filled with loving kindness. May this connection be well. May we be filled with loving kindness. May we be well. May we be safe. May we be loved. May we live with ease."

## CHAPTER 15

# Transitions Big and Small

## *Use Change as an Opportunity to Emphasize What Stays the Same*

*The only constant in life is change.*

—HERACLITUS

Kali texted me during her child's first week at a new middle school in a new town, saying, "I need you to remind me how to sit comfortably with discomfort." Her child had been messaging home, telling his mom he hated the new school, the kids weren't friendly, the teachers didn't like him, and "Can you please just pick me up, Mom? I don't even know why we moved to this ugly town."

Kali's child wasn't in any imminent danger at school, so she needed to pause to respond with BALANCE—just like we'd been practicing together for years. We walked through the steps together.

### Finding Your BALANCE in Your New Situation

"**B**reathe," I said to Kali. It's the fastest, cheapest way to regulate your nervous system. "Breathing," Kali messaged back a few moments later.

"**A**cknowledge your own baggage," I texted. That's when Kali elaborated on her sense of guilt about the move. She'd accepted a new job to be closer to her own ailing parents, and it meant her child had to leave the kids he'd grown up with.

"**L**et go of your guilt," I said, "just for now." "Letting it go," she texted back, "for now."

"**A**ssess the present moment," I reminded her. "What's going on for your child?" She answered right away: "He's upset about the move and feeling uncomfortable in his new surroundings."

"**N**otice," I messaged. And from all the years of working with me, she knew I meant, *notice what's going on in your body and in your child's body or emotional state.* When our kids are physically with us, it can be easier to notice what's going on in their bodies, but even via text, Kali could read between the lines. Did her child really want her to come pick him up? Or would that just reinforce his fear that he couldn't make it through this challenging adjustment? "I was shaking when I first texted," Kali wrote back. "Now my shoulders are just a little tight."

"**C**onnect," I reminded Kali. "See if you can relax your shoulders just a little bit more, and respond."

**E**ngage. That's when Kali texted her child back, acknowledging feelings: "I know this is a big transition for all of us and you didn't pick this move." Then she was able to respond to the request she wanted so badly to give in to but also knew her child could handle. She said, "I know this is hard and I know you can get through this day. I can't wait to see you when you get home."

## Change Is Constant, but Change Is Hard

Parents come to me all the time concerned about regression in their children's development, sleep problems, or concerning social behaviors. If the children are well nourished and well rested, much more often than not we'll discover together that the new challenging behavior has something to do with a transition the child is incorporating. Whether kids are adjusting to a new caregiver, starting a new school, or dealing with the changes that come along with moves or parental separation, a whole range of emotions and behaviors are normal. Even seemingly small transitions like leaving the playground for the day or switching from games time to reading time can be challenging.

No matter what your child or your family is going through, you can validate your children's feelings, remind them of what will stay the same, lean into established routines, and behave in a way that says, "I'm here for you *and* I trust that you can get through this." Because children tend to put themselves in the center of all their experiences, which is developmentally appropriate, they can also easily shift into self-blame if they perceive transitions as negative.

### *Not All Anxiety Is an Anxiety Disorder*

Anxiety is a natural human feeling. Often, the problems with transitions come from fear. Like all humans, children experience fear of the unknown and fears about what's going to happen when they're put in a new situation. Unlike older humans, children don't have tons of experience facing those unknowns and new experiences, and they rely on us to remind them that they can get through the difficult feelings.

Anxiety itself is adaptive and healthy. If your child had never taken a timed test before and feels anxiety that causes them to study hard, that is a perfectly ordered use of that anxious feeling. If a younger child is feeling anxiety about starting a new school and they get up early to make sure all their supplies are in order, they are managing the stressors they do have control over. The way to tell if anxiety becomes what psychologists call *maladaptive* is if the way they are managing stress harms themselves or others.

### Divorce—and Modeling Healthy Relationships

Families with two married parents living at home are referred to as "traditional" and "intact." Families after breakups or divorce are referred to as "broken." This isn't helpful to those of us going through divorces and, if truth be told, there's no real historical basis for calling nuclear families "traditional." The idea of the all-American nuclear family was invented in the 1950s, based on the economics and cultural values of the time. But we are living in a different economic and cultural era, and while about half of marriages survive to see children through high school, the other half don't.

Divorce is one of the big transitions we have to navigate with as much grace as we can muster. When I found out I was getting a divorce, I had a mom-group scheduled for the next day. I didn't want to cancel on them; I'd been with them since my own kids were babies. But how could I even call myself a "parenting expert" when I felt like I'd screwed up what I still saw as an "intact" family?

I took a deep breath and tried to acknowledge my own baggage. I think it's important to tell people you are close enough with about what's going on with you so that they can understand how you are entering the space. So I went ahead and told them: "Look, I just found out I'm getting a divorce, I'm kind of in shock, but I still wanted to show up. I get that this may sound bonkers, but this is where I want to be." If I were a clinical psychologist, this would have been out of turn, but as a developmental psychologist and guide, I get to be more open with my clients. And the other moms in my group didn't miss a beat, as they encircled me with the support the group had been for all of us. They reminded me to soak up that support and look at the science, instead of letting my fears run away with me. I'm still working with this group and to this day I love them!

Later, from a place of BALANCE, I was able to look more calmly at what the science tells us. As it happens, decades of research affirm that kids of divorce do just as well as kids who grow up with two parents at home; it's long-term conflict—whether or not parents live together—that takes a real toll. In fact, whether the high conflict is within a marriage or not, being the child in that **Relationship** taxes long-term health.

We may not be able to control how long our marriages last, but we can control how we handle our part of the uncoupling. Remember to keep any problems between the parents, and avoid dragging the kids into it all. If there are issues between you and your child's other parent, make every effort not to talk about those issues in front of your child. Remember that it's critical for children to feel safe and secure in order to thrive.

Seeing parents argue productively, and make up productively, can be a healthy way to realize that **Relationships** have hard moments and still remain intact. Seeing parents argue and then "take it in the other room," with no further discussion, can leave kids anxious, wondering what happened or what might happen. Seeing co-parents argue when there is no underlying loving **Relationship** can make kids feel the need to take sides, feel unsafe, or be concerned about the welfare of one or both parents.

When you do argue, which you inevitably will, it's more important to close the loop and resolve the argument than to "take it in the other room." Kids notice everything, so they feel safer when you acknowledge what's happening and don't try to sweep it under the rug or pretend everything is fine.

Keep focused on the goal. Supportive **Relationships** help children thrive. Having a secure attachment with a parent buffers children from adversity, supports their development, and allows them to learn and grow. *Every* positive **Relationship** with a trusted adult makes a difference. Remember—perhaps now more than in any other parenting scenario— *more often than not* is what we are going for. Give yourself some grace.

### Moving—and Staying the Same

If you dig the hole deep enough and water consistently, most trees will shake off the shock of a transplant in about a year. Kids aren't so different. The science tells us that moves for children *are* associated with small declines in social skills, emotional well-being, and behavior. But you aren't scarring your kids for life by moving—just be aware that they might need more security reminders during the transition.

The instinct might be to emphasize what's wrong with the current home and what's going to be better when we move (New York sucks! It always rains here! We'll have bedrooms in Ohio! We'll live closer to grandma!). But the research tells us that to help ease the transition, we need to emphasize—to ourselves and to our kids—what will *stay the same*. Make a list, first just for yourself, of everything that will stay the same. Include feelings that won't change, like love; objects that won't change, like specific teddy bears and clothing; and routines that won't change, like family meals or waking up for school. It's the same for the older kids—you just may be swapping posters for teddy bears. Share your list with your kids.

It's a time also to offer all the extra stability you can. Your children are learning to be more flexible and more at home in the larger world, but they need to know that the people they love and depend on aren't going to dissolve. They can best adjust to being transplanted from the secure base if they know that some things—especially your love and support—won't ever change.

## Q & A Session

**Question:** After a lot of back and forth, I'm wondering how and when you'd advise sharing news that we are moving with our toddler. He has no clue, and he is so attached to his little community here. Even though we think he will love our new place and be close to family, he doesn't handle change well!

**Answer:** Toddlers don't have a great sense of time, and talking about something too far in advance may cause unnecessary stress. On the other hand, not talking about something at all and surprising a toddler may also be destabilizing. Here are a few tips to handle this major transition:

1.  Make sure your timing for revealing the news just precedes any noticeable packing.
2.  Explain the news clearly and simply.
3.  Let your child know what will be the same and what will change in your new home. For example, "You will have the same comforter, but a new bed."
4.  Take pictures before dismantling the bedrooms and family rooms, so that you can go back and "visit" later.
5.  Allow your child to express any uncomfortable feelings and avoid trying to convince them not to be upset because of all the great things that are going to happen. This is an opportunity to teach them that they can have mixed feelings—where you are both curious/excited and nervous/sad.

6. Make as few changes as possible. The fact that you're moving inherently means there will be lots of transitions, so try to avoid the ones that you can actually control.

7. Don't spend too much time talking about it—there's no need to fixate.

## Normalize Death and Grief, But Remember that Kids Are Concrete Thinkers

As parents, we can normalize life's patterns by pointing out to our children the rhythms of the seasons, how flowers bloom and die, and the way the leaves fall in autumn; we can also read books that center life in nature's patterns and show death as one aspect of those patterns. American culture treats death in a different way from much of the world. In cultures where death is considered a bad or terrifying thing, the instinct is to talk about it euphemistically. But as parents, we have to make sure we're clear with our kids. When pets and humans die, we can tell our children that their bodies stopped working. It's important to be clear that this beloved pet or person is not coming back. You might expand on that with whatever spiritual or religious beliefs you have. You might share your belief that while Grandma is not coming back, for example, she is watching over the family.

When people die, kids mostly want to know that they're safe and that you're safe. Be careful not to scare children by saying things like, "Grandma went to sleep and she never woke up." Or even, "Fido went to a better place." They died, and we can feel sad about that, and we can cry, but it's important to be clear.

Honor the memories of those lost by collecting pictures, writing poems or letters, and doing other things that may come from your faith tradition—or make new traditions. Rituals of many different types help humans of all ages to process loss. Remind your kids that even when we're grieving a loss, it's okay to have fun and feel a range of human emotions.

## Lean into Routine

Routines and rituals create a sense of home—for both you and your kids. Many of us do love our adventures, but it's the stability of a predictable and grounded base that helps us build courage instead of anxiety. Transitions don't call for rigidity—in fact, those of us who are rigid have a pretty challenging time with change!—but see where you can keep things familiar. Maybe you always have a special meal on Sundays. Keep having it. Maybe at your old home you gave your children a bath every night and your new place only has a shower. Bring the old rubber duckie, and show your child how to have fun and get clean in the new shower stall. Maybe your child is accustomed to reading a book with you before bedtime. Bring in books about the transitions you're going through.

When we can't predict things, we tend to feel anxious. Wiring kids to consider that not knowing opens up possibilities is a perspective that can get us out of the control loop. It's more of an attitude shift that can happen by saying things like, "I wonder what kind of neighbors we'll have?" instead of "I don't know who our neighbors will be, and that's scary."

## Navigating Separation

Starting at around six months and peaking at eight or nine months, and again between twelve and eighteen months, you may notice your baby getting upset when separated from you or another caregiver. If you haven't seen it already, brace yourself for this normal behavior. If you have an older child, remember that separation continues to be a pain point for many children. Learning to navigate the push-pull relationship with parents can take many years—and lots of practice.

Amir's nine-month-old doesn't want her to leave the house. Grandma is babysitting, and if Amir says, "Mommy's going to work—Mommy always comes back. I love you. Bye!" she knows from experience that she'll have to watch her baby break down, reaching out his sweet little arms and crying "Mama." It feels too sad to watch. It makes Amir want to fix her baby's feelings by saying, "Okay, I won't go." She hates walking out the door, knowing her kid is crying. Her instinct? She sneaks out. After doing that more than a few times, she wonders, *Why is my kid so clingy?* And it might well be because her baby never has any idea when she's going to leave.

It's never too late to reroute this kind of dynamic. When a parent does say goodbye, even though it's painful, it provides the child with evidence that they can get through periods of discomfort. It might always be tough when Amir leaves, but her baby will keep having the reinforcement of the experience. Mommy *does* always come back.

Kids are always going to be clingy to some extent—that's part of being a kid. But you can avoid a lot of that anxiety if the message given is that, at random times, you're just going to disappear without saying anything. It's better to say, "If I'm leaving, I'll tell you I'm leaving, and I always come back. I know it's hard for you, but this person I leave you with is safe and loving and I trust them." By learning to accept the discomfort of this separation, you are also teaching yourself that you can get through this. So often, we want to fix the feeling to soothe *ourselves*, but that doesn't really serve our children's growth.

### Help Young Kids Trust You'll Come Back

**Have an upbeat mood.** Your baby is looking to you to see your reaction and to co-regulate with them, so keep it light and casual when you leave (especially if you're feeling upset). Breathe. They need you to model that things are okay as they learn that separations and reunions are a normal part of life. Remember that since this is a normal phase of development, you don't need to apologize on your baby's behalf.

**Plan a distraction for after you leave.** Ask family members or other caregivers to have a few special toys or activities to help your baby recover from separation. Even though your baby's reaction may be intense, it is usually short-lived, and your baby is easily distracted.

**Stay out.** Forgot your wallet? Too bad. Once you've left, try not to return (tip: have someone throw it out the window to you).

Your baby will likely have a much harder time if you return and leave again. This is especially true for parents who try to work in another room or part of the house. Don't expect to be able to pop out for coffee if the baby can see you!

## Rituals to Make Separations Easier

When my daughter was little, there was a crystal hanging from a string in the window of her school, so she would blow a kiss through the crystal and through the window, and I would catch it. Then we got a crystal for home.

Another ritual was "The Kissing Hand," based on the children's book of the same name by Ruth Harper. In the book, a mom and baby raccoon share a family secret of the kissing hand. When I kissed the palms of my children's hands, I told them that, just like in the book, the kiss wouldn't wash off. If they missed me, they could put their hands to their cheeks and say, "Mom loves me."

Once kids age out of these exercises, they still often struggle with separations of longer periods of time, such as when they're at a sleepover or away at summer camp. For older kids, you can offer a soft T-shirt of yours—something they can sleep in or hang on to without worrying about peer judgment.

REFLECTION EXERCISE

*Home Is Where the Heart Is*

Heraclitus called it, back in ancient Greece: "The only constant in life is change." After all these centuries, change hasn't gotten much easier, but there's another adage that has been stitched by countless mothers throughout history: Home is where the heart is. When we practice breathing into the stable homes that are *our bodies* and *our hearts*, we can become more and more at ease with the changing world around us.

Set your timer for as long as you have for this meditation—three minutes or twenty minutes will both suffice. Sit someplace where you can get comfortable, even if it's on the bench at the rest stop in the middle of your cross-country move. Take a conscious breath in while you say silently to yourself: "I'm at home in my body." Feel the breath gather around your heart, put your hand on your heart, and say to yourself: "I'm at home in my heart." As you exhale consciously, say to yourself: "I'm at home in the world."

Repeat:

I'm at home in my body.
I'm at home in my heart.
I'm at home in the world.
Keep breathing.

# The Screen-Time Generation

*Phones, Devices, and Social Media*

> *Kids don't have frontal lobes that are fully functional.*
> *Your frontal lobe is what controls judgment, reasoning, planning,*
> *organization, and thinking of consequences. . . . So parents need*
> *to be their kid's frontal lobe as they navigate the world of*
> *social media and help them exercise good judgment.*
>
> —HEIDI ALLISON BENDER, PhD

We're living in what sometimes feels like an overwhelmingly connected world. Our kids are part of an unplanned global experiment in what happens when we surround developing humans with digital technologies that weren't available even a decade ago, let alone a generation ago.

Some people will tell you the screens are all bad and they're just zapping our children's brains and putting them in touch with drug dealers. Others will insist that screens are the future and we might as well give up on face-to-face connections—they are *so* twentieth century. As with everything in this polarized world of parenting advice, there's space between those two extremes, and leaning into that space is what will best serve you and your kids.

Current research shows that very young children don't learn well from screens. In one experiment, nine-month-old babies who received a few hours of Mandarin instruction from a live human could isolate specific phonetic elements in the language, while another group of babies who received the exact same instruction via video could not. As kids get older, they'll find positive uses for screens—for constructive connections, meaningful content, and faraway educational opportunities that would otherwise be out of reach. You'll also find ways to enjoy screen time together as a family. The trouble comes when screen time starts to get in the way of other connections, or when kids are using screen time to get up to no good.

The American Academy of Pediatrics calls for no screen time at all for kids under two years—except for video chatting—and says kids ages two to five should max out at one hour a day. For older kids, they recommend making a family media plan that can include screen-free zones and times. Parents and children can negotiate the limits and boundaries concerning screen use and rework their plan over time as the kids get older or circumstances change.

Will we get push-back from our kids if we limit their screen time? Sure. But you can let your kids know what your job is, and you can remind them that there are always going to be things in life—like chocolate and screen time—that we sometimes feel we'll never get enough of.

---

### Don't Worry Too Much about Enforcing Screen Time on Holidays

Limiting the use of screens is good for all of us, but if you have a long road trip or flight, or older cousins keep their screens on in a house full of holiday guests, this is nothing to sweat. You may notice the short-term dysregulation that comes from a bunch of changes to routines and new faces, but the long-term impact of a few full days of screen use is not anything to add to your worry plate. Post holidays, go back to your routines and your guardrails. The anxiety and tension of trying to control too much during this temporary time is not worth it! When in doubt, consider the dose and duration. It's okay to be in survival mode on that road trip and then return to the home rules when you get home.

---

## Find the Balance in Your Own Use of Devices

The first time my daughter put together a free-form Lego, she made a Blackberry phone, and I thought, *Okay, I'm not using devices in a way that's going to promote attention.* Of course, it's not just me. The average American adult is now checking their phone about a hundred times a day.

There's no getting around it: the phone sucks attention away from our kids. But I say this with a deep understanding that when we feel isolated, the phone can also help us feel less like we're alone. Our kids need our attention, but we need connection, too. Our work as parents, then, is to find that space between the extremes. We can't neglect our kids, but we can't neglect our own need for adult interactions, either.

As with virtually everything in parenting, developing a healthy-enough relationship with screen time starts with us. Begin by becoming a mentor concerning those devices and screen use. We can't expect to tell our tweens to get their noses out of a device during mealtime when they've spent their whole lives watching us scroll and eat. Do what you might require of your tween when the time comes: set times you are *off* your phone, and make it clear you're available to your kids to pay attention. That may mean that you decide mealtime, reading time, and playtime are phone-free; or it may mean you commit to your first fifteen minutes walking in the door are screen-free and then you can announce, "I'm going to check on work for ten minutes and come back." And then make good on your promise.

Being a social-media mentor means paying attention to how we post, how we comment, and how often we doomscroll. When we post our kids, we want to not only ask their permission (after all, we expect the same of them) but also ask ourselves what our posts convey; take a breath and check in with yourself before you even ask if you can post. Is the message you're posting about your child the kind of message you want them to receive? For example, do you want to post how hot they looked in a bikini or call out all the As on a report card? Maybe not. They may or may not give you permission, but they're watching and learning from you how to use social media.

## Q & A Session

**Question:** My sixth-grader wants all the apps; his friends' parents don't say no, so we're the bad guys. What to do?

**Answer:** Sometimes being a parent and holding to boundaries that you believe are for the best means that you're not popular in that moment (***Rules***). You can always remind your child, "I love you, and I get why this feels crummy to you. I set limits for the purpose of keeping you safe and protected, and when I set a boundary, I make a decision based on what I think is appropriate for your age and your temperament and the environment that you're growing up in. I certainly take into account that this is something that you want, and as your parents, we make the final decision. It's not about not being the bad guy, but more about getting comfortable being the bad guy sometimes" (***Relationship***, ***Rules***). For what it's worth, I don't think you're bad! If *you* do, remember the way out of that feeling: BAD: Breathe, Assess, Deal (see page 10).

### Internet Exposure Comes with Exposure to Mature Content

Kids are being exposed to porn at younger and younger ages. While we don't want to conflate porn and sex any more than we want to conflate sex and gender or gender and sexuality, the fact is that many children are exposed to pornography before they have a concept of nonperformative sex. The minute your child is introduced to the internet, they are open to the possibility of exposure to pornography. It's an uncomfortable conversation for many parents, but you can start young—whenever your child has access to that first tablet—with gentle warnings about what they might see and what to do when they see it.

You can begin the conversation quite simply, so they can recognize porn when they see it and feel comfortable talking about it. I remember when a friend asked her son if he knew what porn was—he was in fifth grade. He said yes. She followed up with, "Tell me what you know." He said he knew it was something he wasn't "supposed to see," but could not say specifically what it was.

When in doubt, check in to see where your child is and start from there. Pornography can be simply defined as pictures, videos, or even cartoons of people with little or no clothes on that focus on the private parts we usually keep covered with a swimsuit. While all parts of a body are good, kids need to know that taking pictures of private parts and sharing them can be unsafe and that sexually explicit material is not something the childhood brain can process. Not all nudity is porn, of course, and the conversation can become more nuanced as kids get older, but art-nudity generally doesn't focus on the private parts and generally isn't hypersexualized.

Pornography is designed to be arousing to the body and addicting to the mind, so kids need to know that there's no shame in having a response to it. That said, porn can rob kids of their own healthy sexual development, turning sexuality into a performance, so it's important to give them some guidelines and direction. Kristen A. Jenson, author of *Good Pictures, Bad Pictures: Porn-Proofing Today's Young Kids*, advises parents to tell very young children to "turn, run, and tell." As kids get older, she advises we teach them to close their eyes, name it when they see it, and tell a trusted adult what they've seen. Kids should also know that if an adult or older teen intentionally shows them porn, that should be interpreted as a red flag and this individual may be attempting to groom them for abuse.

If kids have seen images that they're trying to get out of their minds, you can introduce them to cognitive behavioral theory. That is, every time an image pops into their mind, they can distract themselves with something less problematic. If your child is really into toy cars, tell them to try thinking about toy cars every time the disturbing image comes to mind. If they play the piano, you can have them practice the piano every time the image haunts them.

As kids enter adolescence, remind them that pornography turns people into objects and fuels abuse. Teenagers are natural fighters for justice, so it can help to remind them that watching pornography can be a vote for racism, misogyny, and the all-too-common exploitation of porn performers. Remember to mention that porn also really messes with your sense of what real bodies look like, from penis size to boobs, just like it gives you a completely warped depiction of what a loving sexual interaction looks like. Your child is going to be safer from sexual predators and from sexual extortion if you can have these conversations and if your child feels comfortable coming to you.

## Q & A Session

**Question:** We have limits about screen time, but my kid has a huge meltdown when it's time to turn off the screen, even when I've given wrap-up warnings. What is going on?

**Answer:** If you notice your child is melting down with screen time, plan to have a meeting. Not during the actual heat of the moment, but separately when your child is feeling calm (*Reflection*). You can say, "You know, you've been having trouble letting go of screen time. Let's decide together how much you're going to have, when you're going to have it, and then you can choose whether you turn it off or I turn it off for you. If it's too hard, we'll take a little break from screen time. Too much screen time can make you really tantrum-y after it gets ripped away from you" (*Relationship*, *Reflection*, *Rules*).

Or you might just say, "You know what? We're going to take a little break because it's hard for you to stop using the screen when you've finished. Let's see if having less screen time helps it get easier for you to let go. As you build up your capacity to calmly turn off the screen, we'll be able to add some more time" (*Regulation*, *Rules*).

### Social Media Is an Amplifier

While social media can offer some benefits of connection and shared interests, it can also be highly problematic. In 2023, the surgeon general issued an advisory calling attention to the growing concerns about the effects of social media on young people's mental health. Social media use among adolescents is nearly universal, with up to 95 percent reporting using a social media platform and more than one-third saying they use social media "almost constantly."

A recent study found that kids who habitually check social media had changes in the parts of their brain that control social rewards and punishment. Habitual social media checking impacted the amygdala, one of the emotional centers of the brain that makes us feel and react to fear. The part of the brain responsible for judgment, reasoning, and rewards, called the dorsolateral prefrontal cortex, was also impacted.

Additional research has shown a connection between high levels of social media use and adolescent depression. A recent study from the Oxford Internet Institute found that the negative impacts of social media affected girls and boys at different ages, with girls being most sensitive between the ages of eleven and thirteen and boys between ages fourteen and fifteen.

Still, you can parent your kids without feeling like you're on patrol. You can monitor your child's social media use without shifting into what might feel like surveillance. If your child struggles with body image, self-esteem, or peers, know that social media use can amplify those struggles. If your kid is doing well, if things are feeling good, if you notice that they're looking at bunnies and puppies and recipes online, their social interactions seem healthy, they're getting good sleep, they're not interrupting mealtimes, they're getting their exercise, and life is generally going okay and they just happen to also be on social media, you don't need to panic about the surgeon general's warning. If, on the other hand, you find that your child is bullying or being bullied, they're having body image issues, they're getting poor sleep, or they're depressed, one of the first things you can do is take a look at their social media use, because it may be making them feel even worse in their struggles—and we never want that. Try reducing social media use to one hour per day. After three weeks, see if you and your child notice positive changes.

## REGULATION EXERCISE

### "This Is Hard. This Is Normal. I'm Not Being Chased by a Bear."

Because the science has shown that social media and other digital interactions can send adults and children alike into an unnecessary fight-or-flight response, it's important for the whole family to keep practicing how to turn off that response when you are not in immediate danger. It's healthy to acknowledge the real difficulties you're dealing with *and* to remind your body that you're not in danger.

Set your timer for five or ten minutes. Sit or lie down someplace comfortable, where you can allow yourself to relax. It's okay if you fall asleep during this one, but there's no need to *try* to fall asleep. Gently place your hand on your heart and close your eyes. As you breathe in through your nose, acknowledge to yourself: *This is hard.* Now, exhale through your mouth, reminding yourself: *This is normal.* Now, breathe in and breathe out, focusing on the warmth emanating between your hand and your heart and remind yourself: *I'm not being chased by a bear; my child is not being chased by a bear.*

Keep breathing. With each inhale and with each exhale, you're resetting your nervous system. With your hand on your heart, you're giving yourself an oxytocin hormone love boost. With each affirmation, you're promising your flight-or-flight response that there's no immediate danger, and no need to engage.

Let your shoulders relax. Let your arms and hands relax. As you breathe in through your nose, keep acknowledging to yourself: *This is hard.* Exhaling, remind yourself: *This is normal.* Breathing in and out, focusing on the warmth emanating between your hand and your heart, remind yourself: *I'm not being chased by a bear; my child is not being chased by a bear.*

# Sex, Gender, and Sexuality

### *It's a Whole New World*

*I am no bird; and no net ensnares me:*
*I am a free human being with an independent will.*

—CHARLOTTE BRONTË, *JANE EYRE*

Sex, gender, and sexuality are notoriously uncomfortable topics for parents, but we all have to find our balance between giving our kids the information and resources they need and not being intrusive. Be mindful to talk about love, positive intimacy, and sexual health *at least* as often as you focus on risk and danger.

### Breathe into Your Place of BALANCE

**Breathe:** Remember, there's rich neuroscience behind the power of the breath, and no, you can't skip this step. Take a breath.

**Acknowledge your own baggage:** Ask yourself: "What is this moment about for me?" Beyond worries about sexuality and our kids' safety, these conversations do bring up a certain amount of grief that our kids are growing up.

**Let it go:** Leave the big-picture lessons for later.

**Assess the present moment:** Gauge your child's state of mind—calm, curious, frantic, distraught?

**Notice:** Observe what's going on with your child's body. Ask yourself what your child is trying to tell you—behavior is information.

**Connect:** Let your child know you see them and care about their feelings.

**Engage:** Now that you're in balance, you can decide which response you want to throw your weight behind.

We know these seven, science-backed steps work on mechanisms in the brain-body so we can better manage tense scenarios.

## Sex and Gender

There is so much change in the landscape of the discussions around sex and gender in our culture, I'm just going to lay out the basics as best I understand them, in an attempt to clear up some confusion and leave room to learn more as we grow. Sex and gender can often be confused, so let's be clear about the meaning of the words.

*Sex* refers to biology. The two most common sexes are *female*, who typically have XX chromosomes and ovaries and produce eggs; and *male*, who typically have XY chromosomes and testes and produce sperm. Just under 2 percent of the population has some sort of intersex trait. *Gender*, on the other hand, refers to the socially constructed roles, behaviors, expressions, and identities of girls, women, boys, men, and gender-diverse people. Ideas about gender differ among different cultures and subcultures, and they change over time.

A generation or two ago, for example, many people considered fathers who take a primary role in parenting to be *gender nonconforming*. A generation before that, girls who played sports were also the exception. These days, more and more men are involved in raising their kids, and sports are for everyone. If a man takes his daughter to soccer practice, no one assumes he's a widower. And no one assumes the girl is a "tomboy." Today, gender norms are on the move again as trans and nonbinary identities become more common among tweens, teens, and adults.

Might our children need something from us that's special because of their gender? Sure. But that's mostly because of the socially prescribed roles, biases, and stereotypes that come with being a gender in society.

## Gender and Sexuality

Just like we can't conflate sex and gender, we can't conflate gender and sexuality. *Gender* refers to who someone is as a person, and *sexuality* refers to who someone tends to be drawn to romantically. As parents, we have to come to terms with how we feel about our children's experience of their gender and—usually not until at least early adolescence—their sexuality. This way, we can allow for curiosity and openness, sharing our values with our children in very conscious ways.

Because the culture has changed so much just in the last generation, it's likely that our children are going to have different concepts of gender and sexuality than we had growing up, so we're going to learn at least as much from them as they will learn from us. Practice asking questions at least as often as you impart your own opinions.

It's also worth allowing ourselves space to figure out our feelings so that we can respond most sensitively to our kids, because we know that LGBTQ youth are at higher risk for suicide and depression—and we love them. So, let's not discount that risk because this is hard for us. Let's try to mitigate that risk by providing sensitive caregiving.

## It's a Whole New World of Gender and Sexual Identity

Is your kindergartener drawn to clothes and toys that don't match up with expected gender norms? Does your nine-year-old identify as asexual? Is your middle-schooler using *they/them* pronouns? It's a whole new world of gender and sexual identity, and our kids are going to teach us new ways of looking at it all, just as we taught our own parents' generation. One term I like because it's so inclusive—applicable to anyone experiencing or experimenting with alternatives to traditional gender expectations—is "gender expansive." Introduce the concept or wait for your kids' cues. Ask yourself: *What do I want my children to understand about gender and sexuality and my values around those things?* To make life easier—if you ever feel like an old fogey around binary gender issues (hand raised!), consider getting in the habit of using gender-neutral words like *baby, child, spouse, partner,* and *sibling.*

While it's great to be inclusive and accepting of people of all genders, remember that young children don't have any concept of that. Gender, after all, is a social construction. So, similar to moral development, children's ideas about gender go through a preconventional stage, a conventional stage, and ultimately may enter a postconventional stage.

In the preconventional stage, up until about age two and sometimes until age four, children have no real consciousness of the differences between genders, and they may use pronouns willy-nilly. While contemporary parents often want to affirm their children's identities, there's no need to take your child to the nonbinary support group or the pediatric endocrinologist when they are still in preschool.

By a child's third birthday, they tend to be able to label themselves with a gender identity—usually a boy or a girl. By about age four, kids have typically learned their community's understanding of gender as well, and they will include trans and nonbinary identities in their understanding if those categories have been presented to them and normalized for them. Later, depending on their experiences, they may shift into a postconventional sense of gender and its fluidity. Our job as parents in a changing world is to allow for questions and to allow for the reality that we may not always have the answers.

Because identifying as nonbinary or trans in youth has only recently become normalized in the culture, we don't have a lot of scientific data about it. That said, we have plenty of data that tells us our children need to know we love and support who they are. As with other new cultural phenomena—like social media—there really haven't been any longitudinal studies.

Do trans adolescents do better when they have loving and supportive parents who are open and curious, and who continue to set limits and boundaries, than when they have parents who aren't accepting and don't love them for who they are? Well, we don't have that exact long-term study, but we do have tons of research that shows that's the case for all humans. So, it stands to reason that it would also be true for trans humans, who are not ultimately different from cis humans.

If you feel discomfort because your child's life isn't unfolding the way you imagined it would, remember the practice of sitting with your discomfort. You can take a deep breath and aim to channel your inner grandma-who-has-seen-it-all. You can seek gay-friendly counseling and entertain the reality that your child was born this way and is fabulous just the way they are. You can open up to learning about new experiences and subcultures.

When our kids come to us with anything they might feel nervous about, they're giving us an amazing opportunity to support them. This doesn't mean that you, as the parent, aren't allowed to have your own feelings, but it does mean that you have to manage those feelings. You're still the parent in this dynamic, and your child needs to be able to trust you not to freak out. Instead of saying, "I love you no matter what," which suggests your child has just disclosed a flaw, try saying something specific like, "I love you so much, and your sexuality and your gender are completely unrelated to my love for you."

Or you can say, "Congratulations." If that feels like a stretch at first, practice feeling like you mean it. Whether it's a phase or it's forever, your child still needs a parent who's curious, open, and accepting, and not dismissive. Children need parents who say, "I love you, and tell me about you." They don't need parents who say, "I love you only if you're this one way," or "I love you *even though* you're this way." You can practice saying the positive even if it doesn't come totally spontaneously: "I love you, and tell me about you."

If your child gives you a new name or pronoun they would like for you to use, hold those gifts like something precious. Avoid telling your child that something that feels important to them is just a "phase." Even if it is, it's more important that children are reminded of that unconditional love unrelated to their identities, choices, or even phases. If you're having a big reaction inside, you can be honest about that, too. You can say to yourself or out loud, "I'm having feelings, and I'm looking forward to growing through these feelings." If that sounds goofy, you can laugh at yourself and shift the mood.

If you make a mistake in all of this, be compassionate with yourself. Make a ***Repair*** and ask for a do-over.

## Q & A Session

**Question:** My son likes to wear Wonder Woman and princess costumes even when we encourage him to choose the Spider Man and farmer dress-up clothes. I don't want him to be trans. What should I do?

**Answer:** I cannot tell you how often parents reach out to me about dress-up. I think more parents than are willing to admit it have a feeling that even when their youngest kids dress up in the "wrong" costume for their gender, it's some kind of a flag. Not at all. Young kids dress up, and it's not at all a preview of a desire to "be trans"; but this is a wonderful opportunity to notice how it feels when your child seems to do something outside your expectations (***Reflection***).

How does it feel to face those worries and start the process of realizing that your child is a unique being, whose life and identity will unfold in ways you can't control? What does it mean if they're trans? Even if that may not be your wish for them, imagine how they would feel to get the message that your love for them and your approval are contingent on something so out of their control? Again, young kids dress up, and it's really nothing to read into, but take the opportunity to do some self-exploration if you're uncomfortable.

### How Intrinsic Are Gender Differences?

We know from science that boys and girls and gender-diverse people are all more alike than we are unalike. The science tells us that children—regardless of their gender—need connection, understanding, and appropriate limits and boundaries.

That said, there are slight innate differences between the sexes. Studies show that boys, for example, tend to be fussier than girls as infants. Girls, on the other hand, tend to develop their fine motor skills earlier. Often these minor differences are reinforced by socialization, leading to starker contrasts.

In my parenting groups, I consistently notice that because we expect boys to develop later and more slowly, we tend to coddle our boys a little bit more. As we do that, we tend to expect more of our girls. We use them as examples and say things like, "Noah, look how nicely Hazel is sitting in the circle." Often unconsciously, then, we teach our boys how to be messy and how to make mistakes with more room for error than we allow for in our girls.

By the time our kids are school age, they've been living and breathing cultural norms about emotionality for long enough that our boys do become more comfortable expressing anger and meanness, and our girls do understand that sadness, empathy, anxiety, and kindness are all more culturally acceptable emotions for them.

By elementary school, likely due to minor intrinsic sex differences exaggerated by gendered socialization, girls exhibit more internalizing disorders, like anxiety and depression, and boys exhibit more externalizing issues, like conduct disorders. If your child throws a desk at a teacher, that child is more likely to be male. If your child is dealing with the toxic anxiety of perfectionism, that child is more likely to be a girl.

Our values concerning gender and parenting come into play. Do you want your daughters to be more empathic than your sons? There's nothing wrong with that position, but by consciously thinking about these issues we can be more intentional. It can be helpful to unpack how your own family of origin, era, and culture set you up to think about gender.

Parents come to me all the time, worried that they've been too sensitive with their boys and that those boys aren't going to be able to hack it in a macho community. With girls, on the other hand, it can be helpful to notice whether we're asking them to suppress anger in gender-based ways and, again, if that's intentional or just something we're unconsciously bringing into our parenting. Parents of girls are more likely to worry that their child is growing into a "bitch," in a world where female anger and meanness are unacceptable. Understanding where we ourselves are coming from in terms of our feelings and values about gender norms is an important place to start.

## Puberty Is Normal and Necessary

During puberty, as adolescents develop into sexually mature adults and release hormones that create changes in their reproductive system, the body grows faster than it has since the first year of life. Puberty can sometimes be confusing, uncomfortable, or embarrassing—but it's a normal and necessary process.

In girls, the typical onset of puberty ranges from eight to thirteen years old, averaging around age nine or ten when girls develop breast buds under the areola. Keep in mind that these changes don't necessarily occur at the same time in each breast. Before kids even need bras for coverage, some parents find it makes the transition easier to start with a little jogging bralette.

As puberty progresses, the breast tissue gets bigger and changes in contour. About a year to a year and half later, pubic hair starts to show up. Somewhere between six months and three years after that first downy pubic hair grows in, girls typically get their first period. The average age is twelve and a half. Keep in mind that while period onset has remained more stable, onset of puberty has become increasingly earlier over the past few decades. With increases in estrogen production, girls' superpower of vigilance is activated. This is something that gave our ancestors an increased capacity to go into fight-or-flight or freeze mode to protect youngsters in their care. In the contemporary world, neuroscience has shown that girls and other people with increased estrogen can experience a lot of stress with the internal activation of hypervigilance when they're faced with a perceived threat; online judgment and bullying, for example, can send girls into panic mode.

In boys, puberty tends to get started between ages nine and fourteen, when their testicles start to grow and hormones including estradiol and testosterone start pumping up production. Kids of all genders experience a voice change, but in boys it's more pronounced, and you'll notice the telltale squeaks and cracks before their voices get deeper. Genitals continue to develop, and spermarche—when boys typically start producing sperm—can happen any time between the ages of ten and sixteen, but typically gets started around age thirteen and a half.

Rates of early puberty have been increasing around the world in recent years, especially among African American youth, and developing early can be tough on kids. During early puberty, peers and other adults may see the kids as being older than they are and place higher expectations on them; they may not be quite ready for the risk-taking hormones that are being released or the way people are looking at them. Further, they may just have more sexually mature-looking bodies but not yet through the larger developmental shifts such as menarche and, well, development. If your child seems to be entering puberty before about age eight or nine, talk to your pediatrician about it. Keep in mind they are still developmentally a child, and being treated like a teenager when they're not can disrupt your **Relationship** and other **Relationships** in their lives. The opposite is also true: kids who develop more slowly may experience being treated as less capable and mature then they are.

We tend to focus on girls' hormonal shifts, but by age ten many boys are experiencing the hormonal shifts as well. It's less likely to be as evident physically; you may notice a change in boys' responses and social interactions. Helping kids learn about what's happening with their body and recognizing that changes are occurring is so helpful.

### Normalize Periods and Hormonal Shifts

Other than explaining what a period is, it makes it easier if you've been open about the fact that some people do menstruate. Normalize your own period, if you have one, by leaving tampons or accessories within sight, mentioning casually when you're on your cycle, and just having a generally nonmysterious vibe, saying things openly like, "Oh, I got my period, so I have to grab a tampon." If your child notices blood in a trash can (pardon the uncharming image), you can explain what it is in simple terms, saying something like "I shed the lining of my uterus once a month, and it doesn't mean I'm hurt; I actually can't even feel it!"

## Unshame Masturbation

Parents of adolescents typically know that their kids will be exploring their own bodies and the sensations that feel good to them. This one is super straightforward—no shame, just privacy. The more awkward phone calls come from parents who have toddlers and younger children who are touching themselves in ways that make everyone around them uncomfortable. Here's all you need to get across to children of any age:

1. It is great to get to know the different ways your body feels good when you touch it.
2. Touching your private parts is something to do privately, not in front of other people.

## Bodies Have Smells

Everyone's body smells differently, but there comes a point when your child will run up and give you a hug and likely shock you with their scent. With puberty comes body odor, and it often comes way sooner than you expected. Parents often ask if it's shaming to tell our kids that they've gotten to a point where things need to change. Shame is telling your child they are a smelly human and therefore should hide, but simply saying "Hey, love, there comes a time when body sweat starts to smell, and it's our social contract to just wash those areas and use healthy deodorant. Here are some options for cleansers and deodorants to choose from. I can help remind you until it becomes a habit. This is something all of us do."

## The Sex Talk

When we think about "the sex talk," it can seem like it's a one-and-done endeavor, but we don't have some big conversation only once. We can start with small talks. All kids are different, so unfortunately there is no set script I can hand you, but normalizing your discussions of human sexuality with kids of all ages leads to better health and creates a foundation for gender equality and intimate justice.

You don't have to get everything right in a single conversation—who could?—and you don't have to feel completely comfortable. You just have to open the conversation or find a trusted friend or relative who can be a resource for your child. Trusted friends are game changers in adolescence, and it is so protective to have other trusted adults in your child's life.

Research shows that kids of the current generation are having less heterosexual intercourse than previous generations, but more broadly defined, including defining oral and anal sex as sex, kids are being introduced to sex acts and sexuality at younger and younger ages. If talking to kids about sex and intimacy feels uncomfortable, try chatting on a walk or while the kids are in the car—anywhere there doesn't have to be direct eye contact.

Peggy Orenstein, author of *Boys & Sex* and *Girls & Sex*, did cross-cultural research that has shown Dutch children, as compared to American children, tend to have more helpful information. Interestingly, this isn't because Dutch parents are any more comfortable talking about sex and sexuality; rather, it's that they tend to speak about sex, masturbation, mutual caring, love, and pleasure, while American parents tend to focus on disease and risk. So, consider being more Dutch in your approach, and focus on healthy intimacy, sex, and consent in the context of loving relationships at least as early and often as you bring up sexuality in the context of disease and unwanted pregnancy. Coming from your own place of regulation, be mindful not to overwhelm kids with fears and too much information. Find out what they know, and answer their questions.

## Introducing Consent

*Consent* means agreeing to something. *Sexual consent* means agreeing to sexual activity. You can teach your kids about consent long before you connect the concept to sex. This can be as simple as a child being allowed to tell someone (politely) that they don't want to play in the sandbox. So, teach your kids that it's okay to say no in all contexts. If they don't want to go on a playdate, help your child practice saying no in ways that are kind. If your child has a relative who likes to hug and your child doesn't always like getting hugged, normalize that physical boundary and indicate that they can say no; if the relatives are offended, so be it.

Or you can explain your position to your relatives with kindness while prioritizing your support of your child's decision. To ease the blow, you can, in advance of their arrival, come up with a comfortable way your child can greet a loved one. Will they choose a high-five, a wave, an elbow rub? Each of these are just options—the only thing they *have* to do is find a way to greet that works for them.

Another way to think about and practice consent is to teach your children to accept when someone else has set a boundary. If your friend does not want you to tell you a secret that another friend told them, and you keep pressing them, you're not taking no for an answer. Normalize saying no and also taking no for an answer.

Finally, don't forget that consent can also be taught with simple and respectful behaviors, such as knocking on the bedroom and bathroom door when they are closed. Not only does this knock act as a proxy for asking for consent to enter, but it also has the added benefit of making sure you don't walk in on your adolescent's having a private moment with themselves and ensures they don't witness anything they should not in your bedroom. You're welcome.

## REGULATION EXERCISE

### Walking Meditation

Sometimes it can be even more grounding to do a walking meditation than to do a seated one. To remind yourself that no matter how comfortable or uncomfortable you are thinking about your child's development, no one is being chased by a bear, so start practicing a walking meditation.

You're not exactly taking a walk in a walking meditation, though you will get some steps in. Identify a place where you are going to walk to—the end of the driveway, for example—and take your steps mindfully, paying attention to your breath as you count your steps. Every time you notice that you've gotten to ten, start again from one. Keep breathing. When you've gotten to the place you picked, turn around and count your steps on the way back, breathing with calm.

Repeat three times.

CHAPTER 18

# Finding Your Middle Road

*The Space Between*

> *I would rather be the child of a mother who has all*
> *the inner conflicts of the human being than be mothered*
> *by someone for whom all is easy and smooth, who knows*
> *all the answers, and is a stranger to doubt.*

—DONALD WINNICOTT, MD

Parenting is a massive undertaking, no matter when and how you go about it. I hope these pages have helped make it feel like the undertaking is *manageable*.

So many times, it can feel like every little thing we get right and every little thing we get wrong is going to impact our children in some life-altering way. So I hope you've gained some relief from that and have come to a better understanding of what the science shows us really matters. Yes, as parents, we are our children's first and most important teachers. The big tenets of what matters from the science are sensitive caregiving, temperament, loving support with boundaries, and rupture and repair. The five principles we can keep coming back to are **Relationship**, **Reflection**, **Regulation**, **Rules**, and **Repair**. There are going to be mistakes, and those mistakes are actually *supposed* to happen. Those mistakes serve our kids, and they serve us.

We know that everyday stressors can easily send us into unnecessary fight-or-flight responses, so if you can figure out a system for regaining BALANCE—your parenting passcode—then you're going to be able to access your inner resources to align with the outer knowledge we get from the science—and from our unique children in the context of our unique family's set of values.

## BALANCE Illuminates the Middle Road

**B**reathe: By now you know there's rich neuroscience behind this step, and no, you can't skip it. Take a breath.

**A**cknowledge your own baggage: I hope you're starting to feel this step come naturally. You can ask yourself what this moment is bringing up for you in a mindful way, without self-judgment.

**L**et it go: You can unpack your own baggage later.

**A**ssess the present moment: When you've set aside the baggage, you can stand in the present. Keep breathing into the moment.

**N**otice: What's going on with your child's body? What does that tell you about what's going on for them emotionally?

**C**onnect: Here you're leaning into your *Relationship* with your child and letting them know you see them and care about their feelings.

**E**ngage: Now that you're in balance, the middle road becomes easier to see and follow.

Some days are going to be easier than others, but I hope that with every opportunity you get to practice the principles and breathe into BALANCE, things begin to feel more and more manageable. Beyond the science and honoring our unique selves, well, the rest is noise. Whether you practiced sleep training or you didn't, whether they started eating with sweet potatoes or creamed oatmeal, whether you gave them a sticker to go potty, whether they got into this class or that school, whether they got invited to this or that birthday party, whether they made a varsity team—these things really don't move the needle in the long term, according to the science. Of course, you can acknowledge your children's feelings about any of these things, and I want to acknowledge *your* feelings when there are disappointments and delights along the way. But we can survive our feelings, and beyond those feelings, all these factors and what the world says about them are just noise.

As someone who works as a "parenting expert," maybe I'm not supposed to have so many doubts and internal conflicts of my own. Maybe I'm supposed to know whether I should respond to my tween's panicked text from a two-week sleepaway camp by running to the car and driving through the night to pick her up—or by doing nothing. But every day I take that intentional breath and get into BALANCE. I have to acknowledge my own baggage and calm my "survival brain" reaction; I have to shift into my "sage brain" to the extent that I can and let the space between extreme responses open up. For instance, I decide not to rescue my child from sleepaway camp, but I assure her that I know she can handle this and I offer to meet her for lunch on the Saturday the camp has set up for visiting day. From my place of balance, I'm able to validate my child's feelings, remind her that I know she can get through this, and remind myself that no one is being chased by a bear right now.

## Ask Your Wise Grandmother and Your Best Frenemy

As you've learned through many of the **Reflection** exercises in this book—and through your daily experiences—we all contain multitudes, and we can ask the various parts of ourselves for advice when we need it. When I've got a deep parenting anxiety or conundrum, I like to write letters asking for advice from my inner wise grandmother and my inner bitchy frenemy from high school. Then *I* write their responses.

You do the same. Your inner wise grandmother can be somebody who's real or imagined, but she should sound like someone you really admire and who loves you unconditionally. Once you've written down all your concerns in your letter, write a response from that grandmother in her voice. Then write a response to that same letter of concern in the voice of your totally fraught friend who has some bias and is kind of snarky—someone whom you have a more complex relationship with and who isn't going to make good choices for you. What do they say about your concerns?

When you've got all three letters, look at them and realize you're *all these people*: you're the parent asking for advice, you're the wise grandmother who knows what's best for your family, and you're the snarky frenemy who isn't playing the long game. You've got all that within you, so you can take those concerns and opinions out of your head and put them into practice.

## How Do You Want to Be Remembered?

Looking back, how do you want your kids to remember you? How would you want them to describe who you were as a parent? Get out a journal or a big piece of paper and start writing down your thoughts. You can do this alone or with your parenting partner. What big words jump out at you from the page? Do you want your kids to remember your generosity, the way you beamed when they walked in the room, your ambition at work? All these are wonderful characteristics. At least some of yours are likely to be unique.

Also, how do you want to be remembered by your *grandchildren*? Write down as many thoughts as you can, and then start highlighting the words that repeat or particularly resonate. While some of the characteristics you come up with may harken back to the values exercise presented in Chapter 3. You'll likely notice something a little different emerging here. It's your sense of *purpose* as a parent. Pick three to five repeated words and write them on a notecard. Decorate the card, if you want to. Put it in your wallet. Then, whenever the noise of your parenting experience sounds overwhelming, you can take out this little card and remind yourself.

You're not here to win the most "likes" from friends or acquaintances. You're not here to get everything perfect on the first try—if that were even possible. You're here to be yourself and to parent in a way that honors your purpose, your family's values, and the century of developmental psychology that has shown, with wonderful consistency, what really matters. As parents, we are born at the same time we find out we're becoming parents. We might feel, or others might tell us, that our job is to create a child who is a certain way or to fix a child who doesn't meet our expectations. But the science reminds us that much of our success in child-rearing rests on our own growth, on our own newfound motivation to evolve. Sometimes this means we need to reparent ourselves and give ourselves the sensitive care we didn't experience when we were young.

I hope I've shown through these pages that by doing that—by centering your own mother-tree mindfulness and development—you position yourself to better support your children, to better offer them sensitive caregiving, to better accept, love, and get to know them—to raise them and help them flourish into exactly who they're meant to be.

## ACKNOWLEDGMENTS

There are candle lighters in this world, and I am so blown away by the people in my life who have taken any opportunity to help light mine. I'm deeply grateful to my agent, Pilar Queen, for telling me I was going to write a book and for every minute thereafter. To United Talent Agency, including Charlotte Perman and of course Blair Kohan, for casually telling me that I was going to host a podcast and changing my course.

Thank you to the entire Simon Element team: Richard Rhorer, Doris Cooper, and my extremely patient editor extraordinaire, Leah Miller—thank you for shepherding this book through the process and for being the first to take me on. Thank you to Patrick Sullivan for this meaningful cover and to Emma Taussig, Elizabeth Breeden, Ingrid Carabulea, Clare Maurer, and Jessica Preeg for making such a huge effort to get this book out into the world.

Thanks to my developmental editor and mind reader Ariel Gore; my brain feels less cluttered just writing your name. And to Lauren Lavelle, who makes the overwhelming seamless and, dare I say, a pleasure. To Casey Morris, who keeps me running. To Ana, Lovely, Almie, Ryan, Raf, Grace, and Tess, for the support that made my work possible over the years.

Thanks to the ever-dreaming Krupp team: Heidi Krupp, Mia Humphreys, Gwen Nathan, Jan Major, and Kathy Giaconia.

Thank you to Dear Media, especially Jeff Berman, Paige Porte, and my producer Christiana Morgenroth. Thanks to Brian Peoples and Dylan Wade. Thanks to my youngest contributor, Violet Affleck, for going so far above and beyond both in years and in skills. Thanks to my ASG (authors support group), Vanessa Bennett, Cara Natterson, and Jennifer Wallace.

I'm especially grateful to all the brilliant experts and podcast guests who have contributed so much to the field, to my work, and to this book. I cannot name you all individually here, but thank you to every single one. One of the great joys of doing what I do is the colleagues I get to call friends, from whom I have learned so much and received endless support: Samantha Boardman, Tina Payne Bryson, Stephanie Carlson, Lisa Damour, Tracy Dennis-Tiwary, Anna Johnson, Rachel Simmons, Joshua Sparrow, and Dan Siegel, and of course deep gratitude to Bronwyn Charlton and our seedlingsgroup, which started it all. To all the beloved parents in my groups, you are inspiring. And to the OGs of the groups: Ali, Christine, Courtney, Eleanor, Ferebee, Jasmine, and Jenny—so many green flags, so much love! To all the folks who listen to the *Raising Good Humans* podcast, thank you for your trust.

Gratitude to the MMTCP community for teaching me so much about mindfulness and meditation. Thank you to the whole Mount Sinai Parenting Center team, including of course my cofounder, pediatrician and visionary Blair Hammond; my executive director, Carrie Quinn; and my beloved work wife, Mariel/Meredith Benjamin: we are securely attached. To the supportive friends, new and old, who took the time and care to give meaningful feedback and support, including Drew Barrymore (who at every chance has lit my candle), Margie Block, Barbara P. Bush, Melissa Meister, Selby Drummond, Colin Farmer (the best LT-LD-LC-CB), Danyelle Freeman, Jennifer Garner (not just for Violet!), Pilar Guzman, Brett Heyman, Natalya Hudis, Dana Klein and brood, Beth Kojima, Elise Loehnen, Sabrina Mallik, Crystal Meers, Alexandra Shiva, Dana W. Jones, Julianna Margulies, Rebekah McCabe, Noa Meyer, Kelly Patricof, Eve Rodsky, David Lauren, Gigi Stone, Jessica Chaffin, Zoe Reinis, Julie Rudd, Lara Shrifman, Jessica Yellin, Elisabeth Weed, and my Marco Polo crew.

Thank you to my family, especially Papa Jack: it was a defining event to grow up witnessing such a community of resilience; to my father, for, among many things, teaching me to lean into science; to my sister, Elana; to my meticulous stepfather; and, of course, my mamoosh, who truly embodies the 5 Rs. Of course, more than anything, thanks to

Penelope and Vivian: have I mentioned how much I love the *exactly you* that you are? Thank you for helping me with so much of this book, from cover to content! Also, thank you for the humor and graciousness with which you navigate having a mother who constantly talks about mothering and works while doing so. I love you. I love you.

I get questions about potty training, sleep learning, and screen time from parents all the time. There are as many different ways to approach these issues as there are unique, good parents, so if the following procedures make your life easier, have at them; and if they don't, ignore them. They are strategies that have worked for some parents—no more and no less.

I find that these are the kinds of challenging moments when parents don't care if there is real science behind the minutia; they just want to be told what to do. While I still won't say one method is necessarily better than the next, I'm happy to chime in with some procedural tips that tend to be supported by experts and are helpful to caregivers too tired to comb through an entire book.

## Potty Training for Beginners

Potty training is a huge point of contention in a lot of families and can be so stressful that it's a time associated with increased child abuse, so it's especially important to walk yourself through the seven steps of BALANCE if you notice you're being triggered or are simply too exhausted to think straight automatically. Take that needed breath. There are a number of toilet-training methods, but what's most important is to find the one that works for your unique family—and one that causes you the least stress. I encourage many of my parenting clients to wait until there's a school break or a low-stress vacation when they can take on the process and, as with all transitions, can wait six to eight weeks between major changes.

## Dashed Plans, Regression, and Bedwetting Are Normal

No matter our method, potty training doesn't always go according to plan, of course. There are power struggles, disruptions owing to life, regression, and those kids who don't seem to have trouble peeing in the potty, but just won't poop in it.

If your child is withholding or refusing to use the potty, the whole exercise may have turned into a power struggle. Remember: the only thing kids can control is what goes into their body and what comes out, so when you find yourself in a power struggle, it's best to abandon the project until your child feels more comfortable. Take a break for at least a couple of weeks to reset the struggle. During this resetting time, don't talk about the potty, don't praise or criticize. Breathe in, breathe out, and even if you have trouble believing it yourself, say, "I have no investment in this."

This will help to alleviate the control issues and allow a reset of the trust and cooperation between you and your child. It can take time for kids to figure this out, and as parents, it's just your job to lead them through the process, not to get them to succeed on a particular timeline.

Regression is a common problem, but most periods of regression are transient. Respond with connection and compassion. Some regression may stem from challenging emotional times in the family, while some may have no apparent explanation. If there's anything you can do to alleviate the stressors or transitions in your child's life, that may be helpful. For example, if you have a new baby, but can arrange for some special one-on-one time with your older child without the baby, that may ease the pain. If your child seems stressed out about bathroom practices at their preschool, consider making time to meet with the caregiver to discuss ways they can help the child maintain potty behaviors during the day in a familiar way.

At the same time as you show compassion, you must also *be clear about your expectations* that your child continue using the potty. Express confidence that your child will be able to get over this hurdle. Typically, when this is approached with compassion, calm, and clear expectations, the regression doesn't last very long. If accidents persist for a few weeks or more, or if the child seems distressed, take a month off. Having to pause potty training isn't harmful or indicative of anything other than a later start time for your child.

Bedwetting is also considered normal through age six. Ten to twelve hours is a long time to go without using the toilet, and some kids are deep sleepers, have small bladders, or have other issues that make it hard to stay dry through the night. I know it sounds renegade to say this, but keeping kids in pull-ups for sleep, if needed, can decrease your frustrations at having to wake up in the night to change wet sheets and pajamas. And by the way, bedwetting is pretty heritable, so if you or your co-parent were bedwetters, then it shouldn't come as a total shock.

### Nighttime Sleep Training—Or Not: Choose Your Own Adventure

"Sleep training" or "sleep learning" is the process of helping a baby learn to fall asleep and stay asleep through the night. It might sound simple enough, but it can be challenging and emotional. We get mixed messages from the media, family, friends, and even healthcare professionals about how and if we should sleep-train; and when we're already tired, it can feel like we're being pushed to the brink.

Here's what the science really tells us: there are numerous ways that parents across geography, eras, and cultures have gotten their kids to sleep through the night, and the "right" approach is whatever works for your family. As with so many things in parenting, part of me wishes I could give you an extreme "this way is right" response because that would feel in some ways easier, but there simply is no one "right" way.

Quality research has examined and reexamined the long-term effects of nighttime crying on parent-child **Relationships**, the impact of various sleep-training strategies on child development, and the effect of how we go about getting our kids to sleep in relation to parental mood, and it turns out there's no significant difference in any long-term outcome based on sleep training or sleep-learning style.

With that in mind, let's look at three methods you may want to implement. You also don't have to do sleep training at all; it's up to you. You're the parent. If you do want to use one of these strategies, they all start with putting your baby in the crib when they're drowsy, but not yet asleep. The goal is to teach the baby how to successfully soothe themself to sleep. Your role as parent and caregiver is to remove your own interference in this process, in whatever way you're most comfortable, considering what makes sense given your housing situation. The key to all these methods is consistency and patience.

The following strategies are for infants *four months or older* for whom nighttime feeding is no longer needed. If you're breastfeeding, you can use these methods after four months of age to promote sleep during all the night wakings except the once or twice when you're going to feed your baby. If you, other siblings, or both, share a sleep space with your infant, you can still use these strategies at bedtime.

You and the rest of the family can enter the sleep space once the baby has fallen asleep. And keep in mind that you can adapt these methods based on what works for you and your unique family.

When typical routines are interrupted with illness, travel, and other changes, it's normal to occasionally have to "retrain" your kids, but it should get easier each time.

### Cry It Out

The "cry it out" method is the fastest, rip-the-Band-Aid-off way to get your baby to sleep through the night, and to let them learn to self-soothe back to sleep when they do wake up. I'm not going to sugarcoat this method with a nicer updated name. It is *hard*. However, if you're exhausted and can't function, it's a really good option to get you back to sanity and help your infant learn to sleep. "Cry it out" means that after a typical nighttime routine, you put your baby down, give them a little good night, but don't rock them or feed them to sleep, and then you let them fall asleep on their own, come wailing or what have you.

This method removes nighttime parental interaction, involves the most amount of crying, and requires the highest level of persistence. It can be incredibly difficult emotionally, and it may not be practical if you have crabby neighbors within earshot. It takes a lot of commitment to see it through for at least the first several days. But starting and then stopping this method can increase nighttime crying and isn't really recommended.

If your baby is getting so worked up and is crying without those lulls and pauses that sound more like whining or regrouping, it is likely they are not quite ready and it's not the right method for this little one at this time. Another tell that your baby isn't ready is that there does not seem to be any difference in the amount and intensity of tears between day one and day three. Consider giving the baby a few more weeks to develop before continuing the sleep training. Remember that as long as the baby is safe and well, research has never shown any negative impact on the infant from this crying—but it should do the trick within a few days, and intuitively it makes sense not to let it go on beyond that.

### Modified Cry It Out

If letting your baby cry it out breaks your heart too much, and if you don't mind the same level of bothering the neighbors, and if you've got more time and patience to dedicate to sleep training, a gradual version of the "cry it out" method might work for you. With this style, you do attempt to soothe a crying baby when they're falling asleep, but you use set time intervals and limit direct interaction. Here's how it's done:

1.  After the typical bedtime routine, place your baby in their crib, drowsy but awake, and then leave the room.

2.  After five minutes of crying, return to soothe your infant, but don't offer breast or bottle. Continue to leave and return throughout the "falling asleep" process. You may offer limited soothing like shushing or placing your hand on the infant's belly. Ideally, you want to find ways to soothe without picking the baby up. If you feel like you have to pick your baby up to soothe them, avoid interacting with smiling or direct gaze, and limit their talking to shushing in their ear. After your infant is calm, put them back in the crib, again drowsy but awake, and leave the room. With this method, you do not soothe your baby to sleep; you

soothe them to help them regain a sleepy state. Ultimately, you want them to learn to self-soothe when it is time to fall asleep.

3.  After each soothe visit, start the clock again and wait to return at increasing time intervals—like ten minutes, then fifteen, and so on.

4.  Each subsequent night, wait longer before returning to soothe your baby.

### Camping Out

The "camping out" method means that you sit close to the baby's crib as they're falling asleep and move farther away until, eventually, you're out of the room. Generally, this is the slowest sleep-training method. It may take several weeks. Keep in mind that being present in your infant's sleep space while not attending to them directly may be frustrating for them and emotionally difficult for you, but it's a good alternative for those of us who don't feel comfortable leaving a crying baby without adult support.

Here's how to do it: After the typical bedtime routine, place your baby in their crib, drowsy but awake. Then, calmly sit or lie near the infant's crib. You can put a comfy chair or even a mattress down so you'll be comfortable. You can even do some intentional breathing through the process. You can touch your baby through the crib, but avoid offering feeding, rocking, or cuddling. Again, you're trying to help baby learn to self-soothe here, so you do have to refrain from too much helping along, but you want to do enough that they are not so dysregulated that it backfires.

Gradually, over the course of up to several weeks, you move physically away from the crib—and eventually out of the room. You can do this by slowly moving the chair or mattress away from the crib, until you're literally out the door.

## Q & A Session

**Question:** My sleep-trained toddler has totally regressed and is crying and calling "Mama!" for an hour when he used to sleep. I can't take it anymore. Save me from this nightmare! P.S.: We were just on vacation and he has a new nanny in the picture.

**Answer:** I'm so sorry you're going through this. The changes you mention are super-common causes of sleep regression. Any change in a child's life can impact sleep. It's okay to soothe your child back to sleep (**Relationship**). He hasn't forgotten his sleep training; he just might just need more support right now. You can also make sure daytime routines are in place (**Regulation**).

Transitioning back from the whirlwind of vacation can throw toddlers off and also encourage them to test the boundaries of home routines. Try carving out a little extra one-on-one time during the day (**Relationship**). At night, you can start with giving extra snuggles and then let your little one know you are going to go brush your teeth and come right back to check on them (**Relationship**, **Rules**). You can do small moments of leaving and coming back a few times and then build your way up to leaving for the night. It's also okay to just give him one of your soft T-shirts, put in some earplugs, and ignore the crying if that's what you need for your own sanity and to be a better parent in the morning (**Rules**).

### Telling Kids They're Getting a New Sibling

When you find out you're pregnant or will be welcoming a new member of the family, you don't have to share that news until it's about to become obvious—either because you're starting to show, which will typically be earlier with a second child, or when other people are going to be talking about it and congratulating you in front of your kids.

Young children under about three years old don't have a sense of time, so it's no use telling them the baby is coming in three or six months. Instead, you might talk about the seasons. For example, "There's going be winter, we're going to have snow. We're going to celebrate a holiday, and then your birthday. Then the flowers will bloom in springtime, and that's when the baby's going to come."

Avoid trying to convince your child how amazing this new baby's going be and how much they're going to love them. Keep their life as similar as possible in terms of routines and even bedding. As with all transitions, it's important to remember that kids prefer boring. Lean into routines. Let your child know that you're open for questions if they want to talk about what's to come. Avoid blaming the preparation for the baby when there are things you can't do with your child. Of course, it's understandable that you're not going to be able to pick up child number one from preschool if you've got an appointment to sign adoption papers or get an ultrasound, but try not to set up or reinforce the idea that another baby means less attention for the older kids.

Have some empathy if your child expresses mixed feelings. Therapists often use the comparison of a spouse suddenly introducing another love of their life—someone whom everyone seems excited to meet. How would you feel just being *the old spouse*? So, there's no need to manically force-feed your child love and excitement about a baby that may in fact bring up many different feelings. This transition is a reminder that you can't force feelings. Often, you're better off acknowledging that things can be complicated. You can say something like, "Hey, you might have what's called 'mixed feelings,' where you're really excited and also really worried, and that's okay."

## The "Right" Age for a Phone or Social Media

When a kid gets a phone, they're suddenly carrying the world in their pocket. Unless you have controls on that phone, literally anyone with their number, email address, or social media details can contact them. The internet, along with its unregulated content, is just a click away. Before taking this big step, it's useful to ask yourself if your child is showing other skills of independence and self-regulation that would suggest readiness.

Are they walking to school independently?

Are they able to keep their cool when someone upsets them?

Are they doing their homework without much oversight from you?

Are they able to answer a phone, make a call themselves, and leave a polite message?

Are they able to talk to their peers with kindness and consideration?

Are they open with you and other adults in their life when it comes to content or contacts that may not be appropriate?

If the answers are yes, it's likely that your child is getting to the point where they might be able to handle the responsibilities of having their own phone.

I wish I could give a hard-and-fast rule about the exact age this will happen, but it's more about your readiness as the parent and the skills your individual child has that will help them manage the challenges of having a device.

Phones usually come before social media accounts and can be set up with guidelines regarding who children can communicate with while the children are still learning how to navigate "stranger danger" with their devices. Research on brain science has shown that girls and other people with estrogen can more easily go into a "survival brain" amid the perceived threats of online judgments and bullying. Estrogen has, from an evolutionary perspective, served as a superpower to help women protect their children with vigilance, but in today's world it's all too common for estrogen to send a message of hypervigilance to a tween's developing brain that can blow threats out of proportion.

For children of all genders, based on what we know about neurobiology and the ways in which the tween and teen brains change and reformat as they enter adolescence, it's best to wait as long as possible before introducing kids to the stressors of social media—certainly children will benefit by waiting until *at least* age thirteen, although I'm aware that this feels near impossible in many families.

Beyond that, rather than pick an age when a child is suddenly ready for a phone or for social media (and, again, those are different things), think about these two questions; when you can answer them, you can decide whether you and your child are ready. It's not necessarily correlated with one particular age.

1. When are *you* ready to put in the time to guide and support and monitor your new phone user or your new social-media user? Just like with potty training and so

many other aspects of parenting, it's perfectly all right to wait until you've got a lull in your own schedule, when you feel you can handle the added conscientiousness needed.

2.  Does your child have the skills they need to use the phone or the social media in a way that you feel good about? You can ask your child to make their case. And remember, if you let your child have a particular device this month because they have convinced you they're ready, it's perfectly all right to take it away next month if it turns out they weren't as ready as they had hoped.

### *Introduce a Phone Contract*

Each kid is different. For some, a contract makes them feel clearer and more certain about the family's expectations. A contract also alleviates the pressure of coming up with on-the-spot consequences. For others, a contract may feel too rigid and even unnecessary. With these caveats in mind, here are some elements many parents, children, and tweens find helpful to include:

I agree to keep my phone charged.

I agree not to spam my parents or other people. (So many of the parents in my groups can show me screens full of Mom, mom, mom, mom, mom or please, please, please, please, please . . . This is not good etiquette!)

I agree to put my phone away during family time.

I agree not to use my phone at school and to follow my teachers' rules about phone use.

I agree to remove myself from any group chats where people are talking about another peer who isn't there.

I agree not to download any apps without my parents' permission.

I recognize that my parents pay for my cellphone service and have the right to take it away if I don't keep up my end of this contact.

I agree to turn in my phone to the family charging station by ____ p.m. on weeknights and by ____ p.m. on weekends.

Consequences can be developed together, in conversation with your children, but remember to keep them connected to the infraction. A consequence may be that a child loses access to their phone for a particular amount of time. Also, remember to sign and date the contract and have children do the same so that it feels official.

### Create a Social Media Contract

Once your child has shown the independence and maturity to be able to handle having their own phone, they may be ready to add a social media account. As with phones, it can be helpful to create a contract to clarify expectations and limits. Here are some social media agreements parents and kids find helpful:

I agree to ask my parent's permission before joining any social networks.

I agree to allow my parents to set up parental controls and settings on all my accounts.

I agree to give my parents all my social network passwords and not to give them to anyone else.

I agree not to share personal information that could be accessible to anyone I do not know personally, in real life.

Specifically, I will not share my full name, age, address, school, interests, or any other personal information without my parents' permission.

I agree not to post or share photos of myself, my friends, or my family members without my parents' permission.

I agree not to post or share inappropriate or offensive comments or images.

I agree not to meet anyone in person whom I have met on social media.

I agree to be kind. I agree not to make unkind comments to or about anyone else.

I agree not to engage in online bullying, and when I see it, I will report it to my parents or an appropriate adult.

I agree to let my parents know if I'm the victim of online bullying.

I agree to let my parents know if I'm the victim of online blackmail, even if I have to admit to doing something I'm embarrassed about.

I understand that I may lose online privileges if I neglect my academic or home responsibilities.

I agree to be off social media by ___ p.m. on school nights and by ___ p.m. on weekends.

The beauty of contracts is that you come up with them ahead of time, not in the heat of the moment, and can therefore work with your children in times of relative calm to come up with natural and connected consequences. A consequence of violating the social-media contract might be that a child loses access to social media for a particular period of time. Older children may agree to volunteer in an empathy-building program that helps the type of people they may have harmed if they engaged in bullying another person via social media. You and your child can also come up with your own ideas for connected consequences. If a contract feels too rigid or your child has shown the capacity to follow the contract for a trial period, you can ditch it.

## Introduction

Suzanne Simard, *Finding the Mother Tree: Discovering the Wisdom of the Forest* (New York: Alfred A. Knopf, 2021).

Erik Erikson, *Identity and the Life Cycle* (New York: W. W. Norton & Company, 1980).

Susan S. Woodhouse, Julie R. Scott, Allison D. Hepworth, and Jude Cassidy, "Secure Base Provision: A New Approach to Examining Links between Maternal Caregiving and Infant Attachment," *Child Development* 91, no. 1 (2020): e249–65.

## Chapter 1

Rollo May, *The Courage to Create* (New York: W. W. Norton & Company, 1994), 100.

Daniel J. Siegel, *IntraConnected: Mwe (Me + We) as the Integration of Self, Identity, and Belonging* (New York: W. W. Norton & Company, 2022).

Stephen W. Porges, *The Polyvagal Theory* (New York: W. W. Norton & Company, 2011).

Daniel J. Siegel and Tina Payne Bryson, *The Whole Brain Child: 12 Revolutionary Strategies to Nurture Your Child's Developing Mind* (New York: Delacorte Press, 2011), xii.

Albert Bandura, Dorothea Ross, and Sheila A. Ross, "Transmission of Aggression through Imitation of Aggressive Models," *Journal of Abnormal and Social Psychology* 63, no. 3 (1961): 575.

Lisa Damour, "Motivating Your Kids," *Raising Good Humans*, interviewed by Aliza Pressman, August 19, 2022, https://aliza.libsyn.com/s2-ep-76 -motivating-your-kids.

## Chapter 2

Ann S. Masten, "Ordinary Magic: Resilience Processes in Development," *American Psychologist* 56, no. 3 (March 2001): 227–38, https://pubmed .ncbi.nlm.nih.gov/11315249/.

Ann S. Masten, "Resilience from a Developmental Systems Perspective," *World Psychiatry* 18, no. 1 (February 2019): 101–2, https://pubmed.ncbi.nlm .nih.gov/30600628/.

Anna Freud and Dorothy Burlingham, *War and Children* (New York: Medical War Books, 1943), 21.

Robert A. Emmons, "Why Gratitude Is Good," in Josie Robinson, *Give Thanks: A Gratitude Journal* (Minneapolis: Wise Ink Creative Publishing, 2016), 40.

Lia Beatriz de Lucca Freitas, Maria Adélia Minghelli Pieta, and Jonathan Richard Henry Tudge, "Beyond Politeness: The Expression of Gratitude in Children and Adolescents," *Psicologia: Reflexão e Crítica* 24 (2011): 757–64.

Lev Vygotsky, *The Zone of Proximal Development* (New York: Routledge, 1999).

Angela Duckworth, *MX Blog*, March 10, 2021, retrieved from https://www.mx.com/blog/grit-motivation-alignment-character-angela-duckworth-mx/.

Angela Duckworth, *Grit: The Power of Passion and Perseverance* (New York: Scribner, 2016).

Kou Murayama, Andrew J. Elliot, and Shinji Yamagata, "Separation of Performance-Approach and Performance-Avoidance Achievement Goals: A Broader Analysis," *Journal of Educational Psychology* 103, no. 1 (2011): 238.

Carol S. Dweck, "Motivational Processes Affecting Learning," *American Psychologist* 41, no. 10 (1986): 1040.

J. Zhang, K. D. Vohs, and S. M. Carlson, *Imagining the Future Improves Self-Control in Preschoolers* (Minneapolis: University of Minnesota Press, 2022).

Stephanie M. Carlson, "Let Me Choose: The Role of Choice in the Development of Executive Function Skills," *Current Directions in Psychological Science* 32, no. 3 (2023): 220–27.

Phil Zelazo, "Executive Function Skills Are the Air Traffic Control System of the Brain," *Raising Good Humans*, interviewed by Aliza Pressman, January 8, 2021, https://aliza.libsyn.com/2021/01.

Center on the Developing Child at Harvard University, "Executive Function and Self-Regulation," 2014, retrieved from www.developingchild.harvard.edu.

## Chapter 3
Madeline Levine, *Teach Your Children Well: Why Values and Coping Skills Matter More Than Grades, Trophies, or "Fat Envelopes"* (New York: Harper Perennial, 2012).

## Chapter 4
Richard Schwartz and Martha Sweezy, *Internal Family Systems Therapy* (New York: Guilford Publications, 2019).

Fred Rothbaum, Karen Rosen, Tatsuo Ujiie, and Nobuko Uchida, "Family Systems Theory, Attachment Theory, and Culture," *Family Process* 41, no. 3 (2002): 328–50.

A. H. Maslow, "A Theory of Human Motivation," *Psychological Review* 50, no. 4 (1943): 370–96, https://doi.org/10.1037/h0054346.

National Academies of Sciences, Engineering, and Medicine, *Vibrant and*

*Healthy Kids: Aligning Science, Practice, and Policy to Advance Health Equity* (Washington, DC: National Academies Press, 2019), https://doi .org/10.17226/25466.

Pilyoung Kim and Sarah Enos Watamura, "Two Open Windows: Infant and Parent Neurobiologic Change," Aspen Institute, Washington, DC, June 30, 2015, retrieved from https://ascend.aspeninstitute.org.

Shauna Shapiro, *Good Morning, I Love You: Mindfulness and Self-Compassion Practices to Rewire Your Brain for Calm, Clarity, and Joy* (Boulder, CO: Sounds True, 2022).

Eve Rodsky, *Find Your Unicorn Space* (New York: G. P. Putnam's Sons, 2021).

## Chapter 5

Mary D. Ainsworth, *Infancy in Uganda: Infantcare and the Growth of Love* (Baltimore: Johns Hopkins Press, 1967).

John Bowlby, *A Secure Base* (New York: Routledge, 1988).

L. Alan Sroufe, "Attachment and Development: A Prospective, Longitudinal Study from Birth to Adulthood," *Attachment & Human Development* 7, no. 4 (December, 2005): 349–67, DOI:10.1080/1461673050 0365928.

Alan Sroufe, *A Compelling Idea: How We Become the Persons We Are* (Safer Society Press, 2020).

M. Katherine Weinberg and Edward Z. Tronick, "Infant Affective Reactions to the Resumption of Maternal Interaction after the Still-Face," *Child Development* 67, no. 3 (June 1996): 905–14, https://doi.org/10.1111/j.1467-8624.1996 .tb01772.x.

Alan Sroufe, "The Real Attachment Science," *Raising Good Humans*, interviewed by Aliza Pressman, May 7, 2021, https://aliza.libsyn.com/ep-94 -professor-l-alan-sroufe-explains-how-we-come-to-be-who-we-are.

## Chapter 6

A. Thomas and S. Chess, "Temperament and Personality," in G. A. Kohnstamm, J. E. Bates, and M. K. Rothbart, eds., *Temperament in Childhood* (Hoboken, NJ: John Wiley & Sons, 1989), 249–61.

J. Kagan and N. Snidman, "Temperamental Factors in Human Development," *American Psychologist* 46, no. 8 (1991): 856–62, https://doi.org /10.1037/0003-066X.46.8.856.

Bruce J. Ellis and W. Thomas Boyce, "Biological Sensitivity to Context," *Current Directions in Psychological Science* 17, no. 3 (June 2008): 183–87, https:// doi.org/10.1111/j.1467-8721.2008.00571.x.

Francesca Lionetti et al., "Dandelions, Tulips, and Orchids: Evidence for the Existence of Low-Sensitive, Medium-Sensitive, and High-Sensitive Individuals," *Translational Psychiatry* 8, no. 24 (2018), https://doi.org/10.1038 /s41398-017-0090-6.

Clyde C. Robinson, Barbara Mandleco, Susanne Frost Olsen, and Craig H. Hart, "Authoritative, Authoritarian, and Permissive Parenting Practices: Development of a New Measure," *Psychological Reports* 77, no. 3 (1995): 819–30, https://journals.sagepub.com/doi/10.2466/pr0.1995.77.3.819.

Diana Baumrind, "Authoritarian vs. Authoritative Parental Control," *Adolescence* 3, no. 11 (1968): 255–72.

Alyssa S. Meuwissen and Stephanie M. Carlson, "An Experimental Study of the Effects of Autonomy Support on Preschoolers' Self-Regulation," *Journal of Applied Developmental Psychology* 60 (January–February 2019): 11–23, https://www.sciencedirect.com/science/article/abs/pii/S019339 7318300303.

Eddie Brummelman, Stefanie A. Nelemans, Sander Thomaes, and Bram Orobio de Castro, "When Parents' Praise Inflates, Children's Self-Esteem Deflates," *Child Development* 88, no. 6 (November 2017): 1799–809.

Kyla Haimovitz and Carol S. Dweck, "The Origins of Children's Growth and Fixed Mindsets: New Research and a New Proposal," *Child Development* 88, no. 6 (November 2017): 1849–59.

Ram Dass and Mirabai Bush, *Walking Each Other Home: Conversations on Loving and Dying* (Boulder, CO: Sounds True, 2022).

### Chapter 7

Thomas Curran and Andrew P. Hill, "Perfectionism Is Increasing Over Time: A Meta-Analysis of Birth Cohort Differences from 1989 to 2016," *Psychological Bulletin* 145, no. 4 (2019): 410–29, https://www.apa.org/pubs /journals/releases/bul-bul0000138.pdf.

Thomas Curran, "Mythbusting Perfectionism," *Raising Good Humans*, interviewed by Aliza Pressman, October 28, 2022, https://aliza.libsyn.com /s2-ep-88-mythbusting-perfectionsm-with-professor-thomas-curran.

Joachim Stoeber, "Frost Multidimensional Perfectionism Scale—Deutsch," 1995, https://www.academia.edu/5427984/Frost_Multidimensional _Perfectionism_Scale_Deutsch_1995_.

Joachim Stöber, "The Frost Multidimensional Perfectionism Scale Revisited: More Perfect with Four (Instead of Six) Dimensions," *Personality and Individual Differences* 24, no. 4 (April 1998): 481–91.

Gail D. Heyman and Carol S. Dweck, "Achievement Goals and Intrinsic Motivation: Their Relation and Their Role in Adaptive Motivation," *Motivation and Emotion* 16 (1992): 231–47.

Kristin D. Neff and Katie A. Dahm, "Self-Compassion: What It Is, What It Does, and How It Relates to Mindfulness," in Brian D. Ostafin, Michael D. Robinson, and Brian P. Meier, eds., *Handbook of Mindfulness and Self-Regulation* (New York: Springer, 2015), 121–37.

### Chapter 8

Sheila M. Eyberg and Elizabeth A. Robinson, "Parent-Child Interaction Training: Effects on Family Functioning," *Journal of Clinical Child and Adolescent Psychology* 11, no. 2 (1982): 130–37.

Frank C. Keil, *Wonder: Childhood and a Lifelong Love of Science* (Boston: MIT Press, 2022).

Jennifer E. Stellar et al., "Self-Transcendent Emotions and Their Social Functions: Compassion, Gratitude, and Awe Bind Us to Others Through Prosociality," *Emotion Review* 9, no. 3 (June 2017): 200–207.

Dacher Keltner, *Born to Be Good: The Science of a Meaningful Life* (New York: W. W. Norton & Company, 2009).

## Chapter 9

Rebecca Distefano et al., "Autonomy-Supportive Parenting and Associations with Child and Parent Executive Function," *Journal of Applied Developmental Psychology* 58 (July–September 2018): 77–85.

## Chapter 10

Max Hirshkowitz et al., "National Sleep Foundation's Updated Sleep Duration Recommendations: Final Report," *Sleep Health* 1, no. 4 (December 2015): 233–43, doi:10.1016/j.sleh.2015.10.004.

Marc Weissbluth, *Healthy Sleep Habits, Happy Child: A Step-by-Step Program for a Good Night's Sleep,* fourth ed. (New York: Ballantine Books, 2009), 21.

## Chapter 11

Tina Payne Bryson and Daniel J. Siegel, *No-Drama Discipline: The Whole-Brain Way to Calm the Chaos and Nurture Your Child's Developing Mind* (New York: Random House, 2016).

Dieter Vaitl, "Interoception," *Biological Psychology* 42, nos. 1–2 (January 1996): 1–27.

Lawrence Kohlberg and Carol Gilligan, "Moral Development," in Alan M. Slater and Paul C. Quinn, eds., *Developmental Psychology: Revisiting the Classic Studies* (Sage Publications, 2012): 164.

Elizabeth T. Gershoff et al., "The Strength of the Causal Evidence Against Physical Punishment of Children and Its Implications for Parents, Psychologists, and Policymakers," *American Psychologist* 73, no. 5 (July–August 2018): 626–38.

Robert E. Larzelere, "Child Outcomes of Nonabusive and Customary Physical Punishment by Parents: An Updated Literature Review," *Clinical Child and Family Psychology Review* 3, no. 4 (December 2000): 199–221.

Elizabeth T. Gershoff, "Spanking and Child Development: We Know Enough Now to Stop Hitting Our Children," *Child Development Perspectives* 7, no. 3 (July 2013): 133–37.

Joshua Sparrow, "Dr. Joshua Sparrow Talks Punishments, Consequences, and Time-Outs," *Raising Good Humans,* interviewed by Aliza Pressman, August 20, 2021, https://www.scribd.com/podcast/520938013/S2-Ep-11

-Dr-Joshua-Sparrow-Talks-Punishments-Consequences-and-Time
-Outs-Renowned-Child-Psychiatrist-Dr-Joshua-Sparrow-Talks-Punish
ments-Consequ.

Daniel J. Siegel and Tina Payne Bryson, *The Whole-Brain Child: 12 Revolutionary Strategies to Nurture Your Child's Developing Mind* (New York: Delacorte Press, 2011), 27.

Martin L. Hoffman, "Power Assertion by the Parent and Its Impact on the Child," *Child Development* 31, no. 1 (March 1960): 129–43.

## Chapter 12

Cheryl L. Rusting and Susan Nolen-Hoeksema, "Regulating Responses to Anger: Effects of Rumination and Distraction on Angry Mood," *Journal of Personality and Social Psychology* 74, no. 3 (March 1998): 790–803.

## Chapter 13

Michele Borba, *Thrivers: The Surprising Reasons Why Some Kids Struggle and Others Shine* (New York: Penguin, 2021), 8.

Gordon L. Flett, "An Introduction, Review, and Conceptual Analysis of Mattering as an Essential Construct and an Essential Way of Life," *Journal of Psychoeducational Assessment* 40, no. 1 (2022): 3–36, https://doi.org/10.1177/07342829211057640.

Gordon L. Flett, *The Psychology of Mattering: Understanding the Human Need to Be Significant* (Netherlands: Elsevier Science, 2018), 217.

Jennifer Breheny Wallace, *Never Enough: When Achievement Culture Becomes Toxic—and What We Can Do About It* (New York: Penguin, 2023).

Carol Dweck, "Carol Dweck Revisits the 'Growth Mindset,'" *Education Week*, September 22, 2015, https://www.edweek.org/leadership/opinion
-carol-dweck-revisits-the-growth-mindset/2015/09.

Britt Hawthorne, *Raising Antiracist Children: A Practical Parenting Guide* (New York: Simon Element, 2022).

Jamil P. Bhanji, Eunbin S. Kim, and Mauricio R. Delgado, "Perceived Control Alters the Effect of Acute Stress on Persistence," *Journal of Experimental Psychology: General* 145, no. 3 (March 2016): 356–65.

Susan Silk and Barry Goldman, "How Not to Say the Wrong Thing," *Los Angeles Times*, April 7, 2013.

## Chapter 14

Samantha A. Sang and Jackie A. Nelson, "The Effect of Siblings on Children's Social Skills and Perspective Taking," *Infant and Child Development* 26, no. 6 (November–December 2017): e2023.

Mary C. Maguire and Judy Dunn, "Friendships in Early Childhood, and Social Understanding," *International Journal of Behavioral Development* 21, no. 4 (November 1997): 669–86.

Carollee Howes, "Friendship in Early Childhood," in K. H. Rubin, W. M.

Sources

Bukowski, and B. Laursen, eds., *Handbook of Peer Interactions, Relationships, and Groups* (New York: Guilford Press, 2009), 180–94.

Debby A. Phillips, Kate H. Phillips, Kitty Grupp, and Lisa J. Trigg, "Sibling Violence Silenced: Rivalry, Competition, Wrestling, Playing, Roughhousing, Benign," *Advances in Nursing Science* 32, no. 2 (April–June 2009): E1–E16.

Gianluca Gini, Tiziana Pozzoli, Francesco Borghi, and Lara Franzoni, "The Role of Bystanders in Students' Perception of Bullying and Sense of Safety," *Journal of School Psychology* 46, no. 6 (December 2008): 617–38.

Imogen Hanvey, Aida Malovic, and Evangelos Ntontis, "Glass Children: The Lived Experiences of Siblings of People with a Disability or Chronic Illness," *Journal of Community & Applied Social Psychology* 32, no. 5 (September–October 2022): 936–48.

## Chapter 15
Paul R. Amato, "Research on Divorce: Continuing Trends and New Developments," *Journal of Marriage and Family* 72, no. 3 (June 2010): 650–66.

## Chapter 16
Vivek Murthy, *Social Media and Youth Mental Health: The US Surgeon General's Advisory* (Washington, DC: US Public Health Service, 2023), https://www.hhs.gov/sites/default/files/sg-youth-mental-health-social-media-advisory.pdf.

Amy Orben, Andrew K. Przybylski, Sarah-Jayne Blakemore, and Rogier A. Kievit, "Windows of Developmental Sensitivity to Social Media," *Nature Communications* 13, no. 1649 (March 2022), https://doi.org/10.1038/s41467-022-29296-3.

Adriana G. Bus, Susan B. Neuman, and Kathleen Roskos, "Screens, Apps, and Digital Books for Young Children: The Promise of Multimedia," *AERA Open* 6, no. 1 (January 2020): https://doi.org/10.1177/2332858420901494.

Sheena Guram and Peter Heinz, "Media Use in Children: American Academy of Pediatrics Recommendations 2016," *Archives of Disease in Childhood: Education and Practice Edition* 103, no. 2 (April 2018): 99–101.

Kristen A. Jenson, *Good Pictures, Bad Pictures: How to Talk to Kids about Pornography* (Kennewick, WA: Glen Cove Press, 2014).

## Chapter 17
Sara Raley and Suzanne Bianchi, "Sons, Daughters, and Family Processes: Does Gender of Children Matter?" *Annual Review of Sociology* 32 (August 2006): 401–21.

Jean Malpas, "Between Pink and Blue: A Multidimensional Family Approach to Gender Nonconforming Children and Their Families," *Family Process* 50, no. 4 (December 2011): 453–70.

Alan D. Rogol, James N. Roemmich, and Pamela A. Clark, "Growth at Puberty," *Journal of Adolescent Health* 31, supplement 6 (December 2002): 192–200.

acceptance, parents' need for, 61–62
accommodations, for sleep, 168–69
acknowledgment of your baggage. *See* baggage, acknowledging your
active reading, 135
adaptive capacity, 24, 29. *See also* resilience
adaptive perfectionism, 118, 119
adolescence/adolescents. *See also* tweens
  neuroplasticity during, 64
  promoting empathy with, 45–46
  promoting gratitude with, 33
  sleep for, 162
  social media use by, 278–79
  supporting autonomy during, 36
  supporting motivation during, 40–41
  trans, 284–85
agency, 26, 224. *See also* autonomy
Ainsworth, Mary, 15, 82
allowance jar, 32
amends, making, 227, 254
American Academy of Pediatrics
  on child separation at US–Mexico border, 29
  on co-sleeping and room sharing, 171
  on screen use, 274
American Psychological Association (APA), 29
amygdala, 12, 13, 278–79

anger, 209, 287
anima/animus, parenting, 72, 73
anxiety
  accommodation for sleeping increasing, 168–69
  in parents, 14, 100
  perfectionism and, 119, 123
  permissive parenting and, 101
  regulation exercise for, 237
  transitions and, 264
apologizing, 204, 214
archetypes, parenting, 72–76
assessment of the present moment, 295
  about your child's food and bathroom issues, 148
  in BAD (breathe, assess, deal) passcode, 10
  BALANCE passcode and, 9
  discipline and, 177, 191, 193
  drama between siblings/friends and, 239
  during transitions, 263
  when approaching conflict, 208
  when talking about sex and gender, 281
  your child in the outside world and, 217
attachment, xv. *See also* secure attachment
  amount of responsiveness from parents for, xix, 80

4

parent(s) and caregivers *(cont.)*
  controlling or coercive, 105–6
  co-parent to balance strength of, 100
  development of, 57
  divorce between, 264–66
  down time for, 66
  dreaming up their own unicorn space, 77–78
  engaging their mom brain, 65–67
  "Good morning, I love you" greeting practiced by, 76
  hierarchy of needs for, 58–60
  inner multitudes of, 70–72
  labeling their moods, 200–201
  as "mother" trees, xvii
  neuroplasticity in, 64–65
  path of development in, xv–xvi
  perfectionism and, 116–17, 118, 120–21, 124
  perfectionism in, 120–23
  phone use by, 275
  play with children. *See* play
  powerful impact on their children, 3–4
  prenatal toxic stress and post-partum depression in, 62–63
  presenting a united front between, 194–95
  reparenting themselves, 68–70
  sacrificing their own needs and interests, 74–76
  seeking advice from inner wise grandmother and best frenemy, 296–97
  self-forgiveness and self-empathy by, 214–15
  sharing activities with children that give them joy, 139
  sharing "wow" moments with children, 136–38

  taking care of, 60–62
  temperament of, 98–99
  transitions experienced by. *See* transitions
"parent-child interaction therapy," 134
"parent gut," myth of, 67–68
parenting
  bringing one's experiences and history to, xiv
  extreme ideas in, xv, xix
  finding the middle road for, xv, 294–97
  nonnegotiables in, xix
  "practice makes perfect" and, 158
  reframing your worries about, 99
  what the science tells us about, 294, 297–98
parenting archetypes, 72–76
parenting styles
  about, 100–102
  bedtime consistency and, 167–68
  discipline and, 175
  quiz on, 102–5
peer modeling, inner efficacy and, 220
peers. *See* bullies and bullying; friends(hips)
peers, being left out with, 249
perfectionism
  about, 117–18
  adaptive, 118, 119
  competition and, 128–30
  examples of parents with unhealthy levels of, 116–17
  gender differences and, 287
  growth mindset and, 124
  losing/disappointment and, 128
  maladaptive, 118–19
  mistakes and, 126–27
  quiz on being a perfectionist parent, 120–21

self-soothing
  inner efficacy and, 220–21
  for sleep, 170, 171
sense of self, 151
sensitive caregiving
  about, 15–16
  for autonomy, 145–46
  boundaries/limits and, 106–8
  child's temperament and, 98–99
  limits and, 107
sensitivity
  differences in children's levels of,
    94–97
  parenting styles and, 102
"serve and return," 15–16, 79
sex and sexuality
  definitions, 282, 283
  masturbation and, 290
  puberty and, 288–89
  sexual consent and, 291–92
  "the sex talk," 290–91
  values about, 283–84
sexual identity, 283–86
shadow, parenting, 72, 73
shame and shaming
  body odors and, 290
  discipline and, 190
  empathy and, 41
  letting go over, during conflict,
    214
  masturbation and, 290
Shapiro, Shauna, 76
sibling(s)
  acting as mediator for conflicts
    among, 246–47
  allowing for boundaries between,
    244
  avoiding comparing and labeling
    with, 242–44
  avoiding playing into good kid/
    bad kid dynamics with, 244

BALANCE practice and, 238–39
benefits of relationships with,
  239–40
conflict among, 245–47
equity among, 258–59
family meeting with, 240–41
humanizing language used with,
  257–58
reducing conflict between, 241
resilience built from relationships
  with, 239
roughhousing with, 245–46
with special needs, 259–60
telling children they are getting a
  new, 307–8
validating feelings about, 245
Siegel, Dan, 11
silent treatment, 158, 201
Silk, Susan, 236
Silly Chins game, 136
Simard, Suzanne, xvii, 216
Simon Says (self-regulation exercise),
  47
singing in rounds (self-regulation
  exercise), 47
skin-to-skin contact, 80
sleep(ing). See also bedtime
  accommodations for, 168–69
  for adults, 162
  attachment and, 81
  for babies, 163–64
  consistent bedtime for, 167–68
  co-sleeping and room sharing for,
    80, 160, 171
  "crying it out" and, 161, 304–6
  environment for, 169–70
  guidelines by age on amount of,
    161–62
  helping child fall asleep
    independently, 170–71
  "motion," 171

visualization *(cont.)*
  in Watch the Kite Float Away
    exercise, 159
  of yourself as a mother tree,
    xvii
voice changes, 288
volunteering
  in empathy-building program,
    313
  by parents at school, 218
  sense of mattering and, 223
  service activities, 232
Vygotsky, Lev, 34


walking meditation, 292–93
walks, gratitude, 32
Wallace, Jennifer Breheny, 223
Wang, Xin, 65
*War and Children* (Freud and
  Burlingham), 28
Watamura, Sarah Enos, 64

Watch the Kite Float Away exercise,
  159
weekends, waking up on, 166–67
What Animal Am I? game, 135
whining, 210–11
white-noise machine, 167
withdrawal, by parent, 158, 201
*Wonder: Childhood and a Lifelong
  Love of Science* (Keil), 136
Woodhouse, Susan S., xix
working memory, 25


yelling
  breaking the cycle of, 70–71
  discipline with, 197
  self-regulation and, 4, 6


Zelazo, Phil, 46
zone of proximal development, 34,
  35, 36

**D**r. Aliza Pressman is a developmental psychologist with nearly two decades of experience working with families and the health-care providers who care for them. Aliza is an assistant clinical professor in the Division of Behavioral Health in the Department of Pediatrics at the Icahn School of Medicine at Mount Sinai Hospital, where she is a co–founding director of the Mount Sinai Parenting Center. Aliza is the host of the award-winning podcast *Raising Good Humans*. She holds a BA from Dartmouth College, an MA in Risk, Resilience, and Prevention from the Department of Human Development at Teachers College of Columbia University, and a PhD in developmental psychology from the Columbia University Graduate School of Arts and Sciences. Aliza also holds a teaching certificate in mindfulness and meditation from the Greater Good Science Center at the University of California, Berkeley. She is the mother of two teenagers.